Overcoming Resistance

A Rational Emotive Behavior Therapy Integrated Approach

2nd Edition

 **Albert Ellis, PhD,** is the founder and president of the Albert Ellis Institute in New York City. He received his MA and PhD degrees in clinical psychology from Columbia University. A former Adjunct Professor of Psychology at Rutgers University and Pittsburgh State College, Dr. Ellis has also been Distinguished Professor of Psychology at the Professional School of Psychological Studies in San Diego. He served as Chief Psychologist of the New Jersey State Diagnostic Center and Chief Psychologist of the New Jersey Department of Institutions and Agencies. He has been a Consultant in Clinical Psychology to the New York City Board of Education and the Veterans Administration, and he has practiced psychotherapy, marriage and family counseling, as well as sex therapy, for almost 60 years. He continues this practice at the Psychological Clinic of the Albert Ellis Institute.

A Fellow of the American Psychological Association, Dr. Ellis has served as President of its Division of Consulting Psychology and as a member of its Council of Representatives. He is a Diplomate in Clinical Psychology of the American Board of Professional Psychology, and a Diplomate of the American Board of Psychotherapy.

Dr. Ellis has published over 700 articles and 65 books, among them *Reason and Emotion in Psychotherapy, A Guide to Rational Living,* and *The Practice of Rational Emotive Behavior Therapy.* He has also served as Consulting or Associate Editor of many publications, including the *Journal of Marriage and Family Therapy,* the *Journal of Contemporary Psychotherapy, Journal of Individual Psychology, Cognitive Therapy and Research, Psychological Reports,* and *The Journal of Rational-Emotive and Cognitive-Behavior Therapy.*

Overcoming Resistance

*A Rational Emotive
Behavior Therapy
Integrated Approach*

2nd Edition

Albert Ellis

 Springer Publishing Company

Springer Publishing Company, Inc.
536 Broadway
New York, NY 10012-3955

Acquisitions Editor: Sheri W. Sussman
Production Editor: Jean Hurkin-Torres
Cover design by Joanne Honigman

02 03 04 05 06 / 5 4 3 2 1

Library of Congress Cataloging-in-Publication Data

Ellis, Albert.
    Overcoming resistance : a rational emotive behavior therapy integrated approach / Albert Ellis. — 2nd ed.
      p. ; cm.
    Includes bibliographical references and index.
    ISBN 0-8261-4912-X (alk. paper)
    1. Resistance (Psychoanalysis). 2. Rational-emotive psychotherapy.
3. Psychotherapist and patient. I. Title.
    [DNLM: 1. Psychotherapy, Rational-Emotive—methods. 2. Cognitive therapy—methods. 3. Therapist-Client. WM 420.5.P8 E47o 2002]
    RC489.R49 E43 2002
    616.89'142—dc21
                                       2002021034

Printed in the United States of America by Maple-Vail Book Manufacturing Group.

For Janet L. Wolfe
Still my best friend, critic,
and invaluable helper after 38 years!

Contents

Acknowledgments

As is the case with all of my books on psychotherapy, I want to mainly acknowledge my many clients who made invaluable contributions to the writing of this book. I have gone out of my way to fictionalize their names and some important identifying aspects of their lives, but my descriptions of the methods I used with them, and of the remarkable work that many of them did to implement those methods are factual. To all my clients, then, my grateful thanks!

Emmett Velten and Kevin Everett FitzMaurice read early versions of my manuscript and made some valuable suggestions. Patrice Ward and Tim Runion slaved away at hot word processors to give my manuscript beautiful order. Finally, most of the authors mentioned in this book, and many more I failed to mention, contributed appreciably to it. Windy Dryden inspired the original edition, as well as aided this one with his many contributions of Rational Emotive Behavior Therapy (REBT). Again, many thanks!

Introduction

This is another book that I have written in present-action language. The first one was my recent *Feeling Better, Getting Better, Staying Better* (Ellis, 2001a), an experiment that turned out well. I got the idea for using this style of writing from a number of sources. It was first proposed by William James and other early psychological writers and then adopted by Robert Zettle (1994) in his chapter, "On the Basis of Acceptable Language," in the book, *Acceptance and Change.* It is also used, I later saw, by William Glasser (1999) in *Choice Therapy.*

Why is present-action language useful: Mainly, in our usual parlance, when we say things like, "I am anxious," or "I am depressed," it is needlessly negative and implies perpetual anxietizing and depressing. As Alfred Korzybski (1933/1991said in *Science and Sanity* the statement, "I am anxious" implies that I am anxietizing right now, that this is my *essential nature,* and that I shall most likely plague myself with anxietizing for some time to come. This is a misleading overgeneralization that tends to maintain emotional problems. "Am" is a dangerous word—especially when used as what Korzybski called "the is of identity." I may legitimately note that I now *do* good or bad deeds (by common social standards), but not that I *am* a *good* or *bad person.* For a *good person* would act well all the time and a *bad person* would act poorly forever. Moreover, he or she would be, by implication, totally bad—have all bad traits and actings—which, of course, is most unlikely.

"I am depressed," moreover, ignores human constructionist tendencies by implying that I was *made* depressed by external circumstances: that I had no control over these conditions, that I view them in an *awful* or *terrible* light, and that I have little or no ability to change my depressed feelings. Quite pessimistic—and not exactly accurate!

To counteract this overgeneralized and iatrogenic tendency, in this book I shall often use language such as, "I depress myself," "I feel depressing," and "I anxietize." This terminology shows that I now depress and anxietize myself—but that I need not do so in the future. It uses verbs and adjectives to describe my (and others') distressing, and avoids the hazards of always using negative diagnostic labels—such as *depression* and *anxiety*—that overgeneralize and imply that I am unable to change my thinking, feeling, and behaving. As you can see, this may be important—especially in a book that is about resisting cognitive-emotional-behavioral change. Humans tend to resist changing enough on their own, without being helped to do so by negatively being labeled for their distressing.

My use of present-action language in this book has its own difficulties. Thus, it looks peculiar and at first may be a little troubling to read. It somewhat limits the number of words that can be used to describe behaving—such as *disturbance, neurosis, personality disorder, psychosis,* and so forth—as it tries to substitute present-action ways of stating these forms of disturbing.

Also, in accordance with my original accepting of thinking, feeling, and behaving as holistically integrated and exceptionally interactional, I shall try to use the important word, *Belief,* to mean Believing-Emoting-Behaving. This fully recognizes its complex quality and makes it appear more prone to change than it otherwise would seem to be. People, as I point out later, *also* feel and behave when they think, they *also* think and behave when they feel, and they *also* think and feel when they behave. Why? Because they do! At least, that is one of my main premises. So when I could say, "Clients have Irrational Beliefs when they feel and act upsettingly," I shall italicize the word *Beliefs* to remind my readers that Beliefs *also* include dysfunctional feelings and behaviors. Sometimes, I shall say, "Clients have strong convictions" or "Clients strongly dogmatize" or "Clients strongly doctrinize" when I would have said, in my previous writings, "Clients have strong Beliefs." In this way, by using emotionally tuned words like "conviction," "doctrinize," and "dogmatize," I take shortcuts for saying "believing-emoting-behaving." This is because "conviction", for example, implies not merely a light or moderate Belief but includes distinct emotional and behavioral elements.

My use of the present-action language is still in its experimental stage, and I may sometimes use it carelessly. If you notice any of my lapses, or have suggestions to make about them, by all means write or email me your suggestions at the address below.

Let me also add a special note to this introduction. In my first draft I included a great many references to my own and other writers' articles and books—as is often done in professional volumes. I found, however, that my frequent references cluttered the text, had to be included in the reference list at the end of the volume and added considerably to the length and cost of the volume. So I quite reluctantly cut down on them. I have, therefore, mentioned full names but not given specific references to well-known authors like Sigmund Freud, Carl Rogers, Fritz

Perls and others. I have also omitted references to many dated items and mainly included a good number of recent citations. I feel frustrated about these omissions, but am doing my best to live rationally with my frustrations. Practicality wins out!

ALBERT ELLIS, PHD
Albert Ellis Institute for Rational
Emotive Behavior Therapy
45 East 65th Street
New York, NY 10021
aiellis@aol.com

Updating the Rational Emotive Behavior Therapy Approach to Overcoming Resistance

1

A great deal of "progress" has been made in the field of psychotherapy since I wrote the first edition of *Overcoming Resistance* over seventeen years ago. I put the word *progress* in quotation marks because, as I shall note later on, much of the new findings in the field and the newer techniques that have been developed are largely variations on previous themes that were originated years, and sometimes centuries, ago; and several of the new methods, even when they work with many people some of the time, have their dubious aspects and in some ways may well do more harm than good. So "progress" has its limitations!

Let me briefly mention some of the significant changes that have taken place in psychotherapy since the first edition of this book was published in 1985.

THE RISE OF MODERNISM

Postmodern philosophy rose to the fore in the early part of the twentieth century, largely as a result of the revolt of many thinkers against the rigidities of modernism. Modernism favors a "realistic" or "objective" outlook and insists that although we cannot fully see underlying "reality," it is definitely there. Immanuel Kant showed that our perception of it is limited but it still exists. It is not reality, but our limited and biased perception of it, that we had better doubt. Therefore, if it does exist, we cannot truly and perfectly say what it is, but we can still deal with it in our everyday and scientific life and make reasonably sure that the bridge that we construct does not fall down and kill us.

Up to around the middle of the twentieth century, psychologists and other scientists were largely logical positivists and tried to discover what was objectively "real." Then Karl Popper and other philosophers of science realized, along with Kant, that absolute truth or reality may not be obtainable—because a hypothesis, however sound, can always be superseded by future findings and shown to hardly be absolutely true. Therefore, Popper modified modernistic science and held that it was more valuable, in our experimentation, to falsify a given hypothesis than to try to verify it. By falsifying it we gained more practical knowledge than by universally trying to uphold it. This was the view I took in the first edition of *Overcoming Resistance,* when I had begun to follow Popper and Michael Mahoney.

Postmodern philosophy, instigated by F. Bretano, Edmund Husserl, Martin Heidigger, and other philosophers and forcefully brought into psychology by Kenneth Gergen and a number of other thinkers, went beyond this and claimed that modernist science was essentially absolutistic and limited and that various kinds of social constructivism were, to put it somewhat oddly, more "realistic." Everything that humans "see" is seen through their own limited means of perception and conception, and therefore there are no universal or scientific "truths."

I partly agreed with this postmodern outlook and in my revised edition of *Reason and Emotion in Psychotherapy* (Ellis, 1994) I subscribed to some of it. After all, I pointed out, Rational Emotive Behavior Therapy (REBT) is opposed to absolutistic thinking and to the use of *unconditional musts;* and the postmodernists largely go along with this outlook and also abjure absolutistic "truths." Therefore, REBT is partly postmodern. In 1997 I published a paper in the *Journal of Mental Health Counseling* (Ellis, 1997) showing that REBT uniquely combines some of the virtues of postmodernist thought with distinctly active-directive, and presumably more efficient, methods of therapy.

Postmodernism itself covers quite a range of thinking, from the radical views of Gergen and his followers to the more moderate views of other thinkers. It has also been brilliantly criticized by a number of philosophers, particularly by B. S. Held (1995), who have shown that it can easily become absolutistic and therefore inconsistent with its own basic premises. I generally follow these critics and still believe that what we call "reality" somehow exists, but—again, with Kant, who has influenced me since I first read his *Critique of Pure Reason* when I was in my teens—I say that we cannot by any means perfectly know it. Anyway, in this revision of *Overcoming Resistance,* I shall show, I hope, how psychotherapists can endorse a good deal of postmodernism, can still stick largely to the scientific method, and can do effective therapy.

THE USE OF NARRATIVE IN PSYCHOTHERAPY

Narrative techniques have always been used in psychotherapy, including REBT. For, in addition to telling themselves self-statements that highly influence their feelings and behaviors, humans—with their propensity to create and use language—seem to have a natural, innate tendency to weave their statements into narratives. They are born—as well as reared—storytellers, as their literature has shown for thousands of years. The Bible, for example, has probably been influential because of its great story-telling aspects, as have other scriptures and narratives. So one of the many cognitive-emotional techniques of REBT has always been the use of stories, fables, allegories, and metaphors to explain how disturbing people operate and how they can more effectively think, feel, and behave. Perhaps influenced by REBT's emphasis on self-statements, Michael White emphasized people's story-telling propensity and their constructivist tendencies to create useful as well as self-disturbing stories. White and his associate's findings have had a powerful influence on psychotherapy since the mid-1980's (White & Epston, 1990). In some ways, helping people to revise their gruesome, self-defeating stories into more optimistic self-aiding stories is another version of REBT's helping them to use rational coping self-statements instead of self-sabotaging ones.

Rational coping statements are often distinct philosophies—for example, "I definitely do not have to be approved by significant others but it would be highly preferable if I were. So let me see how I can arrange to get more approval." People can therefore often contradict much actual and potential emotional and behavioral dysfunctioning. When they replace Irrational *Beliefs,* by which they disturb themselves, with Rational ones, they often become more efficient than when they create self-aiding narratives. But even if this is true, some clients, especially resisting individuals, may be more likely to use the narrative forms of helping themselves than the self-statement forms. Which is more effective for more people more of the time can presumably be empirically tested. But in the meantime, narrative therapy can be useful for some people some of the time—as I shall show in this book.

CONSTRUCTIVE PHILOSOPHIZING

REBT has always been a constructivist or choice-oriented therapy. It has partly followed the Stoic hypothesizing, as expressed by Epictetus over two thousand years ago: "People are disturbed not by the events that happen to them but by their view of these events." Gautama

Buddha, though less clearly, also subscribed to this view and so did some of the early Hebrew and Christian thinkers. REBT is largely a choice therapy—as is William Glasser's Choice Theory. It does not overemphasize the element of agency, will, or intentioning in human affairs, since it also very much considers biological and innate as well as social learning and environmental influences on behaving (Ellis, 1962, 1976, 1994). Its ABC theory of human disturbance repeats Epictetus by holding that A (Adversity) does not by itself create neurotic disturbing Consequences (C). Instead, it is B (people's *Beliefs*) that also importantly contribute to C. Dysfunctional Consequences (C), or emotional-behavioral symptoms, follow from A x B. A pronounced constructivist outlook, as particularly encouraged by Vittorio Guidano, Michael Mahoney, and Michael Hoyt, is an important part of REBT (Ellis, 2001a, 2001b).

REBT, however, is realistic rather than Pollyannaist. It holds that people are innately creative, and are capable of constructing a large part of their emotional destiny. But, unfortunately, they also tend, as Korzybski (1933) has so brilliantly observed, to behave irrationally and have innate tendencies toward destructivism. These are also strong human propensities. By acknowledging them and helping clients change them into flexible preferring instead of dogmatic "musturbating," REBT tries to maximally help them.

Rational Emotive Behavior Therapy (REBT) and Cognitive Behavior Therapy (CBT) aim to be more efficient and more effective than other therapies that are primarily oriented toward changing people's dysfunctional thoughts, emotions, or actions. In any event, the methods of dealing effectively with clients' resistances to be presented in this book will stress REBT and CBT formulations. However, I shall particularly show how these can be added to and integrated with other therapeutic practices, such as person-centered, Gestalt, and psychoanalytic therapy. So this book will be considerably broader and more wide-ranging than most of my other books.

PSYCHOTHERAPY INTEGRATION

Perhaps the most important development in psychotherapy in recent years is the movement toward integration. Actually, this is not so recent, since eclectic therapy has been around for a long time and was, for example, heartily advocated by Frederick Thorne in 1950 over half a century ago. Integrative therapy, however, became really popular in the 1980's, promoted by a good many leading therapists, including Larry Beutler, Marvin Goldfried, Arnold Lazarus, John Norcross, and Paul Wachtel.

How does REBT fit into this psychotherapy integration movement? Very nicely, thank you. Although it has some basic principles that definitely differ from some of the other major therapies, it has always been integrative in its techniques—as its very name indicates. It is one of the most cognitive or philosophic therapies, but it has always asserted that human thinking is holistically blended with feeling and behaving. It therefore employs, along with many cognitive methods, an equal number of emotional and behavioral techniques. What other form of psychological treatment uses a greater variety of methods? None that I know.

In recent years, however, I have come to see that although the popular REBT and CBT methods have been empirically shown—in literally hundreds of studies—to be effective, some techniques that are rarely used in REBT and CBT actually work better for individual clients. This seems to be especially true for some clients who resist making good use of most of the "regular" therapies but who, perversely enough, react well to some unpopular therapies that I practically never use with my regular clients. Some of these "irregular treatments"—such as primal therapy—I consider dangerous and harmful. But I have to honestly acknowledge that occasionally they do seem to help clients who have failed with several "good" therapies.

Since this book is mainly about resistant clients, I have therefore gone out of my way to include some techniques that are taken from therapy systems that, on the whole, I do *not* favor. But since they sometimes work with individual clients for whom my favored REBT and CBT methods just don't seem to be effective, I include them in this revised edition of *Overcoming Resistance*. Clients are different and unique—and resistant ones are often more so. I therefore have tried to be unusually open-minded and integrative in this volume. Let us see how my liberalism in this respect works out, along with my (prejudiced) favoring of REBT and CBT treatment methods. This should be an interesting experiment!

SOLUTION-FOCUSED THERAPY

One of the offshoots of a constructivist outlook is solution-focused therapy (S. de Shazer), which has recently become quite popular. Some of its main techniques and tenets overlap with REBT, since it emphasizes clients' choice of methods they can use to help themselves. Thus, it shows them that once they reduce their disturbing and then fall back to their dysfunctional thinking, feeling, and behaving, they can use the techniques that they have created to help themselves before, and find their ways out of their recurring dilemmas. Solution-focused therapy not only emphasizes clients' going back to prior problem-solving but also takes an optimistic rather than a grimly pessimistic view of perceived Adversities. REBT tries to be equally constructivist but also strives for—though it hardly always achieves—what I call an "elegant" therapeutic solution, whereby clients make themselves not only less disturbed, but less disturb*able*. Solution-focused therapy, I shall show later, has its other limitations. But, as I shall keep emphasizing in this book, "elegant" solutions to feeling better and getting better may be available but not actually be used by resisting clients. Therefore, solution-focused therapy may be effectively employed.

RECENT FINDINGS OF EXPERIMENTAL PSYCHOLOGY

Recent findings in experimental psychology are important to development in psychotherapy and seem to at least partially confirm some of the main theories and practices of REBT. Some of them are summarized in four articles in the July 1999 issue of the *American Psychologist* by Bargh and Chartrand (1999), Wegner and Wheatley (1999), Gollwitzer (1999), and Kirsch and Lynn (1999).

First, these articles emphasize the importance of unconscious processes and automaticity in human behaving. Although conscious processes are important, as REBT and constructivism maintain, automatic or environmentally triggered processes are also quite influential. If humans consciously willed all their reacting, they would act inefficiently and probably not survive for very long. Therefore, they are equipped with automatic processes that free their limited attentional capacity. They have goals of staying alive and being reasonably happy but most of their daily life "is driven by unconscious mental processes" (Bargh & Chartrand, 1999, p. 464). Moreover, the process of automation is, itself, automatic.

Freud, of course, brilliantly emphasized the role of unconscious thinking and feeling in human life; however, he overemphasized deeply hidden, repressed unconsciousness. REBT has always stressed that much of our disturbing is unconsciously motivated but that the implicit thinking that creates it is largely just below the conscious level, not deeply repressed, and can be figured out on theoretical grounds, brought to consciousness, and then intentionally changed. But it also holds that conscious control of unconscious behaving requires not mere insight into the fact that implicit philosophizing leads to disturbing feelings and actions, but that this insight will not in itself change behaving. In addition, one had better see that persistent *work and practice* is required to change and keep changing thinking, feeling, and acting. New psychological findings reaffirm REBT's hypothesizing that work and practice at changing one's thoughts, feelings, and behaviors are required to bring unconscious disturbing processes to the surface and to change them several times—until, lo and behold!—they often can be turned into unconscious or automatic self-helping processes.

The new experimental findings highlight the point, which Powers (1999) has also been making for several years, that not only conceiving but also perceiving is the route by which the environment encourages mental activity and emotional and behavioral consequencing. This tends to confirm the REBT finding that Adversity (A) times one's Beliefs (B) creates disturbing Consequences (C). As Bargh and Chartham put it, "Positive or negative evaluations within the current environment play out changes in his or her mood" (1999, p. 473).

What we call will or intention has many unconscious elements and by itself may not change our behavior. What Gollwitzer (1999) calls effective implementation can lead us to commit ourselves to respond to certain situations in a specific manner. When we form intentions of specifically where and how to get started, automatic processes often take over and lead to action. Health-promoting and disturbance-preventing also benefit from implementation intentions.

Gollwitzer also reaffirms REBT's suggested Insight No. 3: "What makes for strong or weak implementation effect? . . . First, the strength of commitment to the formed implementation intention matters. Second, the strength of commitment to the goal for which implementation of intentions are formed. . . . Implementation does not work when goal intentions are weak" (Gollwitzer, 1999, p. 499). This nicely seems to confirm the REBT theory, expressed in the first edition of this book and repeated in this edition, that emotional *force* is often required for thinking, feeling, and behavioral change.

Kirsch and Lynn (1999) cite their own experiments and clinical experience to show how the role of expectancy is most important in creating disturbed and nondisturbed behaviors. Their work has demonstrated that the effectiveness of the therapeutic alliance increases clients' expectancies and intentions and thus helps them. They note that "a variety of different therapeutic approaches either explicitly or implicitly harness the power of expectancies to establish, shape, and fulfill treatment process" (1999, p. 513).

It is good to know that so much work in experimental psychology recently tends to support several REBT theories and practices, which I originally derived from my clinical experiences with many clients.

The growth of Optimistic and Positive Psychology has also been greatly expanded in recent years, and the January 2000 issue of *The*

American Psychologist, edited by Martin E.P. Seligman and Mihaly Csikszentmihalyi (2000) contains sixteen articles summarizing recent studies. I refer to these studies in my book, *Overcoming Destructive Beliefs, Feelings, and Behaviors* (Ellis, 2001b), as well as to the past twenty-five years of research by Ellen Langer (Langer & Moldovenu, 2000); and I show, as I will mention later in this book, how these researches back up some of the major theories of REBT.

MULTICULTURAL ASPECTS OF PSYCHOTHERAPY AND RESISTANCE TO THERAPY

Up until a few years ago, psychotherapy in the United States and most of the Western world was largely monocultural. It was created almost exclusively for fairly well-educated Caucasian clients. But in the 1980s, critics of this one-sided view pointed out that many clients rightly resisted psychological treatment because their therapists were prejudiced against the minority cultures in which these clients were raised and were seeing in them many "abnormalities" and "dysfunctions" that really stemmed from their healthy disagreements with the dominant white culture (*Counseling Psychologist,* 1996; Ivey, Ivey, & Simek-Morgan, 1997; Yeh & Hwang, 2000).

Since this objection to counseling and psychotherapy in the western world makes good sense, multicultural issues have been prominent in the therapeutic literature—and, as a few critics like Weinrach and Thomas (1998) have asserted, too prominent. REBT considers multi-cultural issues very seriously, especially in regard to resistance in therapy, and I shall deal with this question in detail later in this book.

Some of the Basic Principles of Rational Emotive Behavior Therapy (REBT) and Cognitive Behavior Therapy (CBT)

2

Before I proceed, let me emphasize what I clearly said in my first paper on REBT at the Annual Convention of the American Psychological Association in August 1956 (Ellis, 1958) and repeated in *Reason and Emotion in Psychotherapy* in 1962. What we normally call thinking or believing, "aside from consisting of bioelectric charges in the brain cells, and in addition to comprising remembering, learning, problem-solving, and similar psychological processes, also is, and to some extent has to be, sensory, motor, and emotional behavior. Instead, then, of saying, 'Jones thinks about this puzzle,' we should more accurately say, 'Jones perceives-moves-feels-THINKS about this puzzle.' Because, however, Jones' activity in relation to the puzzle may be *largely* focused upon solving it, and only *incidentally* on seeing, manipulating, and emoting about it, we may perhaps emphasize only his thinking.

"Emotion, like thinking and sensori-motor processes, we may define as an exceptionally complex state of human reaction which is integrally related to all the other perception and response processes. It is not *one* thing, but a combination and holistic integration of several seemingly diverse, yet actually closely related, phenomena (Ellis, 1958, p. 35)."

Yes, I clearly said this in 1956. But in developing the ABCs of Rational Emotive Behavior Therapy (REBT) over the years, I formulated A as Activating Events or Adversities, B as Beliefs, and C as emotional and behavioral Consequences of A times B. This may have confused some readers, who interpreted B as pure thinking and forgot that I have always seen it as a focus on believing or thinking, but as also including very important aspects of emotion and behaving. I have

9

since corrected this oversight, especially in my recent books, *Feeling Better, Getting Better, and Staying Better* (Ellis, 2001a) and *Overcoming Destructive Beliefs, Feelings, and Behaviors* (Ellis, 2001b). In these books, I have italicized *Beliefs,* to remind my readers that they also include emotional and behavioral aspects. I shall do the same thing in this book.

This volume will consider many kinds of resistance to psychotherapy and to self-help therapy and will describe how you, as a therapist, can effectively deal with them. It will present many techniques that you (and of course your clients) can use to overcome resistance. Obviously, however, it will favor Rational Emotive Behavior Therapy (REBT) that I started in 1955 and that has developed into Cognitive Behavior Therapy (CBT) in the 1960s and 1970s. Much experience has been gained with these two main forms of therapy in the last half century and many outcome studies have been done showing that, for the most part, they are effective (Hollon & Beck, 1994; Lyons & Woods, 1991).

My emphasis will be on, but not exclusively, a number of cognitive, emotive, and behavioral techniques, and is therefore similar to what Arnold Lazarus calls multimodal therapy (Ellis & Dryden, 1997; Ellis & Harper, 1997; Ellis & MacLaren, 1998; Ellis, Gordon, Neenan, & Palmer, 1998; Kwee & Ellis, 1997).

First, let me explain the ABCs of REBT, which have also largely been adopted in one form or another by some of the most popular variations of CBT.

It is not natural for people, and especially difficult and resistant clients, to subscribe to the ABC's that are used in REBT and in CBT. Practically all people seem to automatically conclude, for the most part, that when an Adversity (A) occurs in their lives and they (usually quickly) experience dysfunctional Consequences (C), that A directly causes C. Perhaps they are biologically prone to do so, because if they make this assumption and quickly try to change A—e.g., try to run away from a lion or try to kill it—they will save their lives and protect their progeny. So they usually resist making what REBT calls the B→C connection—resist seeing that their *Beliefs* (B's) importantly accompany the A's they encounter and therefore contribute strongly to their C's. REBT says, somewhat uniquely, that Adversity (A) accompanied by *Beliefs* (B) about A result in Consequences (C) of emotional-behavioral disturbance. If you practice REBT and CBT, therefore, and you especially want to do so quickly and efficiently, you had better teach yourself and your clients the ABC's of cognitive structuring and restructuring. This normally includes your stressing the following points:

1. As noted above, B's—clients' *Belief* Systems, which are heavily stressed in REBT—practically always include important aspects of emotings and behavings. I shall therefore keep referring to them as italicized *Beliefs* to keep reminding you of their complex nature.

2. Feelings and behaviors, especially disturbed ones, include A's, B's, and C's. People feel and behave, in the final analysis, the way they perceive and think; but they do so within environmental situations. So they'd better, when they feel and act disturbingly, try to see the situation, see their *Beliefs* about it (B's), and observe their emotional and action-oriented Consequences (C's). It may be possible for them to have "purely" biochemical reactions, such as endogenous depression, or take drugs or medication and directly experience feelings. But even this biochemically induced form of disturbance seems to have cognitive-emotional aspects. Thus, clients often have secondary A's, B's, and C's. If they feel depressed (C), they make their depression into a secondary A, "I am unfortunately depressed." Then they easily tell themselves at B, "I *must not* be depressed! It's awful to be depressed!" and they experience the Consequences (C) of depressing themselves *about* their original depression. Or, in the case where they become endogenously depressed (C) they can tell themselves at B, "It's terrible that I have to take medication for my depression. I'm a weakling for having to take it!" Then again at C they may depress themselves about their depression.

3. Have your clients focus on and try to experience the overall emotion that best captures how they feel about an A that they perceive as unfortunate. Especially, collaborate with them to discover unhealthy negative feelings, such as anxietizing, depressing, and raging.

4. Have them recall in detail other situations in which they have felt that and other disturbed emotions.

5. Encourage them to focus on the specific thoughts that evoked their dysfunctional emotions, especially their absolutistic shoulds, oughts, and musts.

6. Have them change their dysfunctional and unhealthy emotions to functional and healthy ones, such as disappointment, sorrow, regret, or annoyance. This is essentially what they do when they use REBT's version of Maxie Maultsby's rational emotive imagery.

7. Have them discover what thoughts they used to create the healthy instead of the unhealthy emotion.

Notice, again, that this focusing technique helps both you and your clients to concentrate on disruptive feelings, thoughts, and behaviors, and then to focus on changing them to more functional thinking, feeling, and behaving. So the focusing itself, though it mainly seems to be cognitive, actually includes emotive and behavioral elements. As I keep noting in this book and my other writings, thoughts, emotions, and actions are integrally and holistically integrated and include all three important aspects of experiencing.

If clients profoundly believe that Activating Events or Adversities (A's) alone cause their feelings and behavings, they will somehow have to change the Adversities in their lives that "make" them disturbed in order to relieve their symptoms. This can sometimes be done, but it gives them little leeway to feel better when they cannot change these A's.

Therefore, for REBT and CBT to be effective, you had better convince clients of the importance of their *Beliefs* and show them that it is quite possible to change them and thereby improve their disturbing Consequences (C's).

Clients may have many negative *Beliefs* that importantly contribute to their dysfunctioning. Although showing them almost any of these B's and how to change them may significantly help, it is almost always more efficient and pervasive to show them a few of their basic or core B's, which often have several subheadings. Thus, when they are bothered by being rejected by their family members, friends, bosses, and even strangers, showing them their conviction that each of these individuals must approve them is therapeutic. But it would perhaps be more helpful to reveal that their dire needing for *all* or *most* significant people's approval is at the core of these specific irrational B's.

If you use REBT theory, you usually can spot one or more of your clients' core IBs quite quickly. Thus, the most common ones to look for are the three basic demands of most self-disturbing people: (a) "I *absolutely must* perform well and be approved by significant others!" (b) "You (other people) *absolutely must* treat me nicely and fairly!" and (c) "Conditions *absolutely must* be the way I want them to be!" These, in turn, are usually accompanied by "If I do poorly and people and conditions treat me badly, (a) I am a pretty *worthless person!* (b) It is *awful* and *terrible!* (c) I *can't stand* it! (d) The world is a rotten place! and (e) It's hopeless! Bad conditions will always exist for me!"

If you look for some of your clients' core Irrational *Beliefs* (IBs), you will usually be able to quickly find them and to start convincing the clients that they are unrealistic, illogical, and self-defeating.

You can usually show your clients that their basic IBs are importantly interactive and interconnected. Thus, their great fears of failing may lead to anxiety about failing in school, work, sex, love, and sports; and their great fear of rejection may lead to anxiety about being disapproved by family, friends, bosses, and strangers.

Try to show your clients—though this is sometimes difficult because it is contrary to common perception—that they rarely have pure thoughts, pure feelings, and pure behaviors. Practically always, their thinking is accompanied by feeling and acting; their emotions are accompanied by thoughts and behaviors; and their behaviors are accompanied by thoughts and feelings. This is the nature of humans, and they think, feel, and act simultaneously or holistically. If your clients understand this and look for the thinking, feeling, and behaving elements when they are "emotionally" disturbed, they will better be able to deal with their dysfunctioning and to ward off future disturbing.

It is useful to show clients that their feelings, no matter how strong, do not prove that something is factual or valid, nor do their thinking and their behaving. If they strongly think that they are a kangaroo, forcefully feel that they are one, and keep hopping around on the furniture as if they were one, none of this proves that they are really a kangaroo! And if they powerfully think, feel, and act as if God or the Devil is directing them, that hardly proves that He or She is.

Are your clients willing and motivated to change their basic Believing-Feeling-Behavings? If not, you can continue to show them the usefulness of doing so, the pains of not changing them, and the possibilities of happiness and self-actualization if they are determined to do so.

Have your clients put enough work and practice into changing their Believing-Feeling-Behavings? Did they largely distract themselves into doing palliative things, like relaxation techniques, and not continuing to use more forceful and longer-lasting methods? Investigate!

Do your clients, particularly your resistant ones, realize that only they can change their Believing-Emoting-Behavings themselves and that no matter how willing you are to do so, you do not have that power? But *they* usually do!

Do your resistant clients have other powerful and abiding *Beliefs*—such as magical convictions—that are interfering with their changing their main IB's? If so, try to find these and point out their incompatibility with the basic changing of their IB's.

Are your difficult clients convinced that they *can't* change and that their plight is hopeless? If so, this one major *Belief* may halt most of their efforts to make progress. Show them that it just won't work!

As Rian McMullin (2000) suggests, your resistant clients may object to your form of therapy and feel that you, as a therapist, are the wrong person for them. If so, you can tell them that they are free to try another therapist or therapy method; and if that doesn't work out, they can choose to come back to you and your methods.

Sometimes, your clients may have hidden agendas that block their working at therapy. Thus, they may hate their mother or their mate who is pushing them to change. Or they may fear that they'll lose their disability payments if they improve. Suspect that some may have these kinds of hidden agendas, and probe for them.

Doing their cognitive, emotive, and behavioral homework is often crucial to help clients change. Check to see if they do any work outside of the therapy session. Emphasize the REBT major insight that only commitment to steady work and practice is likely to lead to change.

I formulated the theory and practice of rational emotive behavior therapy between 1953 and 1955, after I had been practicing psychoanalysis for six years, and finally abandoned it. I thought that it wrongly over-emphasized childhood conditioning as the main source of human disturbance, as did John B. Watson and the radical behaviorists; that it was exceptionally time-consuming and inefficient; that it rightly emphasized people's unconscious wishes and thoughts but exaggerated the frequency of their deep repressions; that it was too passive and nondirective; and that it was antiscientific, in that it invented complicated reasons for and interpretations of people's feelings and behaviors, and then dogmatically foisted them upon clients and patients without empirically looking for evidence to substantiate them—or, according to Occam's razor, looking for simpler and less debatable explanations.

Even while practicing psychoanalysis from 1947 to 1953, I did my best to try to make it more scientific and more effective (Ellis, 1950, 1956), but I signally failed. My critiques of it were enthusiastically accepted by many therapists who already were skeptical of psychoanalysis, but made practically no inroads on the psychoanalytic establishment. So between 1953 and 1955 I did a comprehensive study of all the major techniques of therapy which then existed (Ellis, 1955a, 1955b) and I also went back to re-reading philosophy, which had been my hobby since the age of 16, to rediscover what philosophers had said that would be useful to psychotherapy.

As a result of this research, I came up with REBT by the end of 1954 and started practicing it in January 1955. Although from the start it included many emotive-evocative and behavioral methods—some of which I had been using since I began to do psychotherapy and sex therapy in 1943—its theory was primarily cognitive and would have been *called,* today, constructivist, as George Kelly phrased it as early as 1955. I derived this theory mainly from philosophers, particularly from Epictetus (1890) who two thousand years ago said very clearly, "People are not disturbed by the events that happen to them but by their view of these events." Other philosophers, such as Gautama Buddha, Epicurus, the Greek stoics before Epictetus, Seneca, and Marcus Aurelius, said essentially the same thing; and in modern times,

Bertrand Russell, Martin Heidegger, Jean Paul Sartre, and many others voiced similar views. Humans, they all agreed, were not merely biological or socially conditioned creatures that had little choice about regulating their own behavior. Instead, to a considerable degree they had some degree of free will or agency and they could choose their own thoughts, feelings, and behaviors—and then could later rechoose or change them.

Following this constructivist line of thinking, I formulated in 1955 the now somewhat famous ABC's of emotional disturbance and its treatment. This theory said that practically all humans were born and reared with the tendency to desire to be happy by themselves, with other people, with a few intimates, educationally, vocationally, and recreationally; and when their main desires were blocked or thwarted, they had the choice of making themselves healthfully disappointed, sorry, and frustrated, and thus encouraging themselves to try harder to get what they wanted or avoid getting what they did not want. Or else they had the choice of making themselves anxious, depressed, enraged, or self-pitying, which were unhealthy or self-defeating feelings in that they mainly interfered with the fulfillment of their desires.

This, I think, was a unique differentiation in the field of psychotherapy—which until that time held that practically all genuine feelings were good and should be faced and released—then people would really get what they wanted and would not deny or repress their emotions. REBT takes a somewhat different view: namely, that negative feelings that people have when their desires are blocked can be healthy and useful or unhealthy and self-defeating—and that it is important that they distinguish between these two kinds of negative feelings, minimize their unhealthy ones and maximize the healthy ones. Then they will disturb themselves relatively little. REBT, more than the other Cognitive Behavior Therapies, particularly differentiates healthy negative feelings, such as concern, sorrow, regret, frustration, and annoyance from unhealthy or destructive feelings, such as panic, depression, and rage. It even considers some profoundly negative feelings, such as intense grief over the death of a loved one, healthy, as long as it is not accompanied by depression (Malkinson & Ellis, 2001). It does not oppose human feelings—but only questions those that tend to be self- and society-defeating.

REBT helps people benefit from therapy by showing them fairly quickly that when they do not get their desires fulfilled at point A (Activating Event or Adversity), and when they experience unhealthy negative feelings such as anxiety and depression at point C (Consequence), it is not mainly A (Adversity) that causes or leads to C (Consequence of disturbed feelings). Rather, it is largely B, their *Beliefs* about A. To be sure, A (Adversity) significantly contributes to their disturbed feelings, but it does not directly cause or create them, as psychoanalysts and behaviorists often contend.

The REBT theory of disturbance holds, therefore, that A x B = C. People in large part create their own neurotic emotions and behaviors not merely by perceiving the A's (Adversities) in their lives, but by viewing them in a self-defeating, irrational manner. When they have rational or self-helping *Beliefs* (B's) they tend to have healthy feelings and behaviors at point C (Consequences); and when they have unhealthy feelings and behaviors about A's (Adversities) they tend to have irrational or unhealthy *Beliefs*. I listed eleven of their main Irrational *Beliefs* (IB's) in my first paper on REBT at the American Psychological Association in Chicago in August 1956 (Ellis, 1958), then kept expanding on them until I described about 50 common Irrational Beliefs.

In the meantime, after practicing REBT for a year, I took a closer look at people's irrational beliefs that presumably helped to make them emotionally and behaviorally disturbed about what happened to them. I came up with a concise summary of them, which I partially derived from Karen Horney (1950), who had brilliantly noted "the tyranny of the shoulds." I gave further thought—and clinical experimentation—to her suggestion and saw that just about all the Irrational *Beliefs* that people invented about the adversities of their lives could be placed under three main headings—all of them absolutistic or unconditional musts:

1. "I would not only prefer to perform well at tasks that I deem important and win the approval of significant others, but I *absolutely must* do so! Otherwise it is *awful* and I am an ineffective, worthless individual who will always fail and be rejected by important others!" This Irrational *Belief,* when strongly held, leads to anxiety, depression, self-damning, and feelings of worthlessness.

2. "I would not only prefer to have people treat me kindly, considerately, and fairly, but *they absolutely must do so* at all times! Otherwise, it is *terrible* and they are rotten *people* who should be severely punished for their iniquity." This Irrational *Belief,* especially when strongly held, leads to anger, rage, fighting, feuds, war, and genocide.

3. "The conditions under which I live should not only be preferably easy, good, and enjoyable, but *they absolutely have to* be this way at all times! Otherwise, it is *horrible, I can't stand* it, and the world is a *rotten place* in which it is too difficult for me to live!"

This Irrational *Belief* produces low frustration tolerance, depression, whinyness, and inefficiency in changing what one does not like about external conditions.

I realized that although people may have hundreds of IB's that mightily contribute to their disturbed feelings and behaviors, if they escalated their main preferences into absolutistic demands, they were also capable of changing them back into preferences—and thereby minimizing their disturbances.

Thus, if people *want* to do well at, say, tennis, at their job, or at winning the love of a partner, and they foolishly make themselves believe, "Because I very much want to achieve this goal and would be extremely deprived without it, I *absolutely must, no matter what,* achieve what I want!", then they are in emotional trouble, for there is no reason why they *must* get what they want. They easily may not get it at all, or they may get it and then lose it: they do not have the power to actualize their demands under all conditions at all times. They are not "crazy" for *desiring* to achieve their aims, but rather for insisting that it is *necessary* that they achieve them.

I was not, of course, the first theorist to see that raising your preferences, no matter how "normal" they may be, into arrant and arrogant demands, almost inevitably causes people to anxietize about the real possibility of *not* achieving them and to depress themselves after they fail to get them. Karen Horney observed this before me; and Gautama Buddha strongly seemed to note it when he saw, when he became enlightened, that desires don't *have to be* fulfilled. Desires, he said, were not *needs*. Job sort of saw this and was able to tolerate, although not to like, many severe frustrations. The Stoics definitely realized it in the fourth century B.C. However, none of these thinkers were very precise about what were people's common musts and what they had better do to change them to healthy *preferences*.

After using REBT for a year, I observed that even "normal" people frequently raise their strong preferences into absolutistic musts, and that the stronger their preferences are, the more likely they are to make them into dire "necessities." Why? No one really knows; but we can suspect that in the early days of human history, this escalation had some survival value. Thus, if primitive people told themselves, "I *must* get the hell away from this menacing tiger!" instead of, "I suppose it would be *highly preferable* if I did," they would be more likely to survive and have more progeny. Demanding instead of merely preferring that you do well and be approved by other people probably has its evolutionary advantages.

Even today *musts* often have distinct benefits. For if you think you *have to* win the ball game, get a good job, or succeed with a marital partner, you may well be encouraged to work harder than if you merely *preferred* to achieve these goals. Actually, you have two kinds of demanding or musturbating and they are quite different!

You can use a *conditional* must: "I must get this good job, else I will be disadvantaged and that would be unfortunate. So I'd better do my best to get it." This is a healthy, productive must because it accords with social reality and helps you do as well as you can to get the job.

Or you can use an *unconditional, absolutistic* must: "I absolutely must get this job—or else, if I don't, it's *awful,* I'll never get *any* good job, and it will prove that I am an incompetent, worthless individual." This is an unhealthy, unproductive *must* because it will usually make you anxietize and often make yourself *less* effective at getting the job you want.

Conditional musts, in other words, show you realistically what results you will get if you don't get what you think you must—that is, hassles, deprivations, or fewer rewards. Unconditional, absolutistic musts, on the other hand, strongly imply that unless you get what you think you must, you will *never* get what you want, that it is *totally* bad if you never get it, that you are an *inadequate, worthless individual* for not achieving what you "must" achieve, and that you will never be capable of achieving what you demand.

Conditional musts keep you in touch with the rewards and disadvantages of the social group in which you live, and therefore motivate you to achieve the fulfillment of your desires. They are generalizations about the real world, which are largely accurate and therefore will usually aid you.

Unconditional musts, however, lead to unrealistic overgeneralizations which, as Alfred Korzybski showed, often defeat you and render you "unsane." For you can't logically jump from "Because I failed to get a good job this time, perhaps because I went about it poorly" to "I'll *always* fail to get a good job." You also cannot logically jump from "Because the interviewers did not view me as having the competence or characteristics to do this job" to "I *therefore* am an *incompetent person* and will *never* be able to get a good job." This kind of overgeneralization, as Korzybski said, is (a) unrealistic, (b) illogical, and (c) self-defeating. By making your strong desires into "necessities" you tend to sabotage rather than aid in the achievement of your goals.

In the early days of REBT I realized that preference sentences included, or at least implied, a *but.* Thus: "I would like very much to get this job, and will do my best to go get it, *but* I don't *have to* get it, and will merely be distinctly inconvenienced if I don't." Unconditional "musturbatory" statements, however, are inflexible and have no *buts.*

For example: "I *absolutely must* get this job that I am applying for. There is no excuse whatever for my failing to get it. Therefore, if I don't do what I must do and get it, it is *awful* and I am *no good!*" As I have

Absolutistic musts include two self-defeating forms of overgeneralization. First: "It is *awful* if I don't get what I absolutely must!" As I have shown in many of my writings, awfulizing is a foolish and self-defeating overgeneralization. It tends to mean, "Not only is it highly inconvenient for me if I don't get what I want—or do get what I don't want—but it is *totally inconvenient*, as inconvenient as it could *possibly be.*" These are all extreme statements, which you may *believe* to be true, but which are unrealistic exaggerations.

Second, if you try to get what you want and think, "I *absolutely must* get it" and then fail to obtain it, you may easily conclude that you are an *inadequate person* who can *never* succeed, and who will hereafter be deprived of what you want. Korzybski called this "the *is* of identity"—the irrational belief that I *am,* and will *be* for all time, what I *do.* If I *act* badly I am a *bad person;* and if I act *well* I am a *good person.* Actually, you are a person who acts badly *this time*—but has a good chance of changing and acting better *in the future.* You are also a person who acts well this time—but who is highly likely to behave badly in the future—because you are a highly fallible and imperfect person. All humans, as far as we know, are quite fallible and imperfect!

Partly from using the theories of philosophers, and partly from observing that the majority of my clients kept escalating their normal wishes and preferences into absolutistic musts and demands, I formulated the teachings of REBT. These, in a word, amount to showing clients that whenever they panic, depress, or anger themselves, they had better acknowledge that Adversities (A's) *contribute* to their disturbances but do not literally *create them;* and realize that their *Belief Systems* (B's) are also importantly connected with their disturbing Consequences (C's). Once they acknowledge these points, they can then go on to look intensively at their B's, find the absolutistic, dogmatic musts that they almost invariably seem to include in their thinking when they disturb themselves. Then they can Dispute (D) these musts realistically, logically, and heuristically; and act against them emotionally and behaviorally, until they change them back into strong preferences. Whatever they wish and prefer is usually okay—as long as they do not rigidly and unconditionally insist that they must have what they desire and they must not have what they detest—or else it is *awful* and *horrible* and they are *worthless individuals* for not achieving what they presumably must.

I stated the above both in my first REBT paper in 1956 and in my first book for professionals on REBT, *Reason and Emotion in Psychotherapy*

(Ellis, 1962). For by then I had learned from psychological findings that thinking, feeling, and behaving are not disparate processes, but are actually holistically intertwined. Reread the first two paragraphs of Chapter 2 to see what I said about this in 1956.

My description of the integration of thoughts, feelings, and behaviors in 1956 I now hold more than ever. As I tell my clients and the professionals I train, there really is no such thing as a pure thought, a pure feeling, or a pure action. We give these processes different names, but we forget that they all include important elements of the other two. Thus, when an Adversity occurs in our life, we perceive it and evaluate it, else we would not be able to react to it at all. We may not clearly or consciously perceive it and evaluate it—but on some level we do so. What is more, we perceive it and assess it in a prejudiced manner—in the light of previous experiences with it, the feelings that we have acquired about it, and the actions we have taken before with stimuli of this kind. We also have biological or innate tendencies to react in certain ways to this Adversity—such as innate tendencies to think and feel that it will distinctly harm us (if it is a fall from a height) or will harm us only slightly (if it is a slight bit of tripping while dancing). So we perceive and assess Adversities in a highly prejudiced manner, and our prejudices include innate and learned thinking, emotional, and behavioral aspects. We do not merely see and think about this Adversity. Our perceptions and our thoughts are complex processes that have important feeling and behavioral elements.

Once we assess an Adversity we quickly have a pleasant or unpleasant feeling—or a combination of both kinds of feelings. When we assess a fall from a tree as "bad" or "dangerous," we have a negative feeling (such as displeasure or fear) and when we assess it as "adventurous" and "exciting," we have a positive feeling (such as pleasure or curiosity). But our negative feelings—"This fall is bad! I hate this fall from a tree!"—include thoughts, such as "This is a dangerous fall. It might really cripple me!" and lead to healthy behaviors, such as exploring to see if we have any broken bones, getting up, and calling for help, as well as unhealthy feelings of horror.

The point I am making is that when any Adversity occurs, we react *emotionally* (e.g., with fear or anger) and *behaviorally* (approaching it and trying to deal with it or retreating and trying to remove it). Since our perceiving and thinking about the Adversity lead to our feelings and actions about it, my original formulation of A (Adversity) times B *(Beliefs)* equals C (Consequences) seems to be a simple and effective formula. Actually, however, it is somewhat misleading. As I have just noted, our thoughts, feelings, and actions are all complex and to a considerable degree include cognitive, emotional, and behavioral elements.

Even the stimuli that we encounter—the Adversities of our lives—do not just exist as encapsulated events in the outside world, but usually exist in our prior history—which has many cognitive, emotional, and behavioral aspects. Our fall from the tree occurs in the context of prior falls, our witnessing other people fall from trees, our pains and hurts when we have fallen before, the actions that were taken when we fell, and how others reacted to our previous falls. In other words, the Adversity that happened to us exists in the *context* of our history, our memory of that history, our previous feelings and behaviors about that history, and many other factors of which we may or may not be aware. Even if an apple falls from a tree it has a prior history and context—for example, it is a large or small apple, it is a strong or weak one, it falls on grass or on stones. So it has some history and context. However, we are humans, not objects. Therefore we bring to any Activating Event or Adversity a whole host of *historical* and *contextual* factors; and just about all these factors include perceptions, thoughts, feelings, and behaviors.

A (Adversity) and B (Beliefs about the adversity) are both complex; and B is far more complex than I first described it, and as other ancient and modern thinkers have written about it. Again, like all thinking and cognitive processes, it has important intrinsic emotional and behavioral elements.

Take a fairly simple instance of the ABC's of disturbance. You try to pass an important test and you actually fail it—so the A (Adversity) consists of your having the goal of passing the test and the Consequence (C) is actually failing to reach that goal.

At B you usually hold two types of beliefs about failing the test. Your *rational Beliefs* (RBs) may include, "I don't like failing this test, it may prevent me from achieving my goals. I strongly wish I had passed it, and it's too bad that I didn't, but it's not the end of the world, and I can always try to pass it next time, and at the very worst I'll be inconvenienced but not destroyed." These preferential *Beliefs* describe reality, and will likely give you the Consequences (C) of feeling healthily sorry and disappointed, and then behaving functionally by preparing to study harder for the next test that you take.

If, however, you feel very upset about failing this test and you phobically avoid all important tests for most of your life, your Adversity (A) remains the same—failing the test—but your B's and C's are quite different. At B you may irrationally and demandingly conclude, "I *absolutely must not* have failed this test! I'm a total idiot for failing it! I'll never be able to pass a test like that again, so I might as well give up and stop trying!" This set of Irrational *Beliefs* (IB's) will very likely produce the Consequence (C) of your anxietizing, depressing, and phobically withdrawing from test-taking. In other words, you have a choice, mainly at B (your *Belief* System) of reacting healthily and undisturbedly to A, the failed test, or reacting unhealthily and distressingly to it.

True—but a little too simple. For B not only includes your cognitions about A, but several emotional and behavioral processes. When you tell yourself, "I absolutely should not have failed this test. I'm a total idiot for failing it!" you are really strongly desiring to pass the test, powerfully thinking you're an absolute idiot for failing it, and greatly overgeneralizing about your idiotic behavior and thus making yourself into an "absolute idiot." You have not merely cognitions about failing the test, you have what Abelson (1963) called "hot" cognitions. Your cognitions have a pronounced emotional as well as a cognitive quality. In fact, we could say that whenever you evaluate something as "good" or "bad" for you, you are *emotionally* assessing what is happening in your life, and not merely cognitively assessing it. Your evaluations of the "good" and "bad" things that happen to you are, on some level or other, emotional assessments. They include *feelings*.

By the same token, when you fail an important test and tell yourself, "I'm a total idiot for failing it! I'll never be able to pass a test like that again, so I might as well give up and stop trying to pass any tests!" you are indeed stating a cognition—and, as I said before, a *strong* cognition. But you are also, with this cognition, having a definite action-tendency. Your cognition is behavioral as well as cognitive. You are predicting how you will *act* in the future regarding test-taking. Your thought readies you for withdrawal and inaction—which are, of course, behavioral responses.

From what I have just said, it would appear that the cognitions or *Beliefs* which encourage you to anxietize and depress yourself about failing an important test and also lead you to phobicize about and withdraw from future test-taking, not only particularly create emotions and behaviors—as the theory of REBT holds—but they also actually include distinct emotional and behavioral elements. This tends to confirm the original REBT theory, postulated by me in 1956, that thinking, feeling, and behaving are by no means disparate or pure aspects of human functioning. They are all complex processes that significantly include each other. Moreover, the stimuli that we humans attend to— the Activating Events of our lives—themselves are never pure or "objective." Since we come to these stimuli with goals, values, and desires—particularly the desire to keep living and to be reasonably happy during our existence—they are not really value-free but are approached in a prejudiced manner that makes them "good" or "bad" stimuli. Failing an important test, for example, is only "bad" because our goal is to pass it. It is not "objectively" or "factually" bad for all people at all times under all conditions. Someone who really doesn't want to be an accountant but would rather be an artist may not find failing a CPA exam "bad" but may consider it "good."

What I have just said to some degree supports the postmodern and social constructivist position that absolute truth (reality) never really exists, because we also always view so-called reality in a prejudiced, subjective way. This does not mean that we have to take a completely radical relativistic view and say that there is *no* reality and that we cannot really perceive anything *at all*. Absolute reality may not exist—or at least, as Kant pointed out, we cannot absolutely prove it. But *social* reality—the idea that we are humans who live with other humans and *had better* establish some laws and rules which will probably help us to live more successfully with them—does seem to exist and can be seen with some degree of probability. But not certainty!

What I more fully recognize now is that in my previous REBT formulations, I did not give sufficient emphasis to the "hotness" or "coolness" of our cognitions. When Adversities occur in our lives we indeed may have Rational *Beliefs* that are preferential and flexible, and we may have Irrational *Beliefs* that help us behave unhealthily and anxietize and depress ourselves. But what we call our preferential *Beliefs* are not merely cool cognitions or "objective" assessments of Adversities. Instead, they are warm or hot Beliefs; and as such they include emotional and behavioral elements. What I said in 1956 seems truer than ever: When faced with Activating Events that favor or disfavor us, we think about them and assess them, but we think about them in relation to our goals and desires. Since goals and desires are, almost by definition, emotional, behavioral, and cognitive, our assessment of our being blocked or thwarted also is cognitive, emotional, and behavioral.

Why do I sometimes use the term Believing-Emoting-Behavings to describe the B's in the ABC's model? To show that feeling and acting are quite involved in believing. But since this is a somewhat awkward term, in this book again I shall usually employ the italicized terms *Believings* or *Beliefs* to emphasize that they include all three of the thinking-feeling-acting components.

In accordance with not viewing the B's in REBT as pure cognitions, I shall try in this book to integrate what I have previously called REBT cognitive techniques with their emotional and behavioral aspects. When I use the Disputing of Irrational *Beliefs* and other cognitive methods of REBT, I shall also try to show their emotive and behavioral aspects. When I describe REBT emotive techniques, I shall simultaneously try to include their cognitive and behavioral aspects. When I describe REBT behavioral methods, I shall also emphasize their cognitive and emotive aspects. I shall try to do the same thing with the non-REBT techniques that I describe. When I refer to using some of the techniques of Gestalt therapy or Rogerian therapy with people who resist therapy, I shall try to show how they can be used in combination with REBT behavioral and cognitive methods as well as those usually recommended by other systems. Thus this book will focus strongly on the integrated use of REBT and some other popular therapy methods, and will fairly consistently show how all these methods, even those that have what I consider some irrational aspects, can be used with clients who refuse to use some of the more "rational" aspects of therapy that REBT normally favors.

I shall also show how the elegant methods of REBT are highly preferable in helping clients not only *feel* better but also *get* better in a profound philosophic sense. But when, for one reason or another, these more "elegant" methods do not work, less elegant (or even "irrational") techniques of psychotherapy may be the only ones that are effective. I shall show how these can be used along with some of the best methods of REBT (Ellis, 2001a, 2001b).

I believe that this second edition of *Overcoming Resistance* will show significant differences from the first edition in many respects. It is not that it abandons some of the original principles of REBT, but rather adds to and expands upon them. Let us see how this works out!

Common Forms of Resistance 3

Resistance to personality change has been observed for many years by philosophers and more recently, by Freud and other psychotherapists who followed him. Various writers give different definitions of resistance, but I personally like Turkat and Meyers' (1982, p. 158) definition: "Resistance is client behavior that the therapist labels anti-therapeutic." Albeit a little too simple, this definition also seems realistic. I shall devote this chapter to examining the main kinds of resistance, in what ways they usually arise, and how you can help overcome these resistances in your clients.

HEALTHY AND "NORMAL" RESISTANCE

Clients sometimes healthfully resist change, with some amount of justification; for example, when they feel that their therapist mistakenly see them as having "unconscious" motives (such as repressed hostility for their parents) that they don't really have. Rather than allow themselves be led up the garden path, these clients refuse to accept "discoveries" and interpretations about them, and healthfully resist or flee from treatment. According to the ABC theory of REBT, these clients often *Believe*, "My therapist thinks that I have strong repressed feelings of hatred for my mother, but I don't agree with this interpretation. Too bad that he is wrong, but I cannot always expect my therapist to be right." The client thus rationally disagrees with the therapist, and is not disturbedly fighting her and rebelling against her. In disagreeing with the therapist, the client is healthfully resisting what may well be poor therapy. In such an instance, the one who has the real problem—and is resisting doing effective treatment—may be the therapist! This kind of healthy resistance to specific kinds of interpretations that the therapist tries to impose on the client is probably common, and may prevent therapists from actually harming clients—who, we might say—escape in the nick of time!

RESISTANCE THAT IS "NATURAL"
TO THE HUMAN CONDITION

As I shall contend throughout this book, resistance that stems from clients largely refusing to change their dysfunctional behavior is exceptionally common and may be a strong part of the human condition. As therapists, we preferably should study not only why so many clients who spend considerable time and money in therapy resist changing themselves, but also why many people, inside and outside psychotherapy, actually *do* modify themselves. Thoroughgoing self-modifying is exceptionally difficult for most people much of the time. When it does occur, it often stems from special motivating conditions, such as the following:

1. Many people are so handicapped and miserable because of their disturbing of themselves—e.g., disabled alcoholics—that they are motivated by their sad condition to work hard at self-changing efforts.
2. Some people actually change for the wrong reasons—for example, to prove how superior and noble they are or to spite relatives and friends whom they hate.
3. Some people make a hobby of and are vitally absorbed in growing and changing and devote a large part of their lives to working—sometimes very creatively—at this pursuit.
4. Some self-disturbing individuals devote themselves to membership in change-oriented groups or ideologies, such as self-help groups, cults, or religions.
5. Some people quite sanely and rationally recognize that making themselves disturbing—e.g., addicting themselves to smoking or drinking—is just too painful and self-defeating, especially in the long run. They therefore decide that they had better forcefully work at improving their self-distressing.
6. Some people easily and enjoyably take to the adventure and work of changing themselves and therefore consistently work hard at and have relatively little difficulty changing.

On the other hand, almost the whole history of personality changing shows that it is quite difficult to start and to maintain it, and that without special incentives and motivations, people will rarely do so; or else do so for a while and then fall back to their previous troubling of themselves (Alway, 1999; Ellis, 1976; Prochaska, DiClemente, & Norcross, 1992).

We can realistically say that with the exception of a few individuals who decide to change and then find it rather easy to do so, the great majority of people find it difficult to change and to stay changed. When they actually restyle themselves, they seem to be saying several Rational *Beliefs,* such as, "I wish that changing myself and overcoming my personality problems were easier than it seems to be, but unfortunately it isn't. However, no matter how hard change is, prolonging my disturbing feelings and behaviors is highly self-defeating: therefore, I'd better work really hard to overcome them!" These Rational Beliefs will help people to resist resisting change. They will also help them go back to the drawing board if they relapse and keep working at modifying their dysfunctional thoughts, feelings, and behaving.

In addition to these rational convictions and actions, however, many clients frequently—and, in a statistical sense, normally—have several Irrational *Beliefs* that result in their resisting changing. Although these are indeed ineffective and self-defeating, it is extremely difficult for most people who want to change to relinquish them. They include:

1. "It's not only hard for me to change, but it's *too* hard! It absolutely *should not be* that hard! How awful! I guess I'd better give up trying to do so!"
2. "To try to change myself and *fail* at making this change would be horrible! I *must not* fail! I couldn't stand it—it would really prove what an inadequate person I am. So I'd better not risk this potential failure, and instead simply give up trying to change."
3. "The people with whom I closely associate—such as my parents, my mate, or my employer—must see how hard it is for me to change and should definitely be more helpful! How terrible that they don't! I'll be darned if I'm going to change for such rotten and inconsiderate people!"

In other words, what may be called people's normal resistance to change tends to include the three major Irrational *Beliefs* that also partly cause their emotional and behavioral upsetness. These *Beliefs,* once again, are:

1. "I must do well at the important projects I undertake; if not, I am an inadequate person!"
2. "You must aid me and take care of me when I want you to do so; if not, you are no good!"
3. "Conditions must be easy for me and I must get what I want without too much difficulty and effort; if not, life is awful and I must be miserable."

When people resist changing in the course of psychotherapy or on their own, they commonly have various forms of these three irrationalities

(Leahy, 2001). Very frequently, they have the third one, which leads to low frustration tolerance. They decide to change, are determined to do so, and may even have begun the process, but then find it very difficult. When they view this difficulty as being too hard and too much to undertake, they will likely decrease or discontinue their change efforts, whether in the context of psychotherapy or self-help.

I want to emphasize again that low frustration tolerance (LFT) is one of the most common instigators of people's emotional disturbing. Forms of it are ubiquitous: people procrastinate on tasks and miss important deadlines; they voluntarily start a project and then give it up when they encounter snags; they seek medical advice and then refuse to abide by it; and fail to start or persist in numerous other beneficial aspects of everyday life. LFT is even frequent when people come up against relatively easy and simple problems, such as doing their homework for a course that they are enjoying. It is hardly surprising that it rears its ugly head when they are confronted with a much more complicated and difficult problem, such as changing some of their habitual or disturbing thinking, feeling, and behaving (Ellis, 1979, 1980; Leahy, 2001).

RESISTANCE RESULTING FROM SEVERE EMOTIONAL DISTURBANCE

While virtually all individuals who try to make basic changes in their disturbed thinking, feeling, and behaving frequently resist doing so to some degree, clients who are severely emotionally disturbed have an even stronger tendency to resist change. Therapists often use the word "impasse" to describe the situation that arises when a client is in therapy for several years and seems to be working at it and still makes little progress. Many of these clients are probably exceptionally disturbed individuals, often psychotic or hampered by severe personality disorders. Because of their biological and other limitations they can be expected to benefit, if at all, only from prolonged therapy. When you are at an impasse with one of these clients you may be mistakenly viewing them as what I call "nice neurotics" instead of personality disordered individuals, which would be a more accurate diagnosis.

My long clinical experience as well as my study of the therapeutic literature has shown me that clients with severe personality disorders, such as borderline personality disorder, by their very nature seem to resist any kind of short-term treatment. They are slow learners, who have been born and reared in rigid cognitive and emotional boxes. They have great difficulty learning to change, no matter what kind of therapy they undertake. In my opinion, they have strong biological as well as social learning tendencies to be the way they are—and these include their strong resistance to change and their requiring, in most instances, fairly long-term treatment (Ellis, 2000, 2001a, 2001b; Cloninger, 2000).

EXTREME LOW FRUSTRATION TOLERANCE

I mentioned above that low frustration tolerance, or horror of discomfort, seems to be an important element in normal resistance. If people were able to decide to change and then easily follow up their decision, they would often do so. But for various reasons they find it difficult to change, and therefore easily give up. Some clients have abysmally low frustration tolerance, which strongly interferes with their making changes, no matter how desirous they are of doing so. As soon as they find the going to be rough, and especially if the therapist works out with them regular homework assignments, they fail to follow the advice that they are paying for. They often agree fully with this advice and enthusiastically say that they are going to follow it, but at the next session, they haven't done what they agreed to do.

The main Irrational Beliefs that clients hold that lead to their low frustration tolerance or discomfort disturbance are:

1. "It's *too* hard to change. It shouldn't be so hard. How awful that I have to go through this pain in order to get any therapeutic gain! Screw it, I won't do it!"
2. "I *can't bear* the discomfort of doing my homework, even though I've agreed with my therapist that it will help me move toward my goals. I'll put it off until I feel more like doing it; or maybe just ignore it."
3. "Life *should be* easier than it is! It's *horrible* when I have to do real work and keep at it persistently to change myself!"

As I shall show later, REBT is expecially interested in exploring this kind of low frustration tolerance, in which clients strongly resist the therapy that they agree to follow, and then actively disputes the Irrational *Beliefs* that fuel their LFT.

FEAR OF DISCLOSURE AND SHAME

One of the most prevalent forms of resistance stems from clients' fear of disclosure. They find it uncomfortable to talk about themselves, to give the gory details of some of the "shameful" situations they got themselves into, and find it "too" hard to confess these thoughts, feelings, and actions, even to a therapist. They therefore resist being open in therapy and getting at the source of some of their most disturbing problems. Many psychodynamicaly oriented therapists insist that clients' resistance consists largely of their holding back deeply unconscious materials. In contrast, REBT and CBT hold that clients who resist therapy because they are afraid to reveal their "shameful" thoughts and feelings usually are aware of these feelings, or else have them just below their level of consciousness in what Freud originally called their "preconscious" minds.

REBT hypothesizes that clients who resist revealing "shameful" acts are usually telling themselves something like:

1. "This act is terrible and blameworthy."
2. "Even my therapist would put me down if she knew that I committed it."
3. "She is right in despising me, for I absolutely *should not* have committed that bad act and am a despicable person for having done it."

In other words, these clients are demanding that they *should not* and *must not* have bad thoughts, feelings, or actions; and that by bringing them out into the open, they will be reminded of the fact that they are worthless individuals and their therapist will also see them as worthless. As I shall show later, by teaching clients not to damn themselves for anything they do, and thereby to acquire unconditional self-acceptance (USA), REBT tackles this kind of resistance early in therapy.

RESISTANCE STEMMING FROM FEELINGS OF HOPELESSNESS

A number of clients resist therapeutic change because they strongly feel that they are unable to modify their disturbed behavior—that they are *hopeless* and *unable* to change (Leahy, 2001). Especially when change comes slowly, or they change but go back to their old dysfunctional behaviors, they irrationally overgeneralize. They tell themselves, "Since I have such difficulty changing, and since I fell back even when I made some progress, I'll *never* be able to change. So what's the use of my trying any longer to improve my depression! I've had it so long and worked so hard to give it up that I might as well face the fact that it is impossible!"

Feelings of hopelessness arise particularly from what REBT calls "secondary disturbance." On the primary level, the individual tells himself that because he must succeed at some performance and failed to do so, he is a completely inadequate individual. As a result of this irrational thinking, he feels severely depressed. But his depression itself constitutes a "poor performance." So he then tells himself, "I *must not* be depressed—it's *awful!* I'm *no good* for being depressed!" He then becomes severely depressed about his depression. This secondary symptom often leads to even more disturbance than his primary one, and he becomes so preoccupied with it that he is then unable to get back to dealing with his primary disturbance. This depression about his depression leads to more and more irrational thinking, and he believes more strongly than ever that he will never be able to get rid of his depression. The result is a feeling of hopelessness.

REBT specializes in showing clients that they very often have secondary symptoms about their primary symptoms, and that if they acknowledge that they have these, and forcefully dispute and minimize them, they will find it much easier to get back to their primary disturbances and deal with them. It thereby works against their making themselves feel hopeless about changing.

RESISTANCE MOTIVATED BY SELF-PUNISHMENT

Many psychodynamically oriented therapists held that clients resist changing themselves because they are so guilty and ashamed about their deficiencies that they think they are unworthy of changing and having a good life. I have rarely found this to be the case with "nice neurotics," but it is more often true of those who suffer from psychosis or severe personality disorders. They are prone to beating themselves so severely for their shortcomings that they may tell themselves, "Because I have done terrible things that I *absolutely should not* have perpetrated, I am a thoroughly worthless individual who does not deserve to be happy, but only to suffer."

REBT particularly combats this form of self-punishment in clients. It teaches unconditional self-acceptance (USA) to practically all clients to help them be minimally disturbed, a process I shall later discuss in detail.

PESSIMISM, DEPRESSIVE OUTLOOK, AND LACK OF RISK-TAKING

Leahy (2001), following Beck and Emery (1985) and other writers on depression and anxiety, theorizes that many resistant clients aim much more to minimize their risks than to healthily maximize their satisfactions because they are hypersensitive to loss and failure. They pessimistically view their present and future lives, and are deathly afraid to change for the better, for fear that it will inevitably be followed by "terrible" losses and failures. They are almost allergic to unconditional self-acceptance (USA) and continually rate their personhood as "bad" if they behave "badly." Therefore, they "safely" avoid risks that may lead to enjoyment (which they minimize) but that may also lead to self-damning (which they maximize).

Some of these pessimists, Leahy (2001) points out, may also be addicted to self-consistency. They see that their depressed and anxious self is what they *are*. They would not feel like "themselves" if they changed. So they "comfortably" and "safely" keep it—at all costs! Ziegler and Hawley (2000) found that on a Pessimistic Explanatory Style Test higher-scoring subjects also scored higher on overall irrational thinking and low frustration tolerance, thus providing support for REBT's theory of personality.

PERFECTION AND GRANDIOSITY

I highlighted the need for perfectionism and grandiosity when I first wrote about REBT (Ellis, 1957/1975, 1958, 1962). Many people strive to be perfect (i.e., superhuman) in order to accept themselves as worthy beings. But since perfect human behavior is just about impossible, they damn themselves for not achieving it, and then often desperately try even harder to achieve it—a common vicious cycle.

Perfectionists find change—with its hazards and imperfections—risky, and frequently avoid it (Ellis, 2001b; Flett & Hewett, 2002). Yet they fear to give it up, lest they relegate themselves to a world of all-or-nothing nobodies (Leahy, 2001). So they continue to hang onto their unrealistic goals while actually, mostly unconsciously, withdrawing from the risks of self-change. It has also been found that cognitive restructuring that interrupts perfectionism seems to reduce this kind of dysfunctional resistance to change.

RESISTANCE MOTIVATED BY FEAR
OF CHANGE OR "FEAR OF SUCCESS"

Psychoanalysts from Freud onward have held that resistance often stems from fear of change, from fear of the future, or from fear of success. This is probably correct, in that many self-disturbing individuals have a pronounced need for safety and certainty. Therefore, even though their symptoms are creating great discomfort, they are "familiar" with these feelings and behaviors and are afraid that if they give them up, they may experience even greater discomfort. So, they prefer to stick with the tried-and-true discomfort, and therefore resist changing and plunging into the unknown. More importantly, perhaps, many symptoms—such as shyness and fear of public speaking—protect the clients against possible failure. They will thus refuse to let themselves fall in love and be rejected, or stop themselves from making a speech that might be laughed at. For if they surrendered these avoidances, they would risk subsequent failure and disapproval. Some clients would tend to find this relatively short-term discomfort *more* catastrophic or awful than retaining for a lifetime their phobic symptoms.

What has often been labeled as "fear of success" is practically always a fear of subsequent failure. Thus, if a teenager with social anxiety stops avoiding people and begins to succeed at socializing, he may:

1. Lose the comfort and indulgence of his over-protective parents.
2. Gain the enmity of his siblings.
3. Risk later failure at the activities in which he has now begun to succeed.
4. Be forced to take on more responsibility and effort than he would like to assume.

He may therefore view his social gains as dangers or failures, and may resist trying to strive for them. Does he really have a fear of success? Or is it really one of subsequent failure? As usual, REBT looks at the fear of changing or of success when it is interfering with personality change and seeks out the Irrational *Beliefs* that are creating these fears. These may be:

1. "I must not give up my symptoms, since the discomfort of change would be intolerable!"
2. "I cannot change my neurotic behavior and do better in life, because that would be too risky; I might encounter greater failures later (as I *must* not do); and if I did, that would be awful!"

These and similar *Irrational* Beliefs seem to underlie the fear of change and fear of success, and are revealed and ameliorated with REBT and CBT sessions. Thus, this kind of resistance to change is minimized.

RESISTANCE RESULTING FROM REACTANCE AND REBELLIOUSNESS

A number of clinicians have observed that some of their clients react and rebel against therapy because they see it as an infringement of their "freedom." They may especially rebel against active-directive therapy, even though they have specially sought it out. To deal with this form of resistance, some therapists have invented methods of para-doxical therapy, to try to "trick" these perversely rebellious clients into giving up their resistance (Ellis, 2001a; Erickson & Rossi, 1979; Frankl, 1960; Hayes, Strosahl, & Wilson, 1999).

When clients resist because of reactance, REBT looks for the Irrational *Beliefs* that lead to their resistance, such as:

1. "I have to control my entire destiny, and even though my thera-pist is on my side and working hard to help me, I *must not* let him or her tell me what to do."
2. "How terrible to be directed by my therapist! I cannot *bear* being led by the nose in that manner! I should have absolutely perfect freedom to do what I like, even if my symptoms are killing me!"

In the face of this kind of resistance, REBT and CBT help clients uncover and dispute their Irrational *Beliefs.* They may also use humor and paradoxical intention, such as giving a client the homework assignment of deliberately failing at encountering other people or fail-ing at some task to show him or her that failure is not world-shattering (Ellis, 1999; 2001a).

RESISTANCE MOTIVATED BY RECEIVING SECONDARY GAINS

A number of therapists have noted that many clients are reluctant to give up their disturbances because they are receiving gains or payoffs from them. Thus, a factory worker who hates his job and develops a psychosomatic back problem may resist psychotherapy because if it succeeds, he will be forced to return to the work that he hates.

Psychodynamic therapists often assume and emphasize the deeply unconscious and often repressed reasons for secondary gain. Thus, a woman who says she very much wants to lose weight actually does not lose it because she unconsciously realizes that if she loses it, her hus-band will find her more attractive, and will demand more sex from her.

When we analyze secondary gain resistance in terms of REBT and CBT we often find that it is not as deeply repressed as psychodynami-cally oriented therapists often believe. It may result from several con-scious or semiconscious Irrational *Beliefs,* such as:

1. "Because my mother shouldn't keep bothering me about losing weight and is a rotten person for doing so, I'll fix her wagon by remaining a fat slob!"

2. "Because I really believe that sex is disgusting and that having it would make me disgusting and impure, I will remain pure and good by avoiding having relations."

Using REBT, we can once again find and dispute these underlying Irrational *Beliefs* that block clients from working to give up their dysfunctions even when they are having helpful sessions with an effective therapist.

RESISTANCE STEMMING FROM CLIENTS' HIDDEN AGENDAS

Therapists have often pointed out that a number of clients enter therapy with a hidden agenda—that is, with goals that they fail to verbalize to their therapist or other family members who are in therapy with them. Thus, a husband may have no real intention of working on a better relationship with his wife, but may push her into therapy so that she can become better prepared to agree to a divorce. Or a teenager may agree to have therapy to get the therapist to influence her parents to be less strict with her, and may not be at all interested in changing herself (Leahy, 2001).

Clients who resist therapy because of their having some hidden agenda sometimes actually have quite Rational *Beliefs*. Thus, a man may tell himself, "I wish my wife were sensible and strong enough to work with me toward an amicable divorce, but, unfortunately, she isn't. So I'll use this marital therapy in the hope that she'll become more mature and strong, and then we'll be able to part on better terms." Other clients may have Irrational *Beliefs* that keep them from revealing hidden agendas to the therapist. A woman in marital therapy may tell herself, "If I confess to the therapist that I think my husband is disgustingly unattractive and that I really don't want to have sex with him, the therapist will think that I am very immature and favor my husband in the sessions that we are having together. So I'll keep this to myself!"

By giving all clients unconditional other-acceptance (UOA), you show them that you, as their therapist, will never condemn them, even when they obviously do some bad acts. REBT thereby provides a therapeutic atmosphere that makes it more likely that clients with hidden agendas will reveal their goals to their therapist, and will be able to see and Dispute their Irrational *Beliefs*. One of my clients hid from me his continually lusting after teenage students, both male and female, because he was sure that I would condemn him for doing this heinous thing. When he saw in the course of our sessions that I fully accepted him with all kinds of foolish and "sinful" behavior, he finally opened up and told me about some of his adventures with his students. I was then able to see that he suffered from an obsessive-compulsive disorder (OCD), explored it with him, and helped him overcome it.

Giving clients unconditional other-acceptance (UOA) or what Carl Rogers calls "unconditional positive regard" does not create miracles and does not induce all clients to disclose their hidden agendas. But it certainly works wonders with some of them!

RESISTANCE TO REBT AND TO COGNITIVE BEHAVIOR THERAPY

Because REBT and CBT almost always give clients some responsibility for the degree of their upsetness and therefore for reducing it, many of them resist accepting these forms of therapy. Others erroneously conclude that if they were partly responsible for their own emotional disturbances they are totally blameworthy, and get stuck in their self-condemnation.

With these kinds of resistant clients, you can tactfully show them that while at least in part they are responsible for their self-disturbing, you are not blaming them for having created their dysfunctioning. You are merely helpfully pointing out their complicity so that they can change their ideas, their feelings, and their behaviors and thus no longer disturb themselves.

This is one of the reasons why it is quite important early in their therapy sessions that your clients be made aware of their secondary disturbances, such as damning themselves for *being* disturbed. If you can show them, over and over again, that although their symptoms are unfortunate and handicapping, they themselves are never bad or rotten people for having such symptoms, they will be better able to accept themselves and not put themselves down for having them.

For years I have shown most of my clients that it is a natural human tendency for people to engage in self-blame, and that there are relatively few among the six billion inhabiting our planet that do not frequently do so. I show them that it is a biological as well as a socially learned tendency of people to criticize and damn themselves for their own behavior. By letting them know that this human condition is exceptionally widespread, they begin to realize that they are in normal human company. In sum, REBT and CBT show clients that they are natural constructivists, and therefore construct a good deal of their disturbed behaviors; but at the same time they are also the kind of constructivist who can see how destructive this behavior is and change it.

The ability to change dysfunctional thoughts, feeling, and behaviors is one of the essences of human constructiveness. REBT thus provides clients with an optimistic and creative outlook even though they may have had a long history of self-disturbing.

UNUSUAL BIOLOGICAL AND NEUROLOGICAL LIMITATIONS LEADING TO RESISTANCE

Some psychotherapy clients, especially those who have a great many sessions over the years, tend to have unusual biological and neurological handicaps. Clients who are mentally deficient, are neurologically impaired, or are severely diseased and/or physically debilitated (e.g., some individuals with advanced states of multiple sclerosis or cancer) may resist therapy. Although REBT does not have miraculous success with many of these difficult and resistant clients, it has special methods of reaching some of them, which will be discussed later. It helps them to stop upsetting themselves about their unusual limitations and handicap, and to accept the challenge of often having to work harder than ordinary clients do to effect therapeutic change. Although REBT and CBT are therapies of choice for bright and effective clients who are capable of making profound personality changes in a brief period of time, they can also be effective with a wide range of clients who are uneducated, less intelligent, severely handicapped, and biologically limited.

RESISTANCE CONNECTED WITH THERAPIST-CLIENT RELATIONSHIPS

Freud pioneered in showing that therapist-client relationships are very important both in creating and overcoming client resistance, encouraging analysts to consider and explore transference and countertransference. As a result, relationship problems between therapists and their clients are probably more common in classical analysis than in many other forms of treatment, because this form of therapy encourages clients to have a lengthy series of sessions, during which a good deal of time is spent exploring. This includes their feelings and behavior toward their analysts. However, relationship factors almost inevitably arise in other kinds of therapy as well, factors which frequently facilitate or impede clients' therapy progress (Leahy, 2001). Some of the main ways in which relationship factors lead to resistance will now be discussed.

Resistance Resulting from Client-Therapist Mismatching

Some resistance arises because the clients are sometimes simply mismatched with their therapist. They may be assigned to, or even choose, a therapist whom they just do not like: someone who, to their idiosyncratic tastes or preferences, is too young or too old, too liberal or too conservative, too active or too passive. Because of this mismatching, they do not have too much rapport with their therapist, and therefore listen less seriously to him or her than to a therapist more to their liking.

Frequently, the beliefs that interfere with their having a good relationship with their therapist are Rational *Beliefs*. They may believe, for example, that "my therapist is too conservative or too radical for me, and therefore we are likely to have some major value differences. Consequently, I would prefer to be seen by a therapist who is closer to my own views." In this case, they might decide whether it would be better to try another therapist with more congruent views.

On the other hand, the client may also have some Irrational *Beliefs*, such as, "I must have a therapist who thinks almost exactly the way I do on practically every issue. This one has some real differences with my views, and I *can't stand* it! Even though she helps me in many ways, unless she completely goes along with my views, we cannot possibly get anywhere!" If your clients have Irrational *Beliefs* that prejudice them against you as a therapist, you may explore these IB's somewhere early in the sessions and see if they can be changed. If they can be resolved, then therapy is likely to be effective; but if they cannot, it may be wiser for you to aid the client in finding a more compatible helper. No matter how competent and confident you are, your Irrational *Beliefs* and prejudices about your clients and your clients' Irrational *Beliefs* and prejudices about you may make it wise for them to find another therapist.

Resistance Associated with Love-Hate or Transference Problems of the Therapist and the Client

Many psychodynamically oriented therapists assume that either the client or the therapist has strong feelings of love or hate towards the other person and that these love-hate feelings stem from their unresolved early family relationships. REBT practitioners we find this assumption highly questionable, since the client and the therapist may have strong feelings of love and/or hate towards each other based on reality factors that have little to do with their childhood experiences. Thus, a young female client who just happens to have an exceptionally bright, attractive, and kindly therapist who would be an ideal mate for her—or for almost any other woman—if she met him socially, may realistically fall in love with this therapist even though he has virtually nothing in common with her father, her uncles, or her brothers. Similarly, this woman's therapist may become enamored of her not because she resembles his mother, but because more than most other women in his life he has been close to, she is truly charming, talented, and attractive. When reality-based feelings that are not really transferred from clients' or therapists' early childhoods occur in therapy and when they lead to intense warm or cold feelings on the part of the therapists and/or clients, they may create difficulties and encourage resistance. Thus, a female client who intensely loves her therapist may resist improving in order to prolong her therapy, and a therapist with a strong positive feeling toward his or her client may also consciously or unconsciously encourage resistance to ensure that the therapy continues indefinitely.

If both the client and the therapist were to keep their strong feelings of liking or disliking for each other in a preferential mode, therapy might well proceed with little difficulty. A female client who is realistically attracted to her therapist could tell herself, "Under normal conditions, if he were not my therapist, I'd like to date him, and perhaps later get into a serious relationship with him. But I don't have to do so any more than I have to have an affair with an attractive husband of one of my best friends. So, let me forget about my attraction to the therapist and get on with the real reason we're here, which is to help me overcome my difficulties." However, this same client could also tell herself that "Because I am so attracted to my therapist, I *absolutely must* have intimate personal relations with him, and it is *too much* to bear, and I *can't stand it* unless I do!" If Irrational *Beliefs* of this nature exist on the part of therapists or their clients it would be desirable to discover and minimize them to prevent the therapy from being derailed.

Resistance Sparked by the Therapist's Counter-Transference Problems

Therapists may, of course, be highly influenced by their early childhood relationships, such as their great love or great hatred for their mothers. If so, they may overgeneralize, which is what transference usually is, and hate or love all clients who resemble their mothers. In such cases, they had better discontinue their sessions with a client against whom they are prejudiced or even for whom they have deep-seated loving feelings, and strongly tackle their transference feelings with the help of another therapist until they resolve them (Ellis, 2001c).

Most warm feelings as well as distinctly cold feelings that therapists may have for their clients are somewhat reality-based. As noted above, therapists may feel unusually warm and friendly toward the kind of client whom, if they met socially, they would naturally be attracted to. By the same token, they may be cool, reserved, and even hostile toward the kind of client whom, again if they met socially, they would tend to withdraw from. Both their very warm and hostile feelings toward their clients are not merely counter-transferent in the psychoanalytic sense but are frequently part of the human condition. Therefore, you had better survey both your hot and cold feelings towards your clients, seriously evaluate whether they are likely to interfere with therapy, and possibly avoid seeing those clients toward whom you have extreme positive or negative feelings (Ellis, 2001c).

Resistance Related to the Moralistic Attitudes of the Therapist

Some therapists are so moralistic that they can hardly stop condemning their clients for their evil or their stupid acts. Even though they are in a "helping profession," they frequently believe that their seriously disturbed clients *absolutely should not* be the way they are—especially if these clients abuse their therapist, come late to sessions, refuse to pay their bills, and otherwise behave obnoxiously. As a result, many therapists overtly or covertly damn their clients and consequently help the clients damn themselves and become even more distressed. And understandably, many clients with decidedly moralistic and damning therapists may become quite resistant. See chapter 11 for more details on therapists' problems.

REBT combats this kind of moral condemnation of clients by stressing what Carl Rogers calls "unconditional positive regard" or what REBT therapists call "unconditional other-acceptance," which I shall discuss in more detail in later chapters. Let me note here that moralism often includes two distinct Irrational *Beliefs*: (1) "This client is acting very badly, both in and out of therapy; *should not* act that way; and *must* be stopped from doing so!" (2) "This client is making it *too* hard for me, especially when I am doing my best to help him or her, and definitely must not act that way! I *can't stand* this kind of destructive behavior, and I *can't stand* this client!" By looking for and disputing these two beliefs that may prejudice you against certain clients, you can help rid yourself of this kind of therapeutic moralizing.

CHARACTERISTICS OF NON-RESISTERS

Fred J. Hanna (2001) and his associates have done some important studies to indicate what characteristics and precursors nonresisters are likely to have. After reviewing the literature and interviewing clients to try to discover what traits *resistors* commonly exhibited, he then described certain techniques most likely to persuade and encourage compliance rather than noncompliance with therapy. From my own many years of practice as well as from supervising hundreds of therapists for the past fifty years I tend to agree with most of Hanna's findings and recommendations. I noted some of my own views in the first edition of this book, before Hanna began his research. The following is a list of Hanna's main characteristics of clients who are ready for therapy and my comment on them:

A Sense of Necessity.   Clients have a felt sense of urgency, recognize the importance of or need for some form of change to take place and feel and think they had better try to effect it. I agree, even though Hanna's use of the word *necessity* has dangers. A strong Belief in the *desirability* of change and its advantages for better functioning appreciably helps clients overcome inevitable difficulties and do the work that therapy requires. If, however, clients believe that change is *absolutely* necessary and especially that it *must* occur quickly, they will create anxietizing that may sabotage their efforts to understand how to work at effecting change.

Willingness to Experience Anxiety or Difficulty.   I quite agree, especially with the willingness to accept difficulty. Great anxiety, of course, may deter therapy, and discourage clients from staying with it. But moderate anxiety overlaps with adventurousness. Since therapy usually leads to some anxietizing, clients' willingness to tolerate this is one of the prime factors that helps them to persevere. As for willingness to accept the difficulty, which is desirable in intensive and prolonged therapy, REBT has stressed this from its inception. I frequently quote to clients Benjamin Franklin's aphorism in *Poor Richard's Almanac:* "There are no gains without pains." Willingness to accept this certainly helps!

Awareness.   This is the identification of clients' existing dysfunctioning that effective therapy addresses. Awareness normally becomes enhanced as therapy progresses, but a willingness to let it come is quite important. REBT enhances awareness not only by including exercises that make clients more aware of their feelings and behaviors, but also by making them clearly aware of their accompanying *Beliefs.*

Confronting the Problem.   Hanna (2001) defines this as "acts in which clients use their attentional and other resources to look further and move through difficult problems in spite of their reactions, fears and avoidance." Yes, I have usually found my clients to be confronting, passive, or avoidant; those in the first of these three categories tend to do better at therapy, and those in the third category tend to do worst. Those who actively collaborate with my REBT confrontation and those who keep confronting their problems and possible solutions on their own are usually able to help themselves get better in a relatively short period of time. Determined avoidance of confronting is often indicative of client's having a severe personality disorder.

Effort. This involves clients' deliberately exerting energy toward understanding and applying the therapy. Once again, I agree. Since its start in 1955, REBT has stressed three main insights: (1) Clients don't merely *get* disturbed by unfortunate Adversities (A's) that happen to them. They *also* disturb themselves with their *Beliefs* (B's) about these events. (2) Although they usually first upset themselves during their early childhood, they keep reaffirming their Irrational *Beliefs* to upset themselves today. (3) Understanding and gaining insight into their core Irrational *Beliefs* (IB's) is not enough. Changing them to functional, rational *Beliefs* (RB's) is quite possible—but only by work and practice. This, of course, means effort. See chapters 7 and 8 of this book.

REBT also hypothesizes that since clients usually hold their Irrational *Beliefs* and dysfunctional feelings and behaviors *strongly and forcefully,* they can best change them with *forceful and vigorous* cognitive, emotional, and behavioral disputing. This, of course, involves considerable effort. I and other REBT practitioners, especially Dryden (1999; Walen, DiGiuseppe, & Dryden, 1992) have frequently confirmed the benefits of clients' forceful effort. (See chapter 7.)

Hope. Jerome Frank (1994) has recognized clients' feelings of hope to be a common factor in many different kinds of therapy and has also identified hope as a key factor in the placebo effect. Right on! The conviction, "I definitely *can* change myself!" is a very helpful Rational *Belief,* as opposed to the self-sabotaging one, "I can't change! It's hopeless!"

Along with Adlerian Therapy, REBT uses encouragement to help clients increase their hope that they *can* change their thinking, feeling, and behaving; and, like Glasser's (1999) Choice Therapy, it stresses their *choosing* to do so. In the case of clients who are contemplating suicide, REBT quickly tackles their feelings of hopelessness and often succeeds, in a few sessions, to successfully help them replace it with more hopeful ones (Ellis, 1976). (See chapter 6 of this book.)

Social Support. Social support may be said to be a person's access to confiding and helpful relationships and being able to express oneself in them. As Hanna (2001) notes, this includes the therapeutic relation-ship, in which a therapist's empathy, warmth, support, and the oppor-tunity for emotional expression, play vital, positive roles.

Although I believe in the importance of support by therapists and friends, for several years I have had some concerns about it as well. It indeed helps people to *feel* better when a therapist, relative, or friend shows real interest and listens to and supports them. But in order for clients to experience a profound philosophic-emotional-behavioral change, and thereby to *get* better, they require considerable *internal* help. By too easily settling for external support, they may cavalierly refuse to do the difficult internal work. Also, as I point out in chapter 6, when clients feel better as a result of external support, they usually believe, "I'm okay *because* my therapist (or friend or relative) approves of me" (and not because I *un*conditionally accept myself). They there-by achieve *conditional* self-acceptance (traditionally called *self-esteem*) and may seriously impede their giving themselves unconditional self-acceptance (USA).

Social support may often encourage clients to feel better *and* get better. However, don't count on it! It may be much less helpful than many researchers—practically all of whom measure clients' feeling rather than getting better—ostensibly show. In sum, social support is promoted by REBT—but with some cautions!

These characteristics of non-resistors of therapy described by Hanna interact with and partly include the other important factors of change. But they all tend to show that many clients enable themselves to get started on therapy because of their own characteristics—interac-tion with their therapists' knowledge, techniques, and talent.

All these characteristics of clients' cooperativeness can also be enhanced by various therapist methods. As Hanna (2001) suggests, therapists can (1) intensify the motivation of clients, (2) augment their involvement in the therapeutic process, (3) enhance their sense of the feasibility or possibility that change can and will occur, and (4) remove obstacles to change. Brogan, Prochaska, and Prochaska (1999) also stress the importance of therapists' considering clients' stage of accepting change when trying to help them stay in therapy.

Prochaska and DiClemente came out with their original model of stages and levels of change in 1983 and 1984 and have kept revising it (Prochaska, DiClemente, & Norcross, 1992). It has been widely adopt-ed by psychotherapists, including REBT addiction specialist Michler Bishop (2001). It is especially useful in the treatment of addictive behavior because it shows that that clients resist therapy because they are not in a proper *stage* of readiness to use it. To get better and stay better, Prochaska and his associates indicate that most clients have to

go therough the stages of precontemplation, contemplation, preparation, action, and maintenance, and that recognizing what stage they
are in allows you to tailor your therapeutic interventions to this particular client. A great deal of research has tended to support their theory
of change.

Freeman and Dolan (2001) agree with Prochaska and DiClemente,
but also add the stages of noncontemplations and anticontemplations
before that of preparation and also add the stages of prelapse, lapse,
and relapse before the stage of maintenance.

Although, as I just noted, REBT and CBT have used Prochaska,
DiClemente, and Norcross' stage theory for years, I would now recommend that you consider adding to it Freeman and Dolan's extra stages.
Not all resistant clients go through all these stages, but a hell of a lot of
them do! So the Prochaska, DiClemente, and Norcross hypothesis plus
the Freeman and Dolan additions to it are well worth considering as
you try to figure out the reasons for your clients' resistance and decide
how best to help them in the particular stage of change at which they
have now arrived. More research needs to be done in regard to these
change stage theories; but meanwhile you can read up on them and do
your own experiments with experimenting with them.

Because of the findings discussed in this section, Norcross and
Beutler (1997) have come up with a version of prescriptive therapy,
Systematic Treatment Selection (STS). They suggest that therapy
methods can be matched to the client's general personality and coping
styles, such as whether clients have internalizing or externalizing styles.

Therapists who stress clients' personality and coping styles make
real efforts to determine what these styles are and then try to tailor their
therapy methods, which may be selected from different general therapy systems, to the clients' particular styles. Assuming that resistant
clients really have distinct personality and coping styles—which has
not yet been accurately researched and determined—you, as a therapist, would best match your therapeutic interventions and style with
your clients' particular styles. Although Systematic Treatment Selection
is still in a development stage and requires further research, it looks
promising at present and may later lead to improved treatment selection for a good many resistors. I therefore recommend that you keep
following its progress to see how you may use it effectively.

Do REBT and CBT consider clients' particular characteristics to help
them change? Indeed they do, in some of the following ways:

1. These approaches intensify the motivation of clients by (a)
actively persuading them that they can choose many ways of thinking, feeling, and behaving differently; (b) reinforcing them for doing
self-improvement homework; (c) showing them relatively simple and
quick ways of undisturbing themselves, especially, by looking for their

self-sabotaging *musts* and changing them to healthy *preferences;* (d) giving them the *challenge* and *adventure* of making profound and lasting changes; (e) showing clients that some of their therapy goals and ways of implementing them do not exactly help them to *get* better as well as *feel* better. Indicating how they can revise their aims, and strive for the former as well as the latter therapy.

2. They augment clients' involvement in the therapeutic process by (a) encouraging them to collaborate with the therapist in discovering and Disputing their Irrational *Beliefs;* (b) teaching them to do Disputing on their own and to give themselves experiential and behavioral homework; (c) arranging for them to role-play with the therapist, group members, or other people in situations in which they work through their anxiety, depression, or rage; (d) encouraging them to use REBT principles and practices with their relatives and friends and thereby more effectively learn to apply them to themselves; (e) using cost-benefit methods with clients to show them that even though it is hard for them to change, it is usually much harder for them *not* to change.

3. REBT and CBT enhance clients' sense of optimism about being able to change by (a) showing them that they can *choose* to disturb themselves and also choose to undisturb themselves—that when Adversities occur in their lives, they can choose to have Rational *Beliefs* and consequent healthy negative feelings and behaviors or *Irrational Beliefs* and unhealthy negative feelings and behaviors; (b) teaching clients that they have the ability to choose to fulfill and actualize themselves in a variety of possible ways; (c) helping clients to do "dangerous" things despite their anxiety and encouraging them to experience some anxiety until they desensitize themselves to it.

4. REBT and CBT help clients to remove obstacles to change by (a) showing them how to ferret out Irrational *Beliefs* (IB's) and change them to Rational *Beliefs* (RB's); (b) showing clients how to unblock their inhibited feelings and change their dysfunctional feelings for functional ones; (c) showing clients how to change their destructive actions for more constructive ones.

Other ways that REBT and CBT help promote clients' readiness for change are shown throughout this book.

THE CONCEPT OF STRUGGLE BETWEEN THE THERAPIST AND RESISTANT CLIENTS

Butler and Bird (2000) suggest that resistance in therapy properly be seen as "therapist-client struggle." This term, they hold, is a more helpful, relationship-oriented term than resistance, which they view as "linear, blaming, and hierarchical." They show that if the therapist understands the model of clients' struggle and responds to it over the course of therapy, clients will be less resistant and will benefit more from the therapeutic process.

Butler and Bird present a three-factor model of avoiding harmful struggle: Factor 1: Facilitating successful dialogue between the therapist and clients and between clients and their couple/family relators. Factor 2: Empowering client participation in the regulation of change and stabilizing activity through encouraging a therapist worldview and interactional style with clients to a clinical style. Factor III: Enacting the emotional, nurturing, insight, and behavioral work of therapy through client-therapist relationships and interactions as opposed to making the therapist central in this process.

Butler and Bird apply these three factors to couple and family therapy and show how understanding and using them helps reduce client-therapist struggle and often produce less resistance and more effective therapy. As usual, the supporting studies they cite all seem to use as their criteria for effective therapy clients *feeling* rather than *getting* better. These studies do not usually show that when therapists understand and apply these factors, their clients actually get better and stay better. Nonetheless, Butler and Bird's concept of resistance equaling client-therapist struggle is to be seriously considered and somewhat used in your own encounters with resistant clients.

The reason I suggest using them only somewhat is that Butler and Bird seem to forget that resistance consists of at least two kinds of "struggling." First, clients may well be struggling with their therapist's view of therapy, and their thinking, feeling, and behavioral interactions with the therapist. But second, they frequently resist their own determinations and efforts to change. As I note in the beginning of this chapter, clients voluntarily decide, without any therapist, to diet, exercise, read books, play a musical instrument, etc.—and yet still refuse to *comply* with their own decision. They often resist changing themselves because they may have struggles with relatives, friends, and associates that derail them. So while Butler and Bird make some good points in regard to client-therapist struggles, they neglect to mention the *intrapersonal* struggling and low frustration tolerance that leads many clients to resist changing themselves outside and inside of therapy (Ellis, 1994; Leahy, 2001).

ENVIRONMENTAL FACTORS THAT LEAD TO RESISTANCE

Golden (1983) had an excellent article on resistance in *Cognitive Behavior Therapy* listing a number of environmental factors that encourage people to resist therapy. These environmental influences include:

1. Relatives, friends, or associates may deliberately sabotage clients' becoming less disturbing. They may feel threatened or envious when clients use therapy to make themselves more assertive or successful.

2. Associates of clients may inadvertently become benevolent saboteurs of therapy—as when a husband fosters his wife's elevator phobia by walking up and down stairways with her. While seemingly trying to help her, he may actually be reinforcing her anxietizing.

3. Clients may accidentally or willfully acquire disability, welfare payments, or other benefits for being emotionally dysfunctional, which may significantly reduce their incentive to change.

4. People often use pacifiers, such as alcohol or drugs, to prevent them from seeing how self-disturbing they really are and from doing much to help themselves when they acknowledge this process.

5. Therapists may offer clients palliative techniques, such as relaxation and other cognitive distraction methods, that only temporarily help them feel better. Exclusive use of these techniques may interfere with clients' using more effective methods, such as Disputing their Irrational *Beliefs*.

6. Physicians and psychiatrists may cavalierly prescribe psychotropic medicine, such as tranquilizers, when clients even slightly anxietize or depress themselves. This overuse of medication may actually sabotage psychotherapy by taking away clients' incentives to work on themselves more thoroughly.

As the foregoing reasons for resistance show, many clients frequently come to therapy because they are plagued emotionally yet still resist the best efforts of their therapist and themselves to relieve their suffering. In many instances, their so-called resistance is partly attributable to the limitations of their therapist—to his or her poor judgment, inept theories, and ineffective techniques. But clients often have their own reasons for resisting help. As noted in this chapter, these reasons are varied and wide-ranging, and include both Rational and Irrational *Beliefs*. It is up to you, their therapist, to discriminate between their healthy and unhealthy motives for resisting therapy and to show them how to use the REBT, CBT, and other techniques described in this book to minimize their frequent self-sabotaging.

Disputing Core Irrational Beliefs that Underlie Resistance 4

The basic theory of REBT and CBT hold that almost all people have the goals and values of remaining alive and being reasonably happy and free from pain, and thus conquering Adversities (A's) that interfere with these goals. They have a *choice* of making themselves healthfully sad, disappointed, and frustrated, or *un*healthfully anxious, depressed, angry, and self-pitying. They exert this choice largely through their *Belief* system *about* the Adversities that are occurring to them. If they have self-helping or Rational *Beliefs* (RB's), they rarely disturb themselves at C. But if they have self-defeating or Irrational *Beliefs,* they are likely to disturb themselves emotionally and behaviorally. They do not merely *get* upset by the Adversities that occur in their lives. Rather, they partially *make themselves* disturbing *about* these Adversities. They are *constructivists,* who largely *create* their own healthy and unhealthy *reactions* to undesirable A's. Their A's *contribute* significantly to their C's, but so do their *Beliefs.* Thus, A x B = C.

REBT and CBT do not maintain that *all* resisting in therapy results from clients' Irrational *Beliefs.* As I noted in the last chapter, there are other reasons why clients resist. But if and when they are partly responsible for sabotaging their own therapeutic efforts, the IBs that I have been describing may well be at the core of their resistance.

When you find that your clients seem to have the ability to follow your form of therapy, and nevertheless resist it, one of the first things to do is to look for their basic IB's. See if they are putting themselves down and *Believe* that they are unable to change. See whether they seem to be hostile to you and to your therapeutic procedures, and are demanding that you not be the way you are. See whether they have low frustration tolerance about several things in their lives, including psychotherapy, and are therefore viewing therapy as too hard rather than merely as hard.

Also look for what REBT calls the core Irrational *Beliefs* or dysfunctional schemas that accompany people's grandiose demands. Thus, when they demand that they *must* do well and be approved of by others but are not, they frequently conclude that they are inadequate individuals who are incapable of doing well. When other people do not treat them as well as they think they absolutely *should* treat them, they become hostile and conclude not only that the other people's behavior is wrong and bad, but also that they are *rotten, bad people.* When they proclaim that personality change (or anything else) in life *absolutely must* be easy for them, and conditions *must not* be hard and uncomfortable, they frequently conclude that it's *awful, terrible,* and *horrible* when conditions are not the way they *should be,* that they *can't stand it,* and that it is terrible that the rotten world is imposing such conditions on them.

If you wish to use REBT to make inroads against your clients' resistance, your task is to discover their core IB's, have them agree that they actually have them, then help Dispute these dysfunctional convictions until they minimize them. This leads us to D, Disputing, in the ABCs of REBT. D consists of helping your clients debate their *Beliefs* and convince themselves that these beliefs are unrealistic, illogical, and will achieve poor results. As an illustrative example, let us suppose that a client depresses herself and resists therapy because of her beliefs that (1) she *must,* absolutely *must,* succeed in changing herself, or else she is a thoroughly inadequate and hopeless person. (2) Working at therapy is too hard, especially if she has to keep it up for too long, and that it *shouldn't be* that hard. (3) She can easily get away with making herself depressed. You can help her Dispute her Irrational *Beliefs* in some of the following ways.

EMPIRICAL OR REALISTIC DISPUTING

Irrational Belief. "I *must* succeed at changing myself, and everyone, including my therapist, will despise me if I don't." Disputing (D): "Where is the evidence that I *have to* succeed? Will everyone, including my therapist, really despise me if I don't succeed at changing myself?" Answer: Effective New Philosophy (E): "There is no evidence that I absolutely must succeed at changing myself during therapy. Just because it is *desirable* for me to succeed doesn't mean realistically that I *have* to do so. This kind of necessity doesn't really exist in the universe. Some people may despise me if I do not succeed at therapy, but of course not everyone will. Most people will not care whether I succeed or not, and there is no evidence that my therapist will kill herself if I don't!"

Irrational Belief. "I *can't stand* my having to work long and hard at therapy; it's *too* hard." Disputing (D): "Can I really not stand having to work long and hard at therapy?" Answer: Effective New Philosophy (E): "I wish that I could change myself easily and magically, but that kind of magic does not, alas, exist. I definitely *can* stand many things that I don't like, such as doing my therapy homework. I certainly won't die from this hard work and can still in many ways enjoy myself and be happy. Although working at therapy is often arduous and unenjoyable, if that's the way it is, tough! Actually, if I *do* work very hard at therapy, it'll be arduous in the short run, but in the long run, it will help me achieve more enjoyment in life."

Irrational Belief. "Because there is no easy way for me to get better, I shouldn't have to uncomfortably persist at working at it. Life is unfair and horrible. What's the use of living if I have to do so many difficult and unpleasant things to change myself?" Disputing (D): "Where is it written that changing myself at therapy, or doing other disciplined tasks to help myself, *should not* exist and that it is *horrible* if they do? Why is my life not worth living when there is no easy way for me to work at therapy?" Answer: Effective New Philosophy (E): "It is not written anywhere that I absolutely should have an easy time changing myself at therapy, only in my muddled head! It seems evident that because of the way I am constructed and the history of my upbringing, I will often have trouble changing myself through therapy. Too bad! Really unfortunate!—but if that's the way it is, I'd better *accept* it, even if I don't like it. I can still try to live and enjoy myself despite these bad conditions. I can teach myself, as Reinhold Niebuhr recommended, to have the courage to change the Adversities that I can change, to have the serenity to accept those that I cannot change, and to have the wisdom to know the difference between the two" (Pietsch, 1993).

As McMullin (2000) notes, Disputing can be enforced when you show resistant clients that their particular view of the "facts" has a good many alternatives and different possibilities. It could be that Jones viciously and deliberately treated them unfairly. But many alternative hypotheses exist.

USING ANTI-CATASTROPHIZING AND ANTI-AWFULIZING

I don't think I invented the word *catastrophize* but I may well have invented the term *catastrophizing* (along with my later term, *awfulizing*).

In any event, I think I made *catastrophizing* famous as an important element in cognitive-behavioral therapy.

When clients catastrophize and/or awfulize they take some aspect of their environment, healthily view it as "bad" or even "very bad," but then go on to greatly exaggerate its possible frequency and danger. For example, they become fully convinced that the slight cut on their finger will lead to a deadly infection, that an airplane is about to crash into their living room and kill them, and that our entire planet will go up in smoke tomorrow. Resisting clients often engage in many such catastrophizings and refuse to ameliorate them in spite of the low probability of their occurrence and the low degree of damage that would usually result if perchance they did occur.

Rian McMullen suggests an effective anti-catastrophizing and anti-awfulizing method that can be used with exaggeratedly worrying clients. They are first to list an important and frequent form of catastrophizing—e.g., that if they eat a hot dog they will die of botulism. They are then to estimate—from one to ten—how likely this "disaster" will be and also the worst possible outcome that could result. The therapist then discusses with the client how frequent their catastrophizing usually is, how many people suffer from catastrophizing, and what usually happens if the imagined "horror" actually ensues. Based on your clients' own experience, have them estimate whether the catastrophe actually will occur and, if it does, what is the worst thing that is likely to happen.

Having clients go over many times the worst thing that could happen is a favorite REBT method. It helps them realize that just because it *is* the "worst thing," in all probability it will *not* happen. It lets them see that even if it does occur—if, for example, a world war starts up—they can handle it and still have some pleasures and happiness. It encourages them to realize that even death from the "catastrophe" is not *awful,* and will eventually occur anyway.

Many helpers and therapists, since ancient times, have pointed out that unrealistic notions, when rigidly held, frequently contradict each other and thwart the individual's realistic goals. For example, people who strongly want to go to sleep and strongly insist, "I *absolutely must* sleep!" will often keep themselves awake. You can show them their inconsistencies by strong and persistent confrontation, by demonstrating that their contradictory goals just do not work, by giving them paradoxical stories and parables, by explaining how ironic it is that they are steadily thwarting their own goals, and by other dramatic methods (Ellis, 1999, 2001; Hayes, Strosahl, & Wilson, 1999; McMullin, 2000; Rohrbaugh & Shohan, 2001; Watzlawick, Weakland, & Fisch, 1974).

DRYDEN'S DISPUTING OF "LIGHT RATIONAL BELIEFS"—THE "ZIG ZAG TECHNIQUE"

Dryden, who has written and edited more books on Rational Emotive Behavior Therapy than I have, has specialized in following up my distinction between lightly held intellectual insight and strongly held emotional insight. In his *Zig-Zag technique,* clients vigorously dispute their weak Rational—yes, Rational—*Beliefs* until they solidly present evidence for them and thereby come to believe them more strongly. He fully presents this technique in *Rescue to Change* (Dryden, 2001), which includes the following client handout.

1. Write down your healthy belief in the top left column.
2. Rate your present level of conviction in this belief on a 100-point scale with 0% = no conviction and 100% = total conviction, and write down this rating in the space provided on the form.
3. Respond to this healthy belief with an attack that is directed at the healthy belief. This may take the form of a doubt, reservation, or objection to the healthy belief. Make this attacking statement as genuine as you can: the more it reflects what you actually believe, the better.
4. Respond to this attack as fully as you can. It is really important that you respond to each element of the attack. Do so as persuasively as possible and write down the response in the second oblong to the left.
5. Continue in this vein until you have answered all your attacks and cannot think of any more.

    If you find this exercise difficult, you might find it easier to make your attacks gentle at first. Then, when you find that you can respond to these attacks quite easily, begin to make the attacks more biting. Work in this way until you are making really strong attacks. When you make an attack, do so as if you want yourself to believe it. And when you respond, really throw yourself into it with the intention of demolishing the attack and raising your level of conviction in your healthy belief.

    Don't forget that the purpose of this exercise is to strengthen your healthy belief, so it is important that you stop when you have answered all your attacks. Use as many forms as you need and clip them together when you have finished.

    If you make an attack that you cannot answer, stop the exercise and we will discuss how you can best respond to it in a group or individual therapy session.

6. When you have answered all your attacks, rerate your level of conviction in the healthy belief as before. If you have been successful at responding to your attacks, then this rating will have gone up. If it has not increased or has done so by only a little, we'll discuss the reasons for this in group.

LOGICAL DISPUTING

Irrational Belief. "If I don't totally succeed in overcoming my resistance and working at therapy, I am an *incompetent, hopeless person* who will therefore be unable to improve myself through therapy. I am just no good!" Disputing (D): "How does it follow that I am a totally incompetent, hopeless person, who can never stop resisting changing myself? Even if I always resist, and therefore create a hopeless situation, does this logically prove that I am a totally worthless and rotten individual?" Answer: Effective New Philosophy (E): "No, this does not logically follow. I can only prove that I am a person who has so far failed to stop resisting—but not that I have no ability to do so in the future. I do many useful and good things in my life, including some of the things I do in therapy, so I cannot be a no-goodnik as a person. Even if I always failed at therapy and other important things, I would have a pretty miserable life, but it does not logically follow that I would be a worthless, undeserving individual who the powers-that-be are punishing for being so inept. My undeservingness or worthlessness is a groundless theory that I hold about myself and some other humans. Does it ever follow that because I often act inefficiently, including in therapy, I am a totally worthless, undeserving individual? No. If I *think* that I am worthless, I may well make myself more inept; but my bad deeds do not make me a worthless and undeserving person unless I *think* they do. It is a thoroughly illogical jump to conclude that certain of my poor *behaviors* make *me* totally worthless."

Irrational Belief. "It is *awful* and *horrible* that I have to work at self-change." Disputing (D): "In what way is it awful and horrible to work at therapy and to have to work hard to change myself?" Answer: Effective New Philosophy (E): "In no way. It is distinctly difficult and inconvenient for me to work at therapy; I'd rather it be much easier. But when I label this work *awful* or *horrible,* I am illogically concluding that: (1) it absolutely *should not* be as inconvenient as it is; (2) it is *totally* or one hundred percent inconvenient; and (3) if I suffer from this inconvenience, I can't be happy *at all.* These are false overgeneralizations, because:

"Difficult activities such as changing myself in therapy should be exactly as inconvenient as they are—because the fact is, things are the way they now are. It is inconvenient that I have to work to change myself at therapy, but it could be worse—e.g., if my therapist abandoned me, if other people boycotted me, and if I were thrown in jail for not working at it.

"No matter how uncomfortable working at therapy or any other activity is, I still can make myself happy in many ways. When something bad exists and I *define* it as 'horrible,' I anxietize and depress myself, while if I empirically and logically keep telling myself that it is very bad, and do not exaggerate this state into 'horror' or 'awfulness,' I can work at making it better instead of giving up. If I define something as 'awful' instead of only highly disadvantageous and inconvenient, I will almost always make myself suffer, and will also interfere with my dealing with it adequately. Then I may *make myself* almost totally unhappy!"

USING PERCEPTUAL BRIDGING

McMullin (2000) describes several means of perceptual bridging with which you may help clients give up a dysfunctional *Belief* and change it to a functional one. Thus, if clients believe that relatives, friends, or coworkers are deliberately mean and spiteful, you may help them believe, more healthfully, that they are *naturally* negative or childish and not merely with your clients. Or you may appeal to your clients' higher value—such as the Christian value of accepting the sinner but not the sin. Or you may help your enraged clients relabel the "mean" or "spiteful" label they apply to some of their relatives, friends, and coworkers by giving them the less prejudiced label of "assertive," "independent," or "firm."

PRACTICAL OR PRAGMATIC DISPUTING

Irrational Belief. "Adversities should not exist. I can successfully and rightly depress myself about their existing, define their existence as awful and terrible, and rate myself as a worthless individual for not coping with them better." Disputing (D): "Where will it get me if I view the Adversities of my life as horrible and I put myself down for not coping well enough with them? It will practically always lead to anxietizing and depressing. What will my life be like if I keep telling myself that it is *too hard* to change, and that I am *unable,* being an incompetent individual, to change? It will help me to keep resisting. It is very hard for me to deal with great Adversities and not depress myself about them; but it is much harder to deal with them if I view them as *awful,* and think that I am *unable* to cope with them. The same thing goes for my resistance. If I tell myself that changing shouldn't be so hard, then I will make changing much harder. If I convince myself that changing at therapy is beyond the ability of a stupid, inadequate person like me, then I will most probably sabotage any such change. As soon as I raise my desire to change into an absolutistic must, and put myself down for not changing, that will hinder my actually making changes. Downing myself for not changing will increase my difficulty in doing so, and increase my natural tendencies to resist doing other difficult things." Realistic, logical, and pragmatic methods of Disputing are also included in the REBT technique of Disputing Irrational Beliefs (DIBS) which is illustrated in chapters 5 and 10.

The Disputing methods just illustrated shows how REBT attempts to follow some of the most useful methods of scientific analysis by testing the hypotheses that your client absolutely *must* change, that they are worthless individuals when they *don't* change as they presumably must, that they shouldn't have to work very hard at changing, and that they can comfortably get away with maintaining their disturbances and still lead an unanxious life. These hypotheses are illogical overgeneralizations, that are contrary to the facts of human existence. Much of the time they will lead your clients to unnecessarily upset themselves, and then self-defeatingly resist the thinking-feeling-behaving work required for giving up their dysfunctioning. REBT helps them realistically, logically, and heuristically to dispute their self-destructive formulations, and encourages them to keep working at changing them back into rational, self-helping preferences.

James Overholzer (1993, 1994) has published a series of papers showing how the Socratic method of questioning of clients' Irrational *Beliefs* involves systematic questioning, inductive reasoning, and universal definitions and how, when you ably use it, you can help jar the unrealistic, rigid, and impractical thinking of some of the most resistant clients. Indeed you can—sometimes! But if you combine Socratic questioning with firm didactic evidence that these clients' Beliefs *are* inflexible, dogmatic, and lead to poor therapeutic results, you can sometimes achieve better results than if you only use Socratic questioning. Experiment, if you will, with both methods with different clients.

I want to emphasize that the kinds of empirical, logical, and practical disputing that REBT practitioners teach their disturbed clients are of course done "cognitively." Because cognition plays an exceptionally important, and sometimes crucial, part in clients' emotional and behavioral disturbances, their learning to use empirical reasoning and logical methods of undoing the emotional havoc which they frequently construct can be unusually helpful.

However, the main forms of Disputing had better be integrated with active and emotional work by the clients who use them. This work partly consists of their steadily forcing themselves to *strongly* think against their natural and acquired tendencies to think irrationally. When, as a result of this persistent Disputing, they arrive at an Effective New Philosophy (E), their constrictive attitudes often have to be acted upon. They can tell themselves one hundred times that it is *not* too hard to work at therapy, but unless they *un*comfortably *force* themselves to do this actual work, they will not strongly convince themselves of what they only *lightly Believe*. And they are likely to return, almost automatically, to disturbing themselves.

The kinds of activities that can help clients solidify their Rational *Beliefs* include regularly attending therapy sessions and doing their homework assignments, and deliberately performing other usually avoided tasks.

In addition to engaging in behaviors that reinforce their Disputing, clients had also better give an emotional quality to their disputations by doing so rigorously and forcefully. Thus, they may arrive at the Effective New Philosophy that, "I guess there is *no* reason why it must be easy to change," and they will most likely help themselves somewhat. But underneath their new Rational *Belief* often remains the insistent and strongly-held older one, "It really *must* be simple and easy. It's awful and intolerable that it's not!" What is vital is vigorous *emotional* disputing.

For example, a client could say aloud, with feeling, that "There clearly is no damned reason why changing myself must be easy! It's frequently extremely difficult for me and many other people to effect change. In a sense, we *like* not changing, because we heavily dislike the energy and effort it takes us to change. To hell with that! There practically *never* is any self-changing without a great deal of work and effort, and I'd better not delude myself that there is! So, no matter how long I have to keep it up, I'd better work my butt off or else I'll do it cavalierly and temporarily. Too bad that it takes so much consistent effort, but tough— it *does!* As Benjamin Franklin said, 'There are no gains without pains.'"

"Resisting change" often means that clients have a *light* determination to do so and thus only weakly (if at all) dispute their dysfunctional convictions. Unfortunately, relatively few individuals put determined and persistent effort into steadily carrying out their intentions. Perhaps I am taking an unduly pessimistic view of the human propensity for changing, but I think that human history fairly clearly shows that great numbers of people, with and without any therapeutic help, resolve to change themselves, and then either fail to do it at all, or do it for a while, and then retrogress to their unchanged condition. They strongly avow to themselves and others that they are going to change, but then fail to abide by this agreement.

To sum it up: when your clients say that they definitely wish to change and then they resist doing so, it is crucial that you help them discover and challenge the main IBs that interfere with their changing. These usually are under two headings:

1. "Because I desire to change, I *absolutely must* do it well and satisfy myself, my therapist, and others that I have done it as well as it is possible to do it, or else I am *an inadequate individual* who is really not *able* to change."
2. "It's not only quite difficult to change myself but it *shouldn't be* that difficult. It's *awful* and *terrible*. I *can't stand* all the consistent hard work that it will take to change myself!"

Such disputing had better be done in an emotive, vigorous, and forceful manner. In addition, this kind of rational Disputing and the Effective New Philosophies that are achieved by doing it had better be enhanced by forceful and persistent action that implements their Disputing. People usually do not thoroughly change their actions without changing the convictions that impede these actions, but they also do not thoroughly change and maintain the changing of their attitudes without concerted action to back them up. As usual, thinking *and* emoting *and* acting go together, and integrally reinforce each other.

This emphasis is quite congruent with Ellen Langer's important concept and technique of mindfulness (Langer, 1997; Langer & Moldoveneau, 2000). For twenty-five years she and her associates have done considerable research showing that people can choose to think mindlessly or mindfully and that when they choose to do the latter kind of thinking they often achieve dramatic mental and behavioral changes.

Langer defines mindfulness as the process of drawing novel distinctions that keep us activated in the present and that leads to multiple perspectives in problem-solving. It introduces information about things and events in a conditional way and uses language like "I'd like it to be" instead of more common, absolutistic language like, "It can only be," and overlaps with the concepts of Alfred Korzybski and of REBT. It involves several highly cognitive aspects, but it also has emotional and behavioral involvements.

Although your clients, and especially your resistant ones, are often more mindless than mindful in their thinking, you may be able to help them apply the latter kind of thinking to their practical and emotional problems, and thereby foster their solidly changing. Read Ellen Langer and see!

Some Other Methods of Contradicting Irrational Beliefs that Encourage Resistance

5

When I formulated REBT in 1955, I emphasized that irrational beliefs play a major role in the creation of human disturbance, and that people—especially neurotic people—make themselves disturbed mainly by escalating their goals, desires, and preferences into absolutistic *musts* and demands. The three main "musts" that they use to disturb themselves are: (1) *Ego-driven* musts, such as "I *absolutely must* perform very well and be approved by significant others." (2) *Dogmatic* musts that are foisted upon others, such as, "Other people *absolutely must* treat me kindly and considerately, or they are damnable individuals!" (3) Demands that life conditions *absolutely must* be the way I want them to be, such as, "The conditions under which I live *must* be easy and afford me practically everything I want, and not afflict me with things that I do not want." I do not contend that *all* human emotional and mental disturbances are caused by these three *musts,* but rather that, *in conjunction with biological factors and with extreme environmental conditions,* there are few neurotic complaints in which they are not implicated.

When your clients start with the propositions that they *absolutely must* act competently, and *must* win the approval of significant people, they almost automatically follow these musts with various other dysfunctional and self-defeating convictions. When their experiences show them that they do *not* always act competently and that other people sometimes don't approve of them, even when they are behaving well, they often follow their musts with such overgeneralizations and damnations as:

1. "I am an incompetent, rotten person!"
2. "My life will be completely miserable!"

3. "The world is an awful and intolerable place in which to live!"
4. "People will *always* disapprove of me, and therefore I am doomed to lovelessness and loneliness!"

I continued to expand on the main forms of dysfunctional beliefs in the 1960's and 1970's, along with a number of other REBT and cognitive behavior therapy practitioners, such as Beck (1976), Bernard (2000), Burns (1980/1999), Ellis (1994), Hauck (1991), Mahoney (1991), Meichenbaum (1992), Phadke (1982), and Walen, DiGiuseppe, and Dryden (1992).

The core dysfunctional philosophies they describe share many commonalities. For example, when people believe that, "I *must* act competently and *must* win people's approval" (and then act incompetently and incur disapproval), they will often illogically conclude,

1. "I will always act incompetently and make significant people disapprove of me" (overgeneralization).
2. "I am a total failure and am completely unlovable" (overgeneralization, all-or-nothing thinking).
3. "People will always view me as incompetent and will dislike and reject me" (jumping to conclusions, mind reading, fortune-telling).
4. "People see nothing good in me" (focusing on the negative, overgeneralization).
5. "When others do see me favorably, that is because I am fooling them" (disqualifying the positive, non sequitur, "phonyism").
6. "People's disliking me will make me lose my job, become friendless, and make everything go wrong in my life" (catastrophizing, magnification).
7. "When I act well and people approve of me, that only shows that I can occasionally be right, but this is unimportant compared to my great faults and stupidity" (minimization, focusing on the negative).
8. "Because I deeply and consistently feel that I am despicable and unlovable, this proves that I really *am* despicable and unlovable" (emotional reasoning, circular reasoning, non sequitur).
9. "I am a complete loser and a failure" (labeling, overgeneralization).
10. "People are rejecting me solely because of who I am and what I've done; they could not possibly be rejecting me because of their own prejudices or for other reasons" (personalizing, non sequitur, overgeneralization).

Resisting clients—like other clients—pick up their absolutistic evaluations, inferences, and conclusions from their parents, teachers, and others in their environment. But as far as I can see, resisting clients *easily* soak up these dysfunctional convictions and are especially prone to rigidly hold onto them; many of them are probably born with a strong biological tendency to think irrationally. Some of the worst resistors actually may have learned quite *rational* family and cultural standards, such as, "It is *preferable* for me to treat others considerately," and then they overgeneralize, exaggerate, and turn these into musts.

You can teach your clients many ways of Disputing their Irrational *Beliefs*. A simple form of disputing has been outlined by Phadke (1982), in which disputing is broken up into three separate themes: detecting, debating, and discriminating irrational beliefs. First, however, it is necessary to uncover your clients' core musts (schemes).

INFERENCE CHAINING, LADDERING, AND THE DOWNWARD ARROW

Since its inception, REBT has tried to help clients become aware of their "lighter" Irrational *Beliefs* (IB's)—such as their inferences and automatic thoughts—as well as their deeper, core, or schematic IB's—such as their awfulizing and convictions of worthlessness (Ellis, 1962). A powerful method for revealing these basic and powerful IB's is called *inference chaining* (Moore, 1983; Walen, DiGiuseppe, & Dryden, 1992).

In inference chaining, you take the client's inference that an Adversity (A) is unfortunate or bad and show him that he really sees it as a *disaster*. Here is an example from Michael Neenan and Windy Dryden (1999, p. 96).

THERAPIST: What is anxiety-provoking in your mind about your husband dancing with another woman at the party?

CLIENT: He might find her more desirable than me.

THERAPIST: Let's assume for the moment that he does find her more desirable than you. Then what?

CLIENT: He might leave me and go off with her.

THERAPIST: Let's assume that he does do that. Then what?

CLIENT: I'll be all alone in the world and worthless.

THERAPIST: Why would you be worthless because you're all alone in the world?

CLIENT: Because I'm nothing without him.

THERAPIST: So are you most anxious about your husband leaving you because you think you are "nothing, worthless" without him?

CLIENT: Yes, that's what I'm afraid of. [The client's critical A, her husband's departure, and her derivative irrational belief, that she will be "nothing, worthless without him," have been revealed simultaneously.]

The next step is for the therapist to help the client reveal her major demand about the critical A: e.g., "My husband must never leave me because if he does I'll be worthless." This Irrational *Belief* is then disputed using logical, empirical, and pragmatic arguments.

Neenan and Dryden also show how the downward arrow technique of David Burns (1980/1999) and the laddering technique of personal construct therapists can also be used to reveal clients' core irrationalities.

In the *downward arrow* method, clients are asked for the meaning of each automatic thought, in order to reveal its deeper, underlying awfulness. Again, Neenan and Dryden (1999) give a good example of this technique.

In the *laddering* technique, clients are shown that their evaluations of Adversities are bipolar constructs, with favorable and unfavorable aspects and that if they consider *both* sides, they will likely arrive at wider, and presumably more rational, available behaviors. Once again, Neenan and Dryden nicely illustrate the use of this method:

CLIENT: I can't always afford to buy my kids the things they need for school.

THERAPIST: And what does that mean to you?

CLIENT: The other kids at school will have everything and my kids will be going without.

THERAPIST: Let's assume they are going without, what would that mean to you?

CLIENT: If I'm failing my children, then I'm failing as a father. Also what will the other parents think of me when they are providing adequately for their children?

THERAPIST: Let's suppose you are failing as a father, what would that mean to you?

CLIENT: That I'm a very bad father.

Resistant clients are often more defensive than other clients and are initially highly unlikely to acknowledge their deepest Irrational *Beliefs*. Inference chaining, downward arrow, and laddering can be highly effective in "smoking them out" and helping them to acknowledge and tackle their core irrationalities.

DETECTING IRRATIONAL BELIEFS

You can show your client that whenever they feel seriously disturbed or act self-defeatingly, they probably have dysfunctional doctrines, and you can interpolate and help them see the explicit or implicit musts that are included in their convictions. Here, for example, are some common irrationalities, and the fairly obvious musts, which I am placing in parentheses, that clients often implicitly include:

> "I keep failing all the time (as I *must* never fail at important things), and if I fail this time (as I definitely *must* not do), that means that I will *always* fail."
>
> "People see through me and know that I am a phony (because I *have to* perform better than I do), and even when I appear to act well, I am far from perfect (as I *must not* be) and therefore, they are soon going to find me out and *totally* reject me."
>
> "I can't find anything that interests me (because I've *got to* do everything well; and if I do something poorly, that's *awful* and proof that I am an *inadequate person*)."
>
> "Most people do much better than I (as I *should* and *must* do) and lead an enjoyable life (as I *must* also lead). I will never do well enough and lead an enjoyable life; therefore, this makes me an inadequate person!"
>
> "People are utterly rotten individuals when they treat me unfairly (as they absolutely *must* not do)."
>
> "I always fail at important tasks (and I *should not*)."

DEBATING OR DISPUTING IRRATIONAL BELIEFS

Once the irrational beliefs (IB's) of your resistant clients are clearly discovered, you can actively debate and Dispute them by the various techniques outlined in the rest of this book. You'll have a wide range of choices here, because IBs can be disputed mildly or strongly, by empirical data or by logic, by direct statements or by analogy, didactically or dramatically, and in many other ways. Many cognitive behavior therapists dispute or debate in a mild and somewhat Rogerian manner; but REBT advocates that especially with resistant clients, it had better often be done in a much more active, directive, vigorous way. At the same time that you vigorously Dispute clients' IB's, you can show them that you really want them to be healthier and happier and that this is the best way of helping them. As Young (1974) points out, "Disputing can be done in a powerful manner, but at the same time, emphasizes your favorable relationship with the client, and shows her that you are really on her side." If she thinks that you are merely opposed to irrationality for its *own* sake—and not because it creates havoc for her—she may likely resist your Disputing. So try to consistently show her that her dysfunctional *Beliefs* are sabotaging her *own* goals, and that you want to help her to be less self-disturbing.

In this respect, it is important to note the excellent point made by Dryden and Still (1998, p. 77) that "there is no essence of rationality which could enable it to be applied normatively in all contexts." Although REBT uses the scientific concepts of realism or factuality and of logic to show that clients' *Beliefs* are "false," it mainly means that they are *unworkable for the individual client under the conditions that he/she lives in his/her cultural context.* Thus, the belief that, "I must not fail any test I take because if I do I am worthless and undeserving!" is unrealistic—because one cannot *always* succeed; and it is an illogical overgeneralization, because one *isn't* one of her or his *behaviors*. In REBT, we realistically and logically Dispute this belief—but we do so to show that usually (not always) it will lead to unfortunate results. Our using realistic and logical Disputing seems to help most people surrender Irrational *Beliefs;* but they are not *merely* "false" but *also* unworkable.

A special method of Disputing your clients' Irrational *Beliefs* was created by me in the 1970s (Ellis, 1973). It consists of several questions and possible answers that your clients can use, and that you can then check to see if they do so correctly. It is called Disputing Irrational Beliefs (DIBS) (Ellis & Dryden, 1997):

QUESTION 1: What unhealthy *Belief* do I want to dispute and surrender?
ANSWER: I must be as effective and sexually fulfilled as most other women.
QUESTION 2: Can I empirically, logically, and pragmatically support this *Belief?*
ANSWER: No. It is unrealistic because I don't *have* to be effective sexually. It is illogical because it doesn't follow that if I strongly *want* to be fulfilled sexually, I therefore must be. It is impractical because if I think I *have to* be good sexually, I will probably *interfere with* my sex relations.
QUESTION 3: What evidence exists of the accuracy of this *Belief?*
ANSWER: None, only evidence that it would be preferable for me to do well sexually but not that it would be necessary.
QUESTION 4: What evidence exists of the inaccuracy of my *Belief* that I must be as orgasmic as other women are?
ANSWER: The fact that I am and easily can remain less orgasmic than other women are.

QUESTION 5:   What are the worst possible things that could actually happen to me if I *never* achieved the orgasm that I think I must achieve?

ANSWER: I will lose some degree of pleasure and may lose some partners who demand that I be more effective sexually (and who obviously are not for me!).

QUESTION 6:   What good things could I do if I never achieved the heights of orgasm that I think I must achieve?

ANSWER: I could devote myself to other pleasurable things, could find a partner who would accept me as I am, and could unfrantically explore other sex possibilities.

DISCRIMINATING BETWEEN RATIONAL BELIEFS AND IRRATIONAL BELIEFS

REBT hypothesizes that Irrational *Beliefs* rarely exist by themselves, but are preceded by or associated with rational ones. Thus, clients almost always have preferences or desires ("I really want to pass this examination and get my degree") along with their absolutistic commands or musts ("Because I want to pass this examination and get my degree, I *have to* do so, and it would be *horrible* if I didn't!")

REBT holds that virtually all preferences, even somewhat unrealistic ones, are rational as long as long as they are *only* that—preferences. For if people say to themselves, "I would like very much to have a million dollars right now—but if I don't, I don't, and can still lead a happy life without it," they are not going to seriously upset themselves when their preferences are not fulfilled. But if they tell themselves, "I not only want ten dollars right now, but I *absolutely must* have it, otherwise that would be terrible!" they are going to anxietize or depress themselves even when they have $9.95.

Therefore, emphasize to your clients that you are not in the least interfering with, or trying to change their *preferences*. Preferences are sensible and self-helping for the most part, for several reasons:

1. They sustain your clients' lives. Without desires people would hardly live or fare well.
2. They motivate your clients to continue to live and to look for greater pleasure and happiness.
3. They make life considerably less boring than it otherwise might be, and add appreciably to their existence.
4. Preferences aid the discovery of new preferences and new experiences.

Using REBT, therefore, you help resisting clients to clearly discriminate their Rational from their Irrational *Beliefs*. When they recognize their dysfunctional demands and work at giving them up, they can retain their sensible desires and look for ways of fulfilling them. Like some other forms of psychotherapy, REBT has two main aspects: First, it shows people how to give up their self-defeating ideas and actions and stop needlessly interfering with their enjoyments. It then tries to help them lead more creative and self-actualizing lives. But in order to accomplish self-actualizing, your client had better attack the dysfunctional attitudes that interfere with their goals and values and then, with these largely out of the way, try to create several exciting preferences.

USING RATIONAL COPING STATEMENTS AND POSITIVE THINKING

Emile Coué was a pioneer in the use of positive thinking. He realized, as Seligman (1991) has also shown, that a pessimistic outlook frequently leads people to anxietize and depress. Richard Lazarus, Donald Meichenbaum, Robert Schwartz, Shelly Taylor, and several other psychological researchers have also shown that when people have a preponderance of positive over negative attitudes, they tend to be mentally healthier. R. Lazarus (2000) has clearly demonstrated how strong positive coping statements help some of the most difficult clients to overcome their negative views and achieve better mental health. Ziegler (2001) indicated the compatibility of Lazarus' theory and practice with that of REBT.

Your resistant clients not only usually have several unhealthy negative attitudes, but they also tend to hold onto them extremely rigidly. They have a real "talent" for taking realistic negative observations and exaggerating them out of all proportion. Thus, they tell themselves that "I've failed several times to gain a satisfactory love partner; that means that I'll *never* be able to succeed in love." They notice a large dog and tell themselves "Because it could rip me to pieces if it decided to do so, it will definitely do so." With these kinds of unduly pessimistic clients, you can often help them use empirically-oriented positive coping self-statements, such as:

"I know it's difficult to succeed in love with a partner I really want, but if I keep trying, I will probably eventually do so."
"Even though the dog I see is larger than most, there is very little chance that he will bite me. And even if he does, I will hardly die of a few dog bites."

"Yes, this test will probably be quite difficult to pass successfully, but if I keep studying the material and doing my best to pass it, there is a high degree of probability that I will actually do well."

"I may well get rejected for this job that I really want, but if I keep trying at interviews, I will most likely get a fairly good one."

"If I do not run away from social situations about which I anxietize, I will gradually become less tense in them and I will then be able to relate better with others."

These kinds of rational coping statements realistically acknowledge that your clients will often run into difficulties in trying to reach their goals. But they also acknowledge the positive side of trying to get what they desire, and the probability of having much of their wishes fulfilled if they persist in their trying.

Resistant clients do not necessarily invent the unfortunate possibilities, but they over-emphasize how *awful* it will be if these actually occur and thus unduly anxietize and depress themselves. They will often parrot the positive ideas you present, but not really believe them. They say, "Yes, it is possible for me to succeed after a while. But suppose I fail. I *couldn't* bear it!" You can therefore help them repeat the kinds of positive statements listed above, but at the same time to figure out how they can really start believing them.

Thus, you can help your client not only say, "If I only keep trying, I think that I definitely can succeed in learning this material and passing this important test," but you can have them review why this statement is usually accurate. For example, a client can see that several times in the past when she had at first failed to pass a test, she kept studying and studying and then succeeded. She can also talk to other people who at first failed miserably in taking important tests and who later, through consistent study, were able to do remarkably well.

A limitation of positive thinking is that after a while, it may have little effect. In addition, it may also be contradicted by actual reality. In 1920, Emile Coué was one of the world's most famous therapists. His famous statement, "Day by day in every way I'm getting better and better" was successfully used by thousands of individuals who were at first very pessimistic about their ability to change. This kind of positive thinking, however, is palpably inaccurate because practically no one gets better and better day by day, no matter what he or she does. Many devotees of Coué's kind of positive thinking became disillusioned and abandoned it. Optimistic self-statements, consequently, may be very helpful to your resistant clients—providing that they keep them within a realistic range, empirically test them against what happens in the world, and then carefully revise them.

Along with antipessimistic coping statements, you can encourage your clients to tell themselves more philosophic self-statements that tend to undo their negativistic, musturbatory evaluation of themselves, others, and the conditions around them. A common absolutistic philosophy that a large number of difficult clients strongly hold is the Irrational *Belief,* "I have to perform this important task perfectly well, and I'm a terribly inadequate person if I don't!" A counter-attacking self statement that they can say to themselves, and intensely repeat many times, might be "I would very much like to perform this task perfectly well, but I never *have* to do. If I perform it badly, I am a person who does badly, but I never am a bad person. Telling myself that I absolutely must perform it perfectly well will encourage me to think that I am a totally incompetent person when I fail to do so. Therefore, I can desire but not *need* to perfectly well."

Another common Irrational *Belief* that many resistant clients hold is, "My friend treats me inconsiderately and unfairly, as she absolutely should not do, and therefore I *can't stand* her at all—and she is *no damn good!*" A rational coping statement to contradict this IB would be: "Even when my friend treats me inconsiderably or unfairly, she is a fallible human being and has a perfect right to act wrongly. And I *can* stand associating with her, though I very much dislike some of her unjust behavior. Although she sometimes acts in a manner that I consider unfair, she is not a *totally* unfair person and a *horrible* individual!" This kind of philosophy will not only often help your resistant clients to accept "bad people" in spite of some of their bad behavior, but will also help them accept "good people" who may also at times behave badly.

Positive thinking, then, can be useful for resistant clients, but it can also negatively boomerang when it is Pollyannaish, unrealistic, and includes some musturbatory thinking. It also had better include the conviction that if unlikely misfortunes actually *do* occur, clients can handle them and not depress themselves about them.

Your clients' rational coping self-statements can be stated in general form, so they can apply them to many difficult situations they encounter and about which they frequently upset themselves.

Clients can write down their coping statements on three-by-five cards and mindfully think about them (or voice them aloud) several times a day, until they sink them firmly into their heads and hearts. Some typical philosophically oriented statements include the following:

"Nothing is *awful* or *horrible,* though many things are highly inconvenient."

"I never *need* what I want, no matter how much I desire it."

"I will try to be myself and to *enjoy* myself and not think that I have to *prove* myself."

"I will always be a highly fallible human, who will continue to make many important mistakes, and who can always choose to accept myself in spite of making them."

"I can rarely change others, but I can always stop damning them for their mistakes and thereby considerably reduce my own upset."

Because resistant clients often believe that they should not, must not have to work at changing themselves, but should have someone else magically change them, and because they frequently—and strongly— feel that they *can't* change, they are encouraged to use rational self-statements that forcefully attack these ideas and help them to get on with their lives. These include coping statements about therapy, such as:

"Therapy doesn't have to be easy. In fact, I can actually enjoy the difficult challenge!"

"Sure, it's hard to work at changing myself—but it's much harder if I don't!"

"Too bad that I often fail to work on changing myself. This only proves that I am still, and will continue to be a highly fallible person. I can still accept myself with my fallibility—and then work like hell to be less fallible."

"Therapists usually do their best to help their clients. But they, too, have their problems and failings. Tough! Now, how can I experiment with the suggestions that my therapist makes to me, and also find ways to help myself?"

Let me repeat: Even your bright and well-educated clients had better try repeating rational coping statements like those I describe in this chapter—and not do so mildly or occasionally. They preferably should do so, in a positive, strong, vigorous, emotive manner. Resistant individuals can thereby achieve thorough-going rather than inelegant solutions to their problems.

If you, as their therapist, actively and persistently demonstrate to your clients how to forcefully repeat sensible coping statements to themselves, they may be inspired by your energetic tone, and be appreciably more active themselves. Following their repeating their rational coping self-statements to themselves, also encourage them to act upon them as quickly and as often as possible. For example, they can use the coping statement, "Too bad if I am often so lax at changing myself. This only proves that I am still a highly fallible person. However, I can accept myself—and then work like hell to be less fallible." While saying this, your clients can, at the same time, force themselves to take risks at performances, such as sports, that they may easily fail at, and practice accepting themselves with their failing. They can even paradoxically *deliberately* fail at something. The more they back up their rational coping self-statements with actions, the more they will tend to thoroughly believe them.

THE USE OF COST-BENEFIT ANALYSES

When clients are addicted to self-defeating behaviors, such as procrastination or indulging in too much alcohol or food, and are resisting giving up their addiction, teach them how to do a cost-benefit analysis of their dysfunctional behaving. Thus, if they keep smoking cigarettes even when they are determined to stop, it shows them that they are irrationally focusing on the enormous difficulty of stopping, but not consciously focusing on the even greater difficulty of not stopping. They sweep the disadvantages of their harmful addictions under the rug, and concentrate on the advantages of these addictions, such as the immediate gratification and the release of tension that they receive. One of the most powerful and effective REBT methods is to teach addictive clients to make a comprehensive list of the disadvantages of their indulgences, to look at this list several times a day, and to consciously fix them in their heads (Ellis & Velten, 1992/1998).

Here is a typical list of disadvantages of resisting self-change and therapy.

"If I keep resisting changing it will take me longer to change."
"I will keep needlessly suffering as long as I resist changing."
"My refusing to change will cause suffering to some of the people I care for, and will sabotage my relationships with them."
"My therapy will become more prolonged, boring, and expensive the longer I take to change myself."
"Continuing to afflict myself with my symptoms will make me lose considerable time and money outside of therapy."
"If I continue to resist treatment, I may well antagonize my therapist and encourage her to put less effort into helping me."
"My refusing to work hard at therapy and thereby remain irrationally anxietizing and depressing will make me give up many potential pleasures and make my life much duller."

In addition to listing the disadvantages of resisting, clients can also list the advantages of working harder at therapy, and thereby aid themselves in making important personality changes. Writing down, reviewing, and thinking about both the disadvantages of resisting therapy and the benefits of nonresistance can be of considerable help to clients in tackling their resistance.

REBT and CBT often forcefully bring to clients' attention not only their present but also their later probable disadvantages of resisting therapy. You can remind them, "Yes, you can get away right now with not working on overcoming your low frustration tolerance, because your parents are still around to help support you economically, in spite of your goofing. But how are you going to earn a decent living on your own, after they are gone, unless you prepare yourself now? So, you'd better start whittling away at your low frustration tolerance now, so that it doesn't seriously affect you several years down the pike." Or you may remind your resistant clients, "At this point in time you may be able to get away with your drinking and staying up late, and with your other indulgences, but won't they eventually sabotage your health and life enjoyment? Do you really want to keep making yourself fat, tired, and physically ill?"

Using cost-benefit analysis often gets at your clients' unconscious resistance to change, makes it fully conscious, and thereby interferes with it (Leahy, 2001). Clients sometimes may tell you that they are consciously aware that they are resisting therapy, and aware that this resistance does them little good and much harm. But for the most part, they manage to keep this so-called awareness well covered-up, and are, at most, very *slightly* aware of the expenses of resisting. By encouraging them to do clear-cut cost-benefit analyses in writing, and by their making themselves much more conscious of the harm they are wreaking, their changing becomes more likely. Of course, even when clients are fully conscious of the hazards of their dysfunction, they still may perversely resist giving it up. But awareness often increases the chances of their fighting against their resistance.

As ever, when you encourage your clients to do a cost-benefit analysis of their self-sabotaging, you can meld this with emotive techniques to get them to passionately attend to how specifically harmful their indulgences may be. For example, when one of my clients did a cost-benefit analysis of her not working on her Ph.D. thesis, she at first did it in the superficial manner. She listed the current disadvantages of delaying getting her Ph.D., but she failed to list the *long-term* disadvantages. I pointed out that if her five-year period for finishing the dissertation expired, and she was unable to get her degree, she would in all probability work at low-level jobs, and thereby suffer frustration for the next thirty or forty years. When, at my urging, she forcefully went over these long-term disadvantages, the negatives became much more vivid and daunting. As a result, she did more work on her dissertation during the next three months than she had done in the previous three years.

You can similarly have your clients do a cost-benefit analysis of their resisting therapy, bringing to their full attention the present pains of their keeping their neurotic disturbances as well as the many ensuing years that they are likely to suffer. A client with an automobile phobia who refuses to expose himself to riding in cars can be urged to list not only the present disadvantages of this phobia, but he can also be shown that if he continues to resist practicing in vivo desensitization, he will have to avoid riding for fifty years to come. That will be truly handicapping!

Along with helping your clients more clearly see the tremendous costs of their continued resisting, strongly encourage them to *act* against some of those costs. For example, when my socially anxietizing clients fully see how much they are missing in life by not forcing themselves to encounter other people, they frequently agree to doing the homework assignments of actively practicing such encountering—and penalizing themselves when they don't carry them out.

Encouraging clients to do an effective cost-benefit analysis of their various forms of resistance seems to be mainly a cognitive method of therapy, but it also, as I have just indicated, had better include distinct emotive and behavioral correlates.

Robert Leahy (2001) points out that even when they are aware of the value of doing a cost-benefit analysis to see whether they had better wisely change from dysfunctional to more functional *Beliefs* and habits, many clients fail to use it. Instead they unwisely stick to their past investments and committed actions for several possible reasons:

1. They think they have invested "too much" in the past to give it up now.
2. They are emotionally (strongly) committed to the past while intellectually (lightly) see its disadvantages.
3. They are familiar with the past and find it "too hard" and "too risky" to change.
4. They think they *have to* continue and somehow (miraculously!) succeed with the old habits or else they would prove that they were foolish and therefore would be "inadequate" people.

Leahy (2001) has several good suggestions for helping clients give up the "sunk costs" of their past and present behaviors and to counter their beliefs that to change them now would be "too aversive." These methods include:

1. Teach your clients that "sunk cost" ideas are common among humans—and usually lead to greater future costs.
2. Show your clients the emotional and other costs of sticking to and presumably changing.
3. Show your clients the lesser costs and greater benefits of some alternative *Beliefs* and behaviors that you can help them work out.
4. Separate your clients' reasons for their *past* behaviors—e.g., "I really love him and am therefore sure our relationship will ultimately work out"—from the *present* costs of maintaining those behaviors. Ask them if they *now* knew the costs of their actions when they made the decision to make them would they still decide to make them again.
5. Ask your clients what other people would probably do if faced with the decision to change their present dysfunctional behavior.
6. Ask your clients, "What advice would you give to a friend or relative who had to make this decision?"
7. See if your clients have any core Irrational *Beliefs* behind their commitment to sunk costs—such as, "If I faced the fact that I had wasted four years by not changing my relationship (or job) what would it mean?" Often, they will say, "I would be worthless!" and/or "Life would be *awful.*" These core *Beliefs* could then be Disputed.

USE OF MODELING TECHNIQUES

REBT and CBT often use modeling techniques—which Albert Bandura (1997) has shown can help children and adults function better. You can use them with resistant clients by showing them that no matter how difficult they find it to reduce their disturbed feelings, as well as to reduce their anxiety and depression *about* these feelings, they can find friends and relatives who have done so. They can also read and learn about other very disturbed people who have used REBT, CBT, and other therapy methods to considerably help themselves.

Revealing to clients how you yourself were once distinctly disturbed about something and used various cognitive, emotive, and behavioral methods to help yourself may provide an especially good model for some of them. Encouraging them to attend your workshops or listen to recordings of your self-help talks may also be good modeling devices. Many of my own and my colleagues' clients attend my Friday night workshops, where I give public demonstrations of REBT; and their seeing how I help the often quite-disturbed volunteers may help them considerably to effectively use REBT with themselves.

USING COGNITIVE DISTRACTION
AND RELAXATION METHODS

The ancient Eastern and Western philosophers found that when people made themselves anxious, depressed, and enraged they could quickly distract themselves by using yoga, meditation, and other techniques of thinking of something *else*—almost anything else—rather than indulging in their disturbed thoughts. Modern therapists, such as Edmund Jacobson, Herbert Benson, and Robert Fried have used a wide variety of relaxation methods to help clients stop focusing on their anxious and depressed thinking by deliberately and intensely focusing on their breathing, their muscles, a mantra, or on other forms of cognitive distraction.

REBT and CBT use these distraction methods, but point out that they are often palliative and do not permanently change clients' musturbatory philosophies (Ellis, 2000; Ellis & Tafrate, 1997). But they work!—and sometimes with quite resistant clients who will not accept or work at using more elegant methods of therapy. Preferably, however, cognitive distraction methods can be more effective when used *with* more lasting forms of REBT and CBT.

More Methods of Contradicting Irrational Beliefs that Encourage Resistance

6

In this chapter I will consider more methods of contradicting and actively working against Irrational *Beliefs* that you can use with some of your most difficult clients.

USING THE CHALLENGE OF SELF-CHANGING WITH RESISTING CLIENTS

Resistant clients frequently view self-change as too arduous and painful because it requires so much persistent effort and practice. They consider changing themselves as an adversity, rather than as an advantage. REBT and CBT therefore try to help them to reframe the process of self-change as more of an adventure and challenge than a hardship. One of the favorite homework exercises of REBT is Disputing Irrational Beliefs (DIBS), which I described in chapter 5, and in which clients are helped to debate their dysfunctional *Beliefs* and to reframe some of the difficulties of therapy by asking themselves questions like: "What *good* things can I feel or make happen if I work hard at therapy and still don't succeed too well?"

You can also prod resisting clients with questions like "Suppose you pick the wrong therapy techniques and work hard at it with little good results. Why would *that* be great to do?" By this kind of a paradoxical question, they help the resistors to see that: (1) Trying something and at first failing at it is usually better than not trying at all. (2) Striving to change leads to important information about oneself that may result in later success and pleasures. (3) Action can be pleasurable in its own right, even when it does not produce great results. (4) Trying to change oneself and accepting poor results may decrease one's frustration tolerance. (5) The challenge of striving for therapeutic change—like the challenge of scaling Mount Everest—may itself be exciting and enjoyable.

It may not be easy for you, as a therapist, to help some of your clients view changing themselves as a challenge rather than a dreadful chore. But if you can induce them to accept this challenge, it is one of the most effective cognitive, emotive, and behavioral techniques that you can use. You can say to your resistant clients, "Yes, many people are prone to sit on their butts and foolishly resist changing themselves. But anyone fortunate enough to have your intelligence, talent, and ability can overcome this kind of resistance and achieve impressive results. Not that you *have to* use your innate ability to change, but wouldn't it be challenging if you did use it and got much better results?"

Many clients may take this challenge of changing themselves in order to prove what good people they are—in other words to conditionally, rather than unconditionally, accept themselves. It would be better if you encouraged them to change themselves because *it* is good for them, and not because *they* are good for doing so. It is challenging and useful in its own right to work on changing oneself, but somewhat dangerous to do so because it makes one a "better person."

When you help your clients to accept the *challenge* of changing themselves, you also help them emotionally. For anything challenging, such as winning at sports or even choosing the winning team, has an adventurous aspect and is exciting. The challenge to change can give clients distinct emotional as well as cognitive satisfactions.

Moreover, the challenge to change has behavioral advantages. It impels action and tends to lead your clients to possibilities of significantly changing their lives right now and also to acclimate themselves to the kind of actions that will enhance their lives in the future. An exciting challenge *feels* good and is intrinsically action-oriented.

PROSELYTIZING OTHERS

One of the regular REBT cognitive techniques that you can use with your resisting clients is to encourage them to use REBT techniques with other people as well as themselves. For example, as you work on convincing clients that they partly create their own rage, you can give them homework assignments of trying to talk their friends or relatives out of *their* raging. By helping show other people in their lives how they enrage themselves, your clients will more easily be able to talk themselves out of their own raging. This by no means always works, but some of my clients have been very successful in proselytizing and actually talking their friends and relatives out of some of their self-disturbances. When they refer them to me for psychotherapy, I can see that they have been considerably aided by my referring client.

Teaching other people how to use REBT on themselves can help your clients to deconstruct their own disturbances. As John Dewey said many years ago, we learn by teaching others to learn. Some of my clients do so well with using REBT with their friends and relatives that they actually help these people become considerably less afflicting.

USING HUMOR

Many resistant clients, like many regular clients, lose their sense of humor when they neuroticize themselves. They not only take things seriously, but too seriously, and give exaggerated significance to the events of their and other people's lives (Ellis & Dryden, 1997; Ellis, Gordon, Neenan, & Palmer, 1998).

With my clients I try to highlight the irony of how they are thinking and acting against their own interests. In one case, I showed one of my stubborn clients how ironic it was that she railed and ranted against cold weather, and thereby made herself suffer more (physically *and* emotionally) when she was afflicted by it. I showed another of my resistant clients that the more he angered himself about the inefficiencies of the people with whom he was working, the less he was able to devote time and energy to correcting their inefficiencies.

I also frequently tell my resistant clients, "If the Martians ever come to visit us on earth, they'll die laughing at us Earthians. For they'll see bright people like you vainly insisting that they absolutely can do something that they can't do, such as change the ways of their parents, while also insisting that they can't do something that they almost invariably *can* do, such as change themselves. Those poor Martians probably won't be able to understand, and may well fly back to Mars convinced that we Earthians are completely crazy!"

One of the main REBT techniques that I first presented in a paper, "Fun as Psychotherapy," at the 1976 American Psychological Association's convention, is the use of rational humorous songs. These songs are actually cognitive, emotive, and behavioral. Cognitively, in that they usually satirize and attack a major Irrational *Belief*. Emotively, in that they are musical and rhythmical, since they weld evocative well-known tunes to expressive humorous lyrics. Behaviorally, in that they are designed to be sung again and again by self-disturbing individuals, until the singers internalize the philosophies of these songs and begin to think and feel more rationally. By singing one of the songs to themselves, they are less likely to upset themselves seriously in the first place, or are fairly easily and quickly able to un-upset themselves (Ellis, 1977, 1986). Some of my rational humorous songs with which resistors can help themselves include these two tunes, which satirize low frustration tolerance:

WHINE, WHINE, WHINE
(Tune: "Yale Whiffenpoof Song,"
composed by a Harvard man in 1896!)

I cannot have all my wishes filled—
Whine, whine, whine!
I cannot have every frustration stilled—
Whine, whine, whine!
Life really owes me the things that I miss,
Fate has to grant me eternal bliss!
And since I must settle for less than this—
Whine, whine, whine!

BEAUTIFUL HANG-UP
(Tune: "Beautiful Dreamer," by Stephen Foster)

Beautiful hang-up, why should we part
When we have shared our whole lives from the start?
We are so used to taking one course,
Oh, what a crime it would be to divorce!
Beautiful hang-up, don't go away!
Who will befriend me if you do not stay?
Though you still make me look like a jerk,
Living without you would take too much work!
Living without you would take too much work!

Another of my rational humorous songs makes fun of perfectionists:

PERFECT RATIONALITY
(Tune: "Funiculi, Funicula," by Denza)

Some think the world must have a right direction,
And so do I—and so do I!
Some think that, with the slightest imperfection
They can't get by—and so do I!
For I, I have to prove I'm superhuman,
And better far than people are!
To show I have miraculous acumen—
And always rate among the Great!

Perfect, perfect rationality
Is, of course, the only thing for me!
How can I ever think of being
If I must live fallibly?
Rationality must be a perfect thing for me!

Still another REBT humorous song is an anti-depression ditty:

I'M DEPRESSED, DEPRESSED!
(Tune: "The Band Played On," by Charles B. Ward)

When anything slightly goes wrong with my life,
I'm depressed, depressed!
Whenever I'm stricken with chickenshit strife,
I feel most distressed!
When life isn't fated to be consecrated
I can't tolerate it at all!
When anything slightly goes wrong with my life,
I just bawl, bawl, bawl!

A rational humorous song that helps difficult clients be more realistic about themselves and other people is this one:

GLORY, GLORY HALLELUJAH!
(Tune: "Battle Hymn of the Republic" by Julia Ward Howe)

Mine eyes have seen the glory of relationships that glow
And then falter by the wayside as love passions come—and go!
I've heard of great romances where there is no slightest lull—
But I am skeptical!
Glory, glory hallelujah!
People love ya till they screw ya!
If you'd lessen how they do ya
Then don't expect they won't!

The following is a song that can help people zero in on their secondary symptoms, such as their depression about their depression:

WHEN I AM SO BLUE
(Tune: "The Beautiful Blue Danube," music by Johann Strauss, Jr.)

When I am so blue, so blue,
I sit and I stew, I stew, I stew!
I deem it so awfully horrible
That my life is rough and scarable!
Whenever my blues are verified,
I make myself doubly terrified,
For I never choose to refuse
To be blue about my blues!

A rational humorous song that can help resistors' dire need for approval is this one:

LOVE ME, LOVE ME, ONLY ME!
(Tune: "Yankee Doodle Dandy")

Love me, love me, only me
Or I will die without you!
O, make your love a guarantee
So I can never doubt you!
Love me, love me totally—really, really try dear;
But if you demand love, too
I'll hate you till I die, dear!

Love me, love me all the time
Thoroughly and wholly!
My life turns into slushy slime
Unless you love me solely!
Love me with great tenderness
With no ifs or buts, dear.
If you love me somewhat less,
I'll hate your goddamned guts, dear!

There are two shame-attacking and anti-low frustration tolerance songs that can be used by resistant clients:

YOU FOR ME AND ME FOR ME
(Tune: "Tea for Two," by Vincent Youmans)

Picture you upon my knee
Just you for me, and me for me!
And then you'll see
How happy I will be!
Though you beseech me
You never will reach me—
For I am autistic
As any real mystic!
And only relate to
Myself with a great to-do, dear!
If you dare to try to care
You'll see my caring soon will wear,
For I can't pair and make our sharing fair!
If you want a family,
We'll both agree you'll baby me—
Then you'll see how happy I will be!

I WISH I WERE NOT CRAZY!
(Tune: "Dixie," by Dan Emmett)

Oh, I wish I were really put together—
Smooth and fine as patent leather!

Oh, how great to be rated innately sedate!
But I am afraid that I was fated
To be rather aberrated—
Oh, how sad to be mad as my Mom and my Dad!

Oh, I wish I were not crazy! Hooray! Hooray!
I wish my mind were less inclined
To be the kind that's hazy!
I could, you see, agree to be less crazy—
But I, alas, am just too goddamned lazy!

Two of my favorite songs that REBT clients often use to combat their chronic anxietizing are the following ones:

WHAT IF, WHAT IF . . . !
(Tune: "Blue Danube Waltz," by Johann Strauss, Jr.)

I think of what if, what if!
And scare myself stiff, yes stiff, quite stiff!
When things are as certain as can be,
I ask for a perfect guarantee.
I've got to strike out with solid biffs
At all of my sick what if's, what if's,
But what if I fail to prevail—
Oh my God, what if I fail!

I'M JUST WILD ABOUT WORRY
(Tune: "I'm Just Wild About Harry," by Eubie Blake)

Oh, I'm just wild about worry
And worry's wild about me!
We're quite a twosome to make life gruesome
And filled with anxiety!
Oh, worry's anguish I curry
And look for its guarantee!
Oh, I'm just wild about worry
And worry's wild about
Never mild about,
Most beguiled about me!

(New song lyrics by Albert Ellis, copyright by the Albert Ellis Institute.)

Of course, looking at their Irrational Beliefs in a humorous manner will by no means always work with resistant clients. Some of them are almost completely humorless, and may even be offended by a therapist's attempt to humorously talk them out of some of their disturbances and resistances. But if you use humor carefully and diplomatically, it often works where very little else will. Remember, however: it is important not to make fun of any of your *clients,* but just of their irrational *ideas.*

USING PARADOXICAL INTENTION

Many therapists have found that highly resistant and negativistic clients can sometimes be reached by paradoxical intention, which often has a humorous slant. Victor Frankl (1960) and Milton Erickson (Erickson & Rossi, 1979) have pioneered in using paradoxical methods to help resistant clients. Other therapists, such as Jay Haley (1998) and Steven Hayes (Hayes, Strosahl, & Wilson, 1999), have carried on this tradition and have discovered that since resistors paradoxically stick rigidly with their resistance, they can sometimes be helped to surrender it with paradoxical therapy methods.

REBT sometimes uses humorous paradoxical homework, as when a client who resists taking the risks of exposing himself to desensitizing homework is given the paradoxical assignment of deliberately failing in social or in sporting encounters, in order to graphically see that nothing catastrophic or horrible actually happens (Ellis, 1999; Ellis & MacLaren, 1998). You can encourage depressed clients to loudly wail and moan about everything that occurs in their live, including minor adversities. Or, you can have highly anxious people take the assignment of only allowing themselves to worry from 8:00 to 8:15 AM every day. Or, you can insist that resistant clients refuse to do *any*thing you tell them to do—such as refuse to come on time for their sessions or to do any homework assignments. Perversely, resistors may then stop resisting. But don't count on this, since paradoxical intention is a dramatic method of helping people, but by no means works all the time, and sometimes only does so under special conditions.

USING THE PHILOSOPHY OF EFFORT
TO COMBAT RESISTANCE

REBT follows a constructivist, but not a Pollyannaish, philosophy. I usually explain to my clients that they have enormous constructivist tendencies to change themselves, as long as they work and practice consistently at doing so. But I also explain that they have innate and learned self-defeating tendencies that *interfere* with their constructive abilities. I show them that they can easily fall back to their old dysfunctional patterns of behavior even after they change them, and that therefore they had better persistently keep monitoring themselves and keep working to maintain their changes.

A major goal of REBT and CBT, therefore, is to have clients solidly achieve a basic philosophy of *effort*. Its practitioners assume that resistors often indulge in low frustration tolerance (LFT); and one of the main goals of therapy is to help them to strive for fairly high frustration tolerance. Therefore, you had better help resistors to really see that they usually try to take the "easy" way out, and thereby impede the hard work of changing. Their LFT may almost completely block their efforts to change, or as is commonly the case, allow them to change temporarily and then fall back on their old self-sabotaging behaviors.

In view of this fact, you can keep reiterating the virtues of your resistant clients' achieving higher frustration tolerance. This means that you would like them to make an almost Herculean change to get and stay better. Much against their own grain, they had better acquire a profound philosophy of the value of high frustration tolerance. Such a philosophy has two main elements: First, the full realization that they have low frustration tolerance, or what I often call discomfort disturbance, and that it continually handicaps them. Second, to see that no matter how hard it is for them to acquire higher frustration tolerance, it is well worth the effort. Without decreasing their LFT, it is almost guaranteed that they will not only get worse emotional and behavioral results, but will also fail to achieve real growth and self-actualization.

Your clients' LFT is largely unconscious, or at least just below the surface of consciousness, and is automatically practiced and followed. They had therefore better continually bring it to consciousness and fight against it. However, this is unusually difficult for many resistors to do, for they may well have biological and socially learned tendencies to be afflicted with it. This double tendency can still be ameliorated by what Bargh and Chartrand (1999) call "implemented intentions"—that is, when your clients *convince* themselves that this kind of effort is required if they are to lead a satisfactory life.

The natural tendency of many therapists is to notice their resistant clients' low frustration tolerance, but then to make themselves angry about it and respond somewhat blamefully. Unfortunately clients may respond to the therapist's blameful attitude by further blaming themselves—leading to *increased* rather than decreased intolerance of frustration. Therefore, your dealing with the LFT of your resistant clients is a ticklish situation. You had better keep calling it to their attention, but do so in a completely non-damning manner. Show them, again, how self-damaging it is, but emphasize their constructivist propensities, which they can use to ameliorate it.

The anti-LFT Philosophy, or the Philosophy of Effort, which you hope your resistant clients will attain, has both emotional and cognitive aspects. Since LFT is usually very *strongly* maintained, it therefore had better be *powerfully* resisted. This means that a Philosophy of Effort that you are trying to help your clients achieve has to be emotionally as well as reasoningly constructed. In addition, to be meaningful and effective, it has to be steadily acted upon. Thus, when you help a resistant client to strongly see her LFT and powerfully think against it, you'd better give her—or have her give herself—specific behavioral homework that aids in countering it.

One of my clients at first strongly resisted changing his procrastination tendencies: he had not even completed the first chapter of the Great American Novel that he was writing. In therapy, he realized that he was demanding that he write a perfect first novel. He was also telling himself that writing it when he had both a "day job" and a family to care for was much *too* hard—as it *must* not be. He began to realize that if he kept these two contradictory musts, it would probably take him at least fifty years to finish his novel. Because he really did want to write the novel—and even enjoyed writing—he began to strongly dispute his perfectionism and his low frustration tolerance.

The disputing of his Irrational *Beliefs,* however, was not particularly effective until he gave himself the activity homework assignment of making sure, no matter what difficulties arose in life, that he spent at least a half hour every three days a week actually *working* on the novel. After a period of several weeks, when he experienced his perfectionistic and low frustration philosophies eroding, a half hour of writing every day became easy and habitual. So it was his activity homework that ultimately helped solidify his antiperfectionistic and anti-low frustration tolerance philosophies. A strong belief in the Philosophy of Effort can still be effective. But adding to it forthright emotive and behavioral elements makes it far more solid (Hodges, 2001).

You can have your clients very strongly use coping statements, such as "If I do not consistently and persistently work at changing myself, I will keep making myself angry or depressed for the rest of my life!" But you can also collaborate with your client to give them activity homework assignments that will help lead them to a Philosophy of Effort. Encourage them, for example, to agree to write for at least one hour every day on the novel or story they are trying to finish, and if they miss more than one day a week at this writing, make sure that they contribute one hundred dollars to a cause that they find very obnoxious. By getting a good deal of their project actually finished, they may solidly realize how important it is for them to work at it steadily instead of sporadically.

WORKING WITH CLIENTS'
UNREALISTIC EXPECTATIONS

As Donald Meichenbaum has shown, clients often bring unrealistic expectations to the therapeutic process, such as negative expectations about their abilities to change. Consequently, they decide that change is impossible and they give up. If this is the case, you can actively show them how unrealistic some of their expectations may be, and help replace them with more realistic expectations of what can happen in therapy if they push themselves to help *make* it happen.

You can explore such Irrational *Beliefs* as, "My therapist is going to do practically all the work required for my changing, and show me how to easily effect it," or "If I really try to do what my therapist advises and I have difficulty doing so, that means that I'll never change!" If they have ideas like this, you can actively push, encourage, and persuade them to surrender their IBs and stop resisting (Ellis, 1999; Ellis & Blau, 1998; Ellis & Dryden, 1997).

Using emotive techniques, you can humorously show your resistant clients how ridiculous an idea it is that they are going to be able to change without making real effort in *between* sessions. Behaviorally, you can show them how they are making themselves take much more time and effort to change than they would take if they did not resist; and if necessary, you can get them to agree to execute stiff penalties for noncompliance. For example, you can get them to agree to have shorter sessions or to pay more for their sessions if they do not complete the homework assignments that they agreed to do. Emotively, you can encouragingly show them that they can do very well at therapy—providing they give up their unrealistic expectations about it and work regularly in and in between sessions.

DEALING WITH IRRATIONAL BELIEFS
THAT UNDERLIE CLIENTS' PRIMARY
AND SECONDARY RESISTANCES

Clients frequently have primary demands that lead to their anxiety and depression, such as "I must outstandingly accomplish certain tasks, or else I am a worthless individual." They also, as I keep showing in this book, have secondary disturbances, such as "I must not be anxious, and I must not be depressed."

Clients' primary resistance stems largely from their three main musts: (1) "I must change myself quickly and easily, and I'm an incompetent person if I don't!" (2) "You, my therapist, must make it very easy for me to change, and I'll be damned if I'll collaborate with you if you make it hard!" and (3) "Conditions must be good and not interfere with my changing. If they are not, I refuse to help myself change!"

Once your clients resist changing themselves for any of these three irrational reasons, they sometimes *see* that they resist, and develop yet another set of Irrational *Beliefs* about their resistances, such as: (1) "I must not be so stupid as to resist this therapy that I am paying for—I'm really stupid!" (2) "If I rebelliously resist change, and thereby foolishly sabotage my improvement, it's *awful*—I *can't stand* that I'm acting that way!" (3) "I *can't bear* having such low frustration tolerance!"

When clients have these kinds of secondary disturbances about resisting therapy—that is, make themselves guilty or ashamed *about* resisting—they often tend to energetically block themselves and have what might be called "double-bladed resistance" (Clark, 2001). In REBT we look for and try to eliminate secondary as well as primary resistance, and we do so by showing clients their first- and second-order IBs about changing. We then help clients Dispute both these sets of Irrational *Beliefs,* just as we would dispute any other IB's that lead to disturbance about disturbance.

If you use REBT and CBT, therefore, it is often best to begin with helping undo their disturbances *about* their resistance, since these may likely exacerbate their self-blocking. You can then show them how to modify the ideas and feelings that create their *primary* resistances.

ADVANTAGES AND DISADVANTAGES OF QUICK AND ACTIVE DISPUTATION

Quick and active disputing of clients' Irrational *Beliefs* may save you considerable time and effort, and demonstrate to clients that helpful techniques of psychotherapy can be done in a short period of time. People often ask me, "I notice that as soon as you discover your clients' musturbatory thinking, you immediately, rather than gradually, begin to help them dispute it. Doesn't this tend to arouse oppositionalism, and don't you wind up losing clients after a few sessions?"

I usually reply, "Yes, this disputing in the first or second session can turn off some new clients. On the other hand, practically all my clients come to me in considerable emotional pain, and would very much like to reduce or eliminate it in the shortest possible period of time. Therefore, if I fairly quickly help them uncover and dispute their irrational demands, they may be more motivated and encouraged to work on their demands on their own." I find that about one-third of my clients pick up on what I am teaching and quickly start doing their own self-debating, often within two or three sessions.

I would, in fact, consider it almost unethical if I did not promptly try active Disputing with most of my clients, for one thing, to discover who are the quick-acting ones and do my best to benefit them. In my long history of doing REBT (since 1955), I have found that a relatively small percentage of my clients have been turned off by this kind of fast disputing and quit therapy because of it. More often, clients who resist treatment do so for one or more of the other reasons discussed in this book.

When clients *are* to some degree turned off by my vigorously and actively revealing and Disputing their Irrational *Beliefs* in the first few sessions, I usually persist at this kind of Disputing, and assume that it will take several more sessions for them to see its value. But with some highly resistant clients, I do slow down somewhat and do my best to gain better rapport with them before proceeding. I still think, however, that it is advantageous to first risk fast and active disputing, when there is a good chance that many clients will quickly follow my lead. If some of them resist, I still have the option of going less quickly. I do face the fact that early and active disputing of clients' Irrational *Beliefs* will not work in many instances. However, in spite of its risks, beginning disputation during the first or second session has the advantage of uncovering resistances rapidly, showing me that they exist, and sometimes their exact nature. For example, one of my clients had a business partner who indeed seemed to be running their business in an obnoxious and self-aggrandizing manner. After he had described his partner to me at some length, I showed him that in all probability, this partner had a severe personality disorder, was quite narcissistic, and was highly likely to remain that way. Therefore, I quickly convinced my client that his partner definitely *should* be the way he was, because he *was!* It was highly unrealistic for him to expect his partner to be nice and cooperative, when actually he was consistently difficult and *un*cooperative. Since, however, their business was lucrative, it probably would not be in his best interest to end their partnership and try to run a similar business on his own.

This client at first strongly resisted my view that his partner definitely *should* be the way he was, because that *was* his way. For our first three sessions, my client doggedly held to the proposition that it was *wrong* for his partner to act the way he did and he absolutely must not. I kept agreeing with him that it well might be wrong, but that there was no other real choice for the present, because his partner was going to continue to behave the way he commonly acted—narcissistically.

I could see that my client, although highly intelligent, was allergic to accepting same bad facts of life when they indubitably existed, and when, for the nonce, they could not be changed. He rigorously insisted that certain behaviors were right and proper, and that therefore they clearly must take place. No matter how hard I tried, I could not at first get him to budge on this issue. His strong resistance to my active and quick disputing of his Irrational *Beliefs* quickly made clear his *own* absolutistic thinking, and alerted me to the fact that although he was more ethical and less narcissistic than his partner, he, in his own way, suffered from a personality disorder. I assessed him as rigidly moralistic with a strongly held core belief that justice and propriety had to prevail, or else the world was a completely horrible place.

By diagnosing this client's own disturbance quickly, I was able to map out a plan of therapy with him that, although it took several more months to complete, was ultimately on the right track. In cases such as his, even when early disputing at first elicits resistance and opposition, it can also help reveal important aspects of the client's personality and aid the therapeutic process.

DEALING WITH RESISTANCE TO AN ACTIVE-DIRECTIVE THERAPEUTIC APPROACH

REBT and CBT are especially known for their active-directive approach. These therapies teach clients how to strongly challenge and Dispute their dysfunctional Beliefs; push and encourage them (as did Adler) to constructively change; and they give regular homework assignments. Although active-directive therapy has distinct advantages, it also has several important risks and disadvantages. In *Overcoming Destructive Beliefs, Feelings, and Behaviors* (Ellis, 2001b), I point out some of its hazards, and how to minimize them.

As Butler and Bird (2000) have shown, some clients favor therapists who are active-directive, such as blue collar and lower socio-economic level clients, and others do not. Similarly, some clients struggle with their therapists who stress teaching, language discriminations, structuring, and other active-directive methods. These clients may therefore be more resistant to direct confrontation and teaching, even though, in the long run, the process would likely help clients more thoroughly get better and stay better.

What to do? Frankly, there is no perfect answer to this question, since the research studies that have been done have produced indefinite and conflicting results. Although I am distinctly favorable to active-directive procedures, and believe that *on the whole* they produce better results for most people most of the time when adequately used, I by no means use them with *all* my clients *all* of the time. As I said earlier in this chapter, I experimentally start off quite actively, but soon stop or modify my approach if my clients, for various reasons, resist. I then switch to more productive therapeutic procedures that Butler and Bird (2000) and I (Ellis, 2001b) have suggested:

1. I incorporate active-directive confrontation and teaching within a framework of unconditional other-acceptance (UOA). I show clients in many attitudinal, gestural, vocal, emotional, and behavioral ways that I accept them with all of their failings and poor interpersonal and intrapersonal behaviors, convince them that I really care for them as individuals, and am striving my best to help them improve and fulfill themselves. I go out of my way to support them and help instill optimism that they can considerably improve.

2. I teach my clients the value of social interest, as Alfred Adler did, and how it can add to their lives and to human life. I encourage them to see its humanistic and health-preservative advantages.

3. I particularly show my clients the value—almost the necessity—of their achieving unconditional self-acceptance (USA) and of their integrating it with their achieving UOA.

4. I convince my clients that although I think that some thinking, feeling, and behavioral methods of REBT are good for many people much of the time, they are unique individuals who had better try them on themselves and figure out what personal variations will work best for them in their own lives.

5. I encourage my clients to examine for *themselves* and not to take my teachings or suggestions unthinkingly or dogmatically. I show them how to collaborate with me in arriving at workable thoughts, feelings, and behaviors; and ultimately to become able to do so when they are on their own—without a therapist to help them.

6. I show clients that they may be sidetracking some of their main problems when they talk about irrelevant issues or obsess about the past. But I give them some leeway to do this when stopping them would lead them to distinct resistance because they feel they need more time to "vent" or give me their complete history.

7. I watch for clients who feel I am going "too fast," show them that although they *can* improve faster, they don't *have* to do so. I then slow down my pace if I am engendering too much resistance.

8. I encourage my resistant clients to actively dialogue more with me, or with other family and group members who may be in therapy with them.

9. I take special care to show clients from a different culture that I don't disagree with their cultural values and practices—only with their self-defeatingly holding on to them so dogmatically and rigidly that they are working against their own basic interests.

10. I encourage my clients, as Aaron Beck does, to collaborate with me in finding and Disputing their Irrational Beliefs. I show them that when they tell me about Adversities (A) that supposedly "make them" have disturbed feelings and behavioral Consequences (C), I can always figure out, on the basis of cognitive-behaviorial theory, what are their contributing Irrational Beliefs (IB's). But I also show them that if they learn and use this ABC model, they can figure out their IBs with me and by themselves.

11. I break my REBT teaching into mini-lectures, with considerable time devoted to their questions, discussions, and feedback.

12. I intersperse humor with my teaching, but try not to sidetrack us by acting as too much as a sit-down comedian.

DISPUTING THE IMPOSSIBIILITY OF CHANGING

One of the worst forms of resistance is when clients insist that not only is it difficult to change, but that it is *impossible,* and that they absolutely can't change some of their Irrational *Beliefs,* personality patterns, and behaviors. REBT and CBT practitioners can show these clients that this is an unrealistic, anti-empirical view that is not supported by any facts. The facts show that many clients have *tried* to change have not done so, and therefore can legitimately conclude that it is quite difficult for them to do so. But it is impossible to prove that they absolutely cannot, under any conditions, change, when all possible methods have not yet been tried and found wanting. There is no real evidence that the clients *never* can change, and it is unlikely that there will ever be such evidence.

If you use REBT and CBT, however, you can not only employ this realistic, factual refutation of clients' inability to ever change, but you can also employ a more elegant anti-musturbatory form of disputing. Clients who say they can't change usually start with the underlying proposition, "I *must* have the ability to change quickly and easily, and I'm incompetent and pretty worthless if I don't do what I *must.*"

REBT disputes this musturbatory, absolutistic thinking by showing these clients that they *never* have to change quickly and easily— although that would be highly desirable—and that they are people who act incompetently, rather than that they are *incompetent people.* Also,

REBT holds that when clients tell themselves that they can't possibly change, they are frequently resorting to low frustration tolerance. Thus, they insist to themselves, "I *must* easily and quickly change, and I find that I am actually having a hard time doing so. Therefore, it is not only hard, but *too* hard for me to change, and it *shouldn't be* so hard!"

Clients who contend that they *cannot* change frequently have both self-deprecation and low frustration tolerance at the foundation of their negative insistences. They think that they absolutely *must* change in order to be worthwhile individuals, and that they absolutely *must* change without too much trouble. If you help them to unconditionally accept themselves *whether or not* they change, and to have high frustration tolerance despite the difficulty of changing, then these two basic irrational blocks to improving may be eroded.

Moreover, clients' strong view that they can*not* change may be a cop-out that gets them off the hook of working hard to change. It is desirable to help them become aware that their view that they can't change is often a rationalization for not cooperating with their therapy, for not doing their homework, and for not solidly approaching the real difficulties of changing.

When clients keep insisting that they *can't* change, you had better very strongly and emotively show them that as long as they hold on to this idea, their very holding to it will make it almost impossible to change. As I frequently tell my clients, "All you have to do is to strongly insist that you cannot learn to play the violin, or cannot hit a tennis ball well, and your very belief that you cannot do so will become a self-fulfilling prophecy. Whenever you have a powerful belief that you cannot do something, this idea alone makes it practically impossible for you to do that thing. If you have a strong belief that you *can* learn to play the violin, or that you *can* learn to hit a tennis ball well, that will appreciably help you do so. But your belief 'I can't, I can't, I can't' may be deadly for the accomplishment of this performance."

You can forcefully make a similar point to your clients who are afflicted with I can't-ism by encouraging them to do the homework assignment of deliberately selecting some project that they think they absolutely cannot accomplish, and persisting at it until they *do* accomplish it. If they think, for example, that they are incapable of doing one of the REBT shame-attacking exercises—such as walking a banana on a leash—keep after them several times until they actually do this exercise and realize that what they swear is impossible for them to do, they actually are able to do. Also, show them examples from their own life where they thought that something was utterly impossible to accomplish, and then later they were able to accomplish it.

WORKING WITH CLIENTS WHO CLAIM
THAT THEY HAVE INTELLECTUAL INSIGHT
BUT NOT EMOTIONAL INSIGHT

Clients frequently say that they have "intellectual" but not "emotional" insight, and that their "intellectual" beliefs are not helping them to change. In many respects they are probably correct about that. I wrote a paper in 1963 on the difference between so-called intellectual and so-called emotional insight. Since that time, I have tried to help clients distinguish between their *lightly* believing a rational belief and their *strongly* disbelieving it. Or, they can strongly hold an *irrational* belief, and only lightly *disbelieve* it.

Thus, clients often have insight into their resistance, and they even see that one of the main causes of their resistance is their telling themselves that "therapy *should* be easy, and it's *awful* that I find it so hard." Then, after they recognize that they are resisting, and have also *seen* that they have low frustration *Beliefs* that create resistance, do they therefore automatically work at *changing* these Beliefs and *stop* their resisting? Heck, no!

Actually, their insight that they have about seeing that they resist, and their insight into the low frustration tolerance belief behind their resistance, often do not help them *fight* the idea that therapy should be easy. Knowing that they have this Irrational *Belief* doesn't necessarily mean that they will work to give it up. If they had *strong* or "emotional" insight into this kind of resistance, they would not only see that they are demanding that therapy be easy, but also see that they are stubbornly *sticking* to that demand. REBT would urge them to dispute their IB by asking themselves, "Why *should* therapy be easy? How does it follow that because I'd *like* it to be, it *has* to be?" They could then vigorously answer this by saying, "There's no damn reason why it *should* be easy! It often is—and should be—hard, because that's the way it *is*—very hard! My *wishing* change to be easy definitely won't make it so!"

Clients can gain considerable insight and consciously realize, as they hardly realized before, that they keep downing themselves and defaming themselves. They can also have insight into the fact that one of the reasons that they originally created their self-hatred is because their parents were very critical of them and told them that they were no good. These kinds of insights, however, will quite frequently do them little good—since they are "intellectual" and not "emotional" insights— unless they *work* at changing their IB's. They lament, "Despite the fact that I have intellectual insight into my self-hatred and some of the origins of this self-hatred, I still can't stop hating myself. How do I get the kind of *emotional* insight that will make me stop my self-defaming?"

A good question! For their intellectual insight is superficial and hardly gets to the core of their self-hatred. For one thing, even if their parents *did* criticize them severely and encourage them to hate themselves, they were obviously still *agreeing* with their parents. Actually, during their childhood they were probably telling themselves something like, "I *absolutely must* always do the things that my parents think are right, and be accepted by them in order to be a worthwhile person. Since they are condemning and rejecting me, I am no good." This Irrational *Belief* led to their self-hatred during their childhood, and by continuing in the present to hold onto it in regard to their *present* ineptitudes and failures, they are perpetuating it.

What REBT would call "real" insight or "emotional" insight would first of all consist of the insights that they now *partly* have: (1) They were criticized severely by their parents. (2) They accepted this criticism and made it their own. (3) They still irrationally agree with their parents (and other people) that when they do the wrong thing and are considered to be a bad person, that is correct, and they really *are* bad. So these insights are fine, but now they had better do the kind of Disputing that REBT advocates *after* they gain them. Preferably, they would have to Dispute their original convictions that they *had* to follow their parents' rules, were incompetent individuals if they did not follow them, and were damnable if their parents severely criticized them for not following them. They would have to Dispute these IB's and see that their not following their parents' rules was wrong in that it got them into difficulty and engendered severe criticism, but it by no means made them incompetent, worthless, damnable individuals. It merely made them children who were doing the "wrong" thing and were being criticized and penalized for doing it.

Second, the kind of "emotional" insight they would get in using REBT and CBT would show them that they are *still continuing* to believe this parental philosophy and taking it seriously *today*. So, if they still hate themselves today it is because they *continue* their dysfunctional thinking about their poor performances and about other people disapproving of them for such performances.

Third, they would, if they used REBT and CBT, *today* consistently Dispute their remaining Irrational *Beliefs:* (1) That they *have to* perform well at important tasks, (2) that they *absolutely must* be approved by significant others for such performances, (3) that if they don't perform well, and/or they are disapproved of for their performances, they are worthless individuals. These *present* IB's would not only have to be *seen* clearly by clients (and seeing them amounts to "intellectual" insight). But they would also have to actively *Dispute* and *give up*—in fact, strongly *give up*—these IB's several times before they made significant inroads into them.

Real insight, or "emotional" insight, in REBT and CBT means several things: (1) Seeing that one is partly self-disturbing, (2) seeing the possible reasons for this distressing, (3) seeing the Irrational *Beliefs* that go with this disturbance, (4) actively and vigorously Disputing these IB's, (5) replacing them with rational coping statements that consist of preferences, and sometimes strong preferences, but not *demands, commands,* and *absolutistic musts.* In other words, "emotional" insight consists of your clients seeing their IB's, surrendering them, and changing them for rational *Beliefs*—and persistently working strongly (emotionally) and *actively* (behaviorally) to do so. It is highly cognitive, emotive, *and* behavioral!

Once again, effective insight in REBT (as I've noted since the 1950s), consists of three important ideas. Insight number one is your clients' acknowledging that they are disturbed and that, at least in large part, they themselves contribute to this disturbance by their own acquired and innate tendencies to create IBs. Insight number two is clients' realizing that even if they have learned some of their IBs early in life, especially from parents and relatives, if they *still* behave dysfunctionally it is not because of these early influences, but because they *still* convince themselves of their Irrational Beliefs and refuse to change them. Insight number three—and this is perhaps the most crucial to good therapy and overcoming resistance—is the idea that for your clients to change their Irrational *Beliefs* requires *persistent work and practice.* This is often tremendously difficult for them to accept. But without this acceptance, clients rarely change very much!

Leonard Rorer (1999) has given some profound thought to the fact that clients often have "intellectual" but not "emotional" insight and has come up with the idea that they sometimes admit and dispute their IBs without getting at the *core* IB's that they really hold. Thus, when clients say, "Yes, I agree that the world isn't fair," but still strongly feel that it *absolutely should be,* he recommends asking them, "What would the consequence or the cost be of accepting that the world often *isn't* fair?" The clients may then reveal that if they fully accepted the unfairness of the world, they would have to believe that *no* justice existed, that human relations were entirely chaotic, and that they would have to kill themselves. These core IB's—even deeper than their "normal" ones—could then be revealed and disputed.

Rorer also cites the view of Raymond DiGiuseppe (1991, p. 182). "People do not give up ideas, regardless of evidence against the idea, *unless they have an alternate idea to replace it."* If your clients rigidly stick to an Irrational *Belief* despite their "seeing" that it is "false," you can sometimes help them to devise an alternate, Rational *Belief* to replace it. Doyle (2001) and Kinney (2000) also point out that you can use attitude change, for which there is a great deal of instruction in the social psychology persuasion literature, to help clients *really* buy into helpful rational *Beliefs.*

USING WILL POWER TO HELP CLIENTS OVERCOME RESISTANCE

REBT is basically a choice therapy, as are several other constructivist therapies, because it holds that although humans easily and innately tend to often disturb themselves, they have some real choice about not doing so, as well as a definite choice about undoing their disturbances after they have once helped create them. Because it is a choice therapy, REBT definitely accepts will or agency: it holds that people are not entirely determined by either their biology or by external events and teachings, but they have some degree of choice in making or unmaking their disturbing. Although their degree of agency or free will is important, it is also distinctly limited by their biological tendencies and by their environmental restrictions. Biologically, they can't flap their hands and fly. Environmentally, they can't have all their desires fulfilled because many limiting conditions stop them from accomplishing this utopian goal. Although REBT is not absolutistic in its espousal of free will, and to a large degree accepts a soft deterministic position (Bandura, 1997), like most other therapies, its practitioners believe in will or agency, else they would not try to help people change.

While holding that humans have considerable will, and that this helps them help change their dysfunctional to functional thinking, feeling, and behaving, REBT carefully defines the term "will power" to make it more realistic and practical. According to REBT, people have considerable will power when they fulfill the following requirements:

1. They definitely *decide* to change their thinking, feeling, and behaving, specifically from self-defeating to self-helping ways
2. They strongly *determine* to implement their decisions to change
3. They acquire sufficient information on possible ways of changing. They figure out this information themselves, or model themselves after others who have changed, or read or hear about methods of changing, and otherwise inform themselves regarding some of the most helpful techniques for doing so.
4. They take their decision to change, their determination to change, and their gathering information on changing and *act* on them—without persistent action over a period of time, they have *will* but no *will power.* Will largely consists of deciding,

determining, and finding information about changing, but this kind of will is fairly powerless without concerted and consistent *acting* in the direction of change.

5. After people have actually begun to make changes, will *power* consists of *continuing* this process by again strongly resolving to change, getting information favoring change, and—especially— acting on it

6. This complicated process of having will, and especially of having will *power,* never really stops, since maintaining change is often just as difficult as achieving it in the first place, and requires, as REBT insight Number 3 says, "continual, steady work and practice"

As Wegner and Wheatley (1999, p. 482) show, your client's sense of will "is a variable quantity that is not tied inevitably to voluntary action—and so must be accounted for as a distinct phenomenon." You have to *tie it to action* to achieve will *power.*

REBT advises you to make this concept of will power exceptionally clear to your clients, and notably to the resisting ones. Resistors, as I said earlier in this chapter, tend to have light or intellectual insight rather than strong, emotional insight. But in REBT, real insight includes action and practice, and its concept of will power emphasizes that and shows your clients the kinds of things they can do to achieve it. All the will in the world—and even all the determination to change dysfunctional or functional living—falls far short of will *power.* Resistant clients often fervently believe that will without the power is enough. The fact that they resist—hardly change at all or first change and then fall back to their prior dysfunctioning—tends to prove that, at the very most, they may have much will, but little will power.

By all means, keep showing clients the difference between these two concepts, and show them how their Irrational *Beliefs* interfere with their giving power to their will. Once again, the two main dysfunctional insistences that interfere with changing are, first, "It's easy for me to want to change, but hard to back up this determination with active power. In fact, it's sometimes very hard to act on my will and determination. It *shouldn't be* as hard as it is! It's *awful* that it's so hard! I'll wait till it becomes easy!"; and second, "I have to have marvelous will power and use it to change myself. But in case I fail, I am a total failure, have no will power, and am incapable of change!"

These two dysfunctional imperatives, together or separately, allow people to have all the will and the determination in the world without having the will *power* to back it up. See if your resistant clients have these IB's, then teach them how to actively Dispute them, for unless they do vigorously, persistently, they will have plenty of will—and little will power!

When you cognitively show clients how to work at having will power, you had better also emotionally motivate them. *Strongly* show them that humans are constructivists and do have agency and will, and can use these legacies. Encourage them to see that they actualized their intentions in the past and can do so again. Show them the pleasure of using will power and of changing through doing so. Help them experience the *challenge* of self-control—particularly because it is so difficult to achieve and retain. Try to help them achieve the *vital and meaningful goal and purpose of growing and developing despite the great difficulties of doing so.*

Action-wise, try to devise and arrange with your clients some homework assignments and experiments. Show them, with these exercises, that if they stop at the decision and determination stage without going on to implement their will with action, they will most probably stymie themselves. Thus, no matter how many times they decide and determine to stop smoking, they had better stop buying cigarettes, refuse those that are offered to them, throw away partly smoked cigarettes, and otherwise act to stop smoking. Yes, *act!* If, in addition, they penalize themselves in some way every time they smoke, that can be even more effective.

USING BIBLIOTHERAPY, AUDIO-VISUAL, AND OTHER SELF-HELP MATERIALS WITH RESISTANT CLIENTS

The use of bibliotherapy, audiotherapy, and other self-help materials has been a part of REBT since I first originated it in 1955. At that time, I had practically no written material on REBT. But when I started writing articles for popular magazines and for professional journals on REBT, and especially on its use in sex, love, and marital relationships, I thought I might try them on my REBT clients.

In many instances, I found that they enthusiastically read this material, and benefited considerably by it, particularly learned the principles of REBT and used them more thoroughly than they probably would have otherwise done.

I saw that this technique worked especially well with resisting clients. They would have a good session with me, seem to understand some of the principles and practices of REBT we were discussing, but then quickly forget them. When, however, I gave them an article or audiocassette incorporating similar principles and practices of REBT, they would sometimes read these articles or listen to the tapes five or ten times, and then really "get" what I was trying to explain. Many people learn material more thoroughly when they read it than when they hear it, and many serve themselves well by combining hearing and reading.

I began to routinely encourage my clients to use articles, books, tapes, and other self-help materials relating to REBT. I even wrote some special handouts especially for clients. I recommended my own and other authors' books, such as my first book on REBT, *How to Live with a Neurotic,* which was written in 1956 and published in 1957. This briefly and simply explains some of the main practices of REBT and CBT and has proven helpful to my clients and to thousands of other people who have never been my—or maybe anybody else's—clients.

At the psychological clinic of the Albert Ellis Institute in New York, we give our new clients a packet of ten pamphlets explaining some of the elements of REBT, and encourage them to read them as soon as possible. We find that those who do read them, and read them several times, get more help, and more quickly, than those who don't. This is particularly true with resisting clients. Several other therapists have found bibliotherapy and audiotherapy useful, such as Wehrly (1998).

For example, I have four therapy groups that I see every week, each group with a maximum of eight people. The group members learn the REBT from me and my associate therapist. Then they use it, as we encourage them to do, on the *other* members of the group, so that when a group member says, "I feel very depressed about my wife wanting a divorce," the group members, along with the therapists, try to figure out their colleague's Irrational *Beliefs* and show them how to dispute them.

Some new members of the group—or even some old members—hesitate to use REBT principles, so we frequently give them homework assignments either to reread some of the pamphlets we originally gave them, or to read one of our main REBT books—such as my books, *How to Stubbornly Refuse to Make Yourself Miserable About Anything, Yes, Anything* (Ellis, 1988), *How to Control Your Anger Before It Controls You* (Ellis & Tafrate, 1997), *How to Control Your Anxiety Before It Controls You* (Ellis, 2000a), and *How to Make Yourself Happy and Remarkably Less Disturbable* (Ellis, 1999). We also now have a large number of audio- and video-cassettes that we carry in our bookstore and catalog. So, if a client doesn't seem to understand REBT or to use it in the group, we suggest the homework of reading some of the pamphlets or books, or listening to some of the cassettes, and find that resisting clients often learn REBT principles much better than they do in group or individual therapy sessions.

This is probably because resistant clients frequently carelessly listen to the live therapy sessions, and then lightly (if at all) use what they've learned between sessions. When they are assigned to do reading or listening to cassettes, they are more likely to read a pamphlet or a book, or listen to a cassette over and over and over again, and as a result, eventually "get" it. Bibliotherapy and audiotherapy may not always work for resisting clients, but they are definitely one of the best ways of catalyzing the therapy process.

When using bibliotherapy, audiotherapy, and other self-help materials with your own clients, it is highly advisable to include an emotive and an active behavioral aspect. Emotively, you can question your clients and get them to express their *feelings,* especially their negative ones, about the self-help material. How did they react to some of the REBT or other materials that you encouraged them to use? Give them examples of how other people's growth and development have been aided by bibliotherapy and audiotherapy.

An example that I often give to my clients is that of a very self-disturbing woman whom I never actually saw for therapy. She had abysmal low frustration tolerance *and* self-downing and had had a great many psychoanalytic sessions, which had helped minimally. A friend encouraged her to read *A Guide to Rational Living.* She read and reread it several times and really absorbed the idea of unconditional self-accepting (USA). By working on achieving USA, she still had almost as many failures at her job, with friends, and with lovers as she had before—but she learned how not to put herself down as a *person.* She made herself into one of the most adept unconditionally self-accepting individuals I have ever seen—completely from reading the book. She then came to see me for one session, just to tell me how happy she was with achieving USA and how useful REBT was for her.

We also, as I noted before, have some of our resisting clients come regularly to our clinic's Friday Night Workshops where I publicly demonstrate with two volunteers how to use REBT on themselves. Some of the most resisting clients enjoy the workshop very much and get considerable help from watching me work with the volunteer clients.

Audiotherapy, bibliotherapy, and demonstration therapy are best done with a behavioral component. Reading itself is a behavior, and sometimes we have clients read in conjunction with completing the REBT Self-Help Forms (illustrated at the end of this section). Sometimes spouses or friends read aloud REBT pamphlets and books to each other and discuss them, and then "test" each other to see if they're using REBT principles on themselves.

In individual and group therapy sessions, we review the clients' self-help homework, ask them how it affected them, and what they learned from it, what they would like to do now to further their self-change process. Many of the materials they read and listen to suggest a variety of behavioral assignments, such as approaching new people or speaking in public to overcome social anxiety. So we encourage clients to take some of the sample assignments in the self-help materials and try them with themselves.

Sometimes clients may get together—especially some of my group therapy clients—and have regular discussion groups on the REBT techniques they are reading about. Many of them read two or three chapters of *A Guide to Rational Living* (Ellis & Harper, 1997), *How to Live with a Neurotic* (Ellis, 1957/1975), *How to Stubbornly Refuse to Make Yourself Miserable About Anything, Yes Anything* (Ellis, 1988), and *How to Make Yourself Happy and Remarkably Less Disturbable* (Ellis, 1999), then get together to discuss it. Some of them actually arrange discussion groups with friends who may not themselves be in therapy.

People who once had some REBT and then dropped out—often because they were resistant—are still encouraged to keep reading and listening to tapes on their own. Subsequently they may come back to individual or group therapy, or attend an REBT workshop, and report that while "on sabbatical," they've significantly improved. Some clients may actually come to therapy sessions only once or twice a year, but do a considerable amount of tape-listening on their own and, as far as I can see, improve a good deal.

You can select suitable self-help materials specific to your clients' issues. Addicts, for example, often tend to be difficult and resistant and frequently have a dual diagnosis that includes a severe personality disorder. Books that I have found especially helpful with these clients are Tom Horvath's *Sex, Drugs, Gambling and Chocolate* (1998), *When AA Doesn't Work for You* (Ellis & Velten, 1992), and Dryden and Matweychuk's *Overcoming Your Addictions* (2000).

A 35-year-old cocaine addict, who had only benefited slightly from three months of REBT therapy with me, read *Overcoming Your Addictions;* loved its clear, simple, and no nonsense style; and made much greater strides after reading it. "I don't want to insult you," she said, "but some points that the book made about my addictions were even better than the ones you made. And the book gave me more leeway to go at my own pace." Instead of feeling insulted, I was happy about my client's progress and glad that I had recommended the book.

The most commonly used of all the self-help materials that we use at the Psychological Clinic of our New York Institute is the REBT Self-Help Form (Figure 6.1) developed by Windy Dryden and Jane Walker in 1992.

Clients find it extremely helpful to fill out this form regularly and then check with a therapist or a friend knowledgeable in REBT to see if they have filled it out properly, and especially whether they have found and

REBT Self-Help Form

A (ACTIVATING EVENT)

- Briefly summarize the situation you are disturbed about (what would a camera see?)
- An A can be *internal* or *external*, *real* or *imagined*.
- An A can be an event in the *past, present*, or *future*.

IB's (IRRATIONAL BELIEFS)

To identify IB's, look for:

- DOGMATIC DEMANDS (musts, absolutes, shoulds)
- AWFULIZING (It's awful, terrible, horrible)
- LOW FRUSTRATION TOLERANCE (I can't stand it)
- SELF/OTHER RATING (I'm / he / she is bad, worthless)

D (DISPUTING IB'S)

To dispute ask yourself:

- Where is holding this belief getting me? Is it *helpful* or *self-defeating*?
- Where is the evidence to support the existence of my irrational belief? Is it *consistent with reality*?
- Is my belief *logical*? Does it follow from my preferences?
- Is it really *awful* (as bad as it could be)?
- Can I really not *stand* it?

C (CONSEQUENCES)

Major unhealthy negative **emotions:**

Major self-defeating **behaviors:**

Unhealthy negative emotions include:
- Anxiety   • Depression   • Rage   • Low Frustration Tolerance
- Shame/Embarrassment   • Hurt   • Jealousy   • Guilt

RB's (RATIONAL BELIEFS)

To think more rationally, strive for:

- NON-DOGMATIC PREFERENCES (wishes, wants, desires)
- EVALUATING BADNESS (It's bad, unfortunate)
- HIGH FRUSTRATION TOLERANCE (I don't like it, but I can stand it)
- NOT GLOBALLY RATING SELF OR OTHERS (I—and others—are fallible human beings)

E (NEW EFFECT)

New healthy **negative emotions:**

New constructive **behaviors:**

Healthy negative emotions include:
- Disappointment
- Concern
- Annoyance
- Sadness
- Regret
- Frustration

FIGURE 6.1   REBT Self-Help Form.
© Windy Dryden and Jane Walker 1992. Revised by Albert Ellis Institute, 1996.

disputed their core *Irrational Beliefs*. After they use the form several times they can often automatically supplant their irrational beliefs with rational ones—in their heads and, we hope, their hearts.

SOLUTION-FOCUSED TECHNIQUES

DeShazer (1985) introduced a new concept into therapy—and particularly into brief therapy—when he developed solution-focused therapy. The theory of this method is that all clients are constructivists and can therefore be encouraged by their therapists to try out their own solutions to their emotional-behavioral problems and, when they are stuck, to re-use solutions that they have previously used successfully.

As solution-focused therapists Becvar and Becvar (1998) suggest, you can ask your resistant clients several key questions, such as:

What would you be doing if you were not disturbed?

What did you do before when you suffered from your current problem or similar ones, and how did these solutions work?

What pleasures and interests would you like to add to your life?

What fulfillments would you like to enhance?

What are some of the best enjoyments that you think you would like to have?

What are some of your worst problems that you think you would like to reduce or eliminate?

McMullin (2000) has devised a unique form of solution-focused therapy that can be combined with REBT. He gets clients to record all the techniques they have found effective in reducing their destructive feelings and how effective (on a ten-point scale) they are. When I use McMullin's method, I also get my clients to keep a record of all the Rational *Beliefs* or coping statements they have found effective in reducing their self-defeating emotions. These can similarly be rated from 1 to 10 in effectiveness and can be used again many times to see if they retain their effectiveness.

Solution-focused therapy, as I have noted (Ellis, 1996) has its definite weakness, especially since the previous solutions clients created for their problems obviously did not work *permanently*. Therefore, a different and more lasting solution had better be sought. But sometimes it works very well, either in the original de Shazer form, in REBT adaptations, or in other ways. Bishop and Fish (1999) have shown how it can be used together with REBT Socratic questioning, and one of their studies even showed how REBT questioning was more effective than traditional solution-focused questioning.

REVEALING AND DISPUTING HISTORICAL MATERIAL

An extended archeological dig into clients' historical material has been sorely abused by psychoanalytic therapists and has probably wasted more time than any other therapeutic method. Used moderately and wisely, however, it has some distinct advantages. You can use it in some of the following ways to enhance your REBT and CBT work.

1. Your clients' IB's have usually been held for a long time and were formulated under specific past conditions, so showing your clients how they perhaps originated sometimes helps them get in touch with them and understand better why they have become so deeply embedded;
2. Particularly when your clients were abused and treated unfairly in the past, you can collaborate with them to figure out the probable IBs of their past oppressors, help them understand how disturbed these oppressors were, and which IB's led to their disturbances;
3. You and your clients can review significant experiences in their past, figure out what Irrational *Beliefs* they used to upset themselves at that time, and see if they are still destructively holding on to some of them today;
4. You can help your clients to reinterpret some of their old "traumatic events" and devise new *Beliefs* and coping statements about these events;
5. Clients can write a history of some of the most meaningful and most disturbing events in their life and examine the RB's and IB's that seemed to accompany them, enabling them to then see that it was not only these events, but their own rational or irrational interpretations about them, that led to favorable or dysfunctional emotional Consequences;
6. Clients can keep a diary of current significant happenings in their lives and note their emotional and behavioral reactions to these happenings and the important RB's and IB's that accompanied them.

Methods of Overcoming Resisting that Emphasize Emotive-Evocative, Experiential Methods

7

The previous chapters on overcoming resisting have mainly considered methods which emphasize cognitive techniques but which also have distinct interactional, emotive, and behavioral aspects. This chapter will deal with some of the main techniques of overcoming resistance that are used by REBT, CBT, and other therapies and that emphasize emotive-evocative, experiential methods. But, as usual, I will show how these had better be used in conjunction with cognitive and behavioral techniques of therapy.

Although some critics of REBT assumed that it was almost entirely cognitive when I first created it in 1955 and that it later jumped on the emotive and behavioral bandwagons that started rolling in the 1960s, this is inaccurate. REBT has always been what Arnold Lazarus calls a multimodal form of therapy and includes thinking, feeling, and behaving techniques that are used with practically all its clients. As I noted in my first presentation on REBT at the American Psychological Association meeting in Chicago in August 1956, it theorizes that "human thinking and emotion are not two disparate or different processes, but that they significantly overlap and are in some respects, for all practical purposes, essentially the same thing." Robert Plutchik (2000) also largely favors this circumplex model of emotion and cognition, and Richard Lazarus has endorsed it for many years.

In chapter 2 of the first edition of *Reason and Emotion in Psychotherapy* (1962), I also make clear that so-called emotional disturbances, such as anxietizing and angering, largely stem from distorted perceptions and irrational thinking; that many emotive methods such as catharsis and dealing with the therapist-client relationships help clients to change their unrealistic views; and that not only straight thinking but also effective action are required to overcome disturbing feelings.

103

REBT, then, stresses cognizing or philosophizing methods of therapy more than virtually any of the other major cognitive therapies—
including those of Aaron Beck (1976), George Kelly (1955), Michael
Mahoney (1991), and Donald Meichenbaum (1997). But it also, as its very
name shows, is highly emotive, evocative, and dramatic. In this chapter, I
shall describe many of its important emotive-evocative techniques.

UNCONDITIONAL ACCEPTANCE OF CLIENTS

REBT especially follows the philosophizing of Paul Tillich and Carl
Rogers by advocating that therapists give their clients full or unconditional acceptance. They fully accept clients as humans, no matter how
execrable or self-defeating their behavior is—including their behavior
in therapy. With REBT, you can demonstrate to your clients unconditional other–acceptance (UOA) by showing that you never judge them
as persons, no matter what they do. You can distinctly show them that
their behavior may be self-defeating or immoral, but that they are
never inadequate or bad people. This kind of unconditional acceptance
of your clients is, as Rogers particularly noted, probably the best kind
of relationship you can have with them. It encourages them to fully
accept themselves, despite their fallibility, while encouraging them to
honestly face their disturbances, including their resistance to therapy.

Unconditional other-acceptance has recently been researched and
endorsed by R.D. Enright (Enright & Fitzgibbons, 2000) and his
associates (Doyle, 2001; Durn & Glaze, 2001) and has been found to
be significantly related to therapeutic effectiveness. Karen (2001) also
shows how forgiveness of others relieves destructive guilt and adds to
human functioning and happiness. Several research studies here also
show that UOA (unconditional other–acceptance) correlates significantly with USA (unconditional self-acceptance) (Betz, Wohlgemuth,
Harshbarger, & Klein, 1995), and that USA also leads to more effective
therapy and less disturbance (Chamberlain & Haaga, 2001).

One of my 35-year-old male clients, drug addicted and diagnosed
by two psychiatrists as having a severe personality disorder, was quite
obnoxious to his wife and children and equally annoying as a client. He
broke appointments without the required advance notice, was delin-
quent in paying his fee to the Institute's clinic, and continually plagued
me about how little I was helping him and what a bad therapist I was.
Although I firmly pushed him to work on changing his drug taking and
his annoying interpersonal behavior, I virtually never angered myself at
him but steadily showed him that I felt that he could change and
improve even when he insisted that he was hopeless.

After a year and a half of his behaving badly in therapy and in his outside life, he finally saw that I fully accepted him, though not his poor behaving, and his attitude toward me changed remarkably. He acknowledged his failures, stopped putting himself down, withdrew cold turkey from all drugs, worked hard to make some extra money to pay off his debts, and since that time has given away scores of copies of *A Guide to Rational Living* and referred many people to the Institute for therapy and workshops. As he said during one of his final sessions with me, "I know that you have always disliked many of the things I do, but I have always been impressed with your lack of hostility and your great faith in me. I am sure that if I continue to behave the way I've done in the past, you would never want to be anything like a friend. But you have really proved to me, by your manner and tone, that you follow the philosophy of acceptance that you keep writing about in your books." In this case, at least, my accepting this difficult client in spite of his obnoxious behavior finally paid off.

Because I am very active-directive and confrontative with clients, therapists may get the impression that I do not relate specifically to them. A research study by DiGiuseppe, Leaf and Linscott (1993) dramatically refutes this notion, showing that most of my clients take my directions as evidence that I am on their side. McMullin (2000, p. 380) notes:

> One of the world's most experienced cognitive therapists is Albert Ellis. After five decades of working with all kinds of clients in individual and group sessions, he has probably accumulated close to a hundred thousand counseling hours (DiMattia & Lega, 1990).
>
> If you listen to Ellis's many published taped counseling sessions or, even better, his video sessions (available from the Albert Ellis Institute in New York), or if you observe him in one of his many public sessions you will notice the following characteristics:
>
> - He focuses on the client intently. Though he may be before an audience of several hundred professionals, he is constantly observing what his client is saying, feeling, and showing him. (Professionals in the audience who whisper during his sessions do so at their own peril. More than a few have heard, "If the people in the back can't be quiet during this session, we will bring them up here to see what their problem may be.")
> - He drops his agenda to follow the client's present experience. He follows a cognitive framework, but it is a framework based on where the *client* is rather than on where he (Ellis) is himself.
> - He is a directive therapist, teaching, guiding, and instructing his client, but he immediately and quickly stops his comments when the client makes a statement.

- Although he may strongly and assertively attack a belief, he never attacks a client. He shows complete and total respect for the person.
- He takes clients as far as they are willing to go during the session, but doesn't try to push them to his end point before they are ready.
- He shifts directions instantaneously based on his clients' responses.
- He is honest and emotionally transparent. He doesn't hide behind a professional facade or pretend to be distant, removed, and non-emotional. If a client asks him a question he gives an honest answer. For instance, a client might ask, 'Well, what would you do in this situation?' Instead of replying, 'You want to know what I think?' or 'You feel uncomfortable deciding for yourself,' or 'We are talking about you, not me,' Ellis will answer the client directly and honestly.

Similarly, other active-directive practitioners of REBT are usually seen by clients as interested in them and caring for them.

MEETING CLIENT RESISTANCE AND REACTANCE WITH REVERENCE

Cowan and Presbury (2000) put the concept of resistance within a Relational framework and point out that there are often quite healthy reasons why clients resist. They first note that resistance to change is a normal, healthy reaction because resistors might feel threatened and almost fall apart at the seams if their protective devices were suddenly shattered, and thus at first might increase their resistances and other defenses.

This, of course, is true of some clients—but hardly all. Those with serious personality disorders and with rigid defense systems are not likely to be disrupted by direct antiresisting tactics. At the same time, such clients may only make progress by direct confronting and by concerted attacking of their resistance.

Cowan and Presbury correctly point out that resistance almost always involves therapists' *relationship* with their clients and is sometimes hardly the fault of the clients. True. But client-instigated resistance clearly can exist—and, again, is probably much more frequent among those with severe personality disorders, especially those who do not relate very well and are semi-autistic. As Cowan and Presbury (2000, p. 418) wisely note, "Like all models, one size rarely fits all and it is important to reflect on the limitations inherent in this [relationship] approach to therapeutic impasse."

Leahy (2001) considers various kinds of resistance in detail and advocates reverential approach to many clients who feel put off by a tough-minded therapist.

TEACHING CLIENTS UNCONDITIONAL SELF-ACCEPTANCE (USA)

REBT theory holds that there are many cognitive, emotive, and behavioral reasons why humans disturb themselves, and that the main one probably is their damning themselves thoroughly when they do badly and only accept themselves on a conditional basis. As I have noted in my writings, and as Alfred Korzybski (1933/1991) has observed, they promulgate the "*is* of identity": they often correctly rate their thinking, feeling, and behaving on the basis of how well it helps them and their fellow humans, but at the same time they rate themselves, their being, their essence. Consequently, when they achieve bad results, they frequently rate themselves as bad *people,* and when they do well they just as mistakenly rate themselves as good people. These global self-ratings rarely work, since people do literally thousands of "good" and "bad" acts, they frequently change from day to day in these respects, and no matter how well they do today, then still remain in real danger of performing "badly" in the future. Therefore, REBT contends, they frequently make themselves anxietizing, depressing, and self-downing.

It is highly probable that the worst resistors condemn themselves more for their ineffective behaving than do nonresisting clients. This is perhaps because they are more self-disturbed than nonresistors, may suffer from severe personality disorders, or may be less likely to admit the full extent of their dysfunctioning than are other clients. Many of them, such as those with schizoid behavior, may have a strong innate tendency, as well as partially acquired one, to rate *themselves* as well as their *behaving* and to do so in a pronounced negative manner.

For reasons such as these, REBT and CBT especially attempt to counteract the self-damning tendencies of resisting clients—as well, of course, as that of all clients. You do this in several ways, if you use REBT and CBT:

1. You especially work at unconditionally accepting yourself, no matter what are your deficiencies and failings. This attempt enables you to honestly admit your failings, including your failings as a therapist. You can make unusual efforts to fully accept yourself while still rating your therapy *performances,* "To thine own self be true" is one of your main goals, and your achieving this will help you be true to others, including your clients.

2. In order to unconditionally accept yourself, you acknowledge the crucial importance of unconditional self-acceptance to practically all people: it seems to be one of the prime requisites for healthy mental living. And although it may be very difficult, it is hardly impossible to achieve.

3. You remain skeptical of Carl Rogers' conviction that if you unconditionally accept your clients and refrain from negatively judging them as persons, that they will therefore automatically accept themselves. REBT more realistically recognizes that clients may be helped to achieve unconditional self-acceptance by modeling themselves after the unconditional other acceptance of their therapist; but it also acknowledges that they have the choice of conditionally accepting themselves *because* their therapists accept them. Thus, they can mistakenly conclude, "Because my therapist sees that I am a fallible but still worthwhile human and fully accepts me, therefore *I* can accept myself. Because he or she, a choosing person, decides to accept me no matter what, his or her acceptance makes me a worthwhile person and I can fully acknowledge that." Unconditional acceptance by one's therapist doesn't have to lead to conditional acceptance of oneself, but the REBT position is that it very frequently does and, in fact, it rarely leads to *unconditional* self-acceptance. Why? Because the human tendency to conditionally accept oneself, in the light of one's "good" behavior and the approval of other people, seems to be so strongly innate and acquired, that it usually takes prepotency over unconditional self-acceptance.

4. REBT advises therefore, that you work very hard to unconditionally accept all humans, including your resisting clients. You do so by still pragmatically engaging in the human tendency to rate one's own and other people's *behaviors* as self-helping or self-defeating, as "good" or "bad", while at the same time resisting people's tendency to rate their entire worth on the basis of their thinking, emoting, and behaving. Admittedly, you may have a hell of a hard time doing this, and may slip into conditional acceptance on a good many occasions. But do your best to carefully continue to evaluate and measure your clients' functioning without at the same time judging them as humans.

5. While striving to help your clients develop USA, you are actively teaching your clients the value of their achieving it. You continually stress the logical and realistic difficulties—indeed, impossibility—of these clients making accurate global ratings of themselves and others and show them several techniques of refusing to do so.

6. At the same time, you can use a good many indirect or emotive methods of teaching your clients the values and the effectiveness of unconditional self-acceptance. Thus, you can use stories, metaphors, fables, paradoxes, and other emotive-evocative methods and also use direct cognitive ways that some therapists who advocate USA ignore or neglect.

7. You can use the therapy process itself to encourage clients to achieve unconditional self-accepting. Thus, you can show your clients

that when you, their therapist, make a mistake in therapy, you blame your errors but not yourself. You can also show clients, when they are damning themselves for resisting or for making other mistakes in therapy, that they can make themselves feel healthfully *sorry and regretful* about their therapy errors, but definitely not self-downing. You can give clients shame-attacking and other emotive-evocative exercises that encourage them to experientially and behaviorally combat their self-excoriating tendencies. These are described in the next section of this chapter.

In several ways similar to those just described, you can relentlessly explore your clients' self-damning and their highly conditional accepting of themselves, and encourage them to be unconditionally self-accepting (Ellis, 2001a; Ellis & Harper, 1997; Hauck, 1991; Mills, 2000).

USING SHAME-ATTACKING EXERCISES

The "shame-attacking exercises" that I developed in the 1960's are one of the best known and most useful of the emotive-evocative and behavioral REBT methods for helping people surrender their strong self-downing tendencies. In calling them, I realized that what we normally called *shaming* is the essence of a great deal of human disturbance. It is not by any means the only human tendency that leads people to upset themselves and also to upset themselves about their upsetness. As I have already pointed out, low frustration tolerance also contributes mightily to their becoming and remaining disturbing. But self-denigrating or blaming oneself for one's failings, particularly when one exhibits them in the presence of other judging individuals, is hard to beat as a method for sabotaging oneself.

When people feel what is usually called shame, embarrassment, or humiliation, especially when they have acted foolishly or incompetently in the presence of others, they usually acknowledge two things. First, they see that they did "badly" or "wrongly" and that others observed this and agree that they acted "badly." Second, they do not merely acknowledge their errors and ineptness, but they also judge *themselves,* and usually damn their *personhood,* for having done this action and for being disapproved for having done it. They of course can experience self-shaming and self-embarrassing when they are not in social situations, because they can notice their own incompetent behaviors and can excoriate themselves for them. But even when they are being severely criticized by others, and even when these others are trying to make them feel ashamed, they themselves are contributing mightily to the process. As Eleanor Roosevelt said, "No one can insult you without your permission."

Recognizing that self-shaming is ubiquitous among humans and that it has serious emotional consequencing—because one can easily continue denigrating oneself long after the so-called shameful act has ended—I developed several ways of helping my clients overcome it. Most notable of these are, "shame-attacking exercise," which I have assigned to hundreds of clients and encouraged thousands more in my talks and writings to use to effectively tackle their self-shaming. Those who have pushed themselves to regularly do them report having benefitted considerably and learned to greatly reduce their social anxiety.

Shame-attacking is also one of the best ways to teach clients one of the basic theories of REBT. For when they tell me, usually in the first few sessions, that they did something "stupid" and that that "made" them feel ashamed, or that another person "made" them feel humiliated, I quickly stop them and say, "That's really impossible. No one can make you feel almost anything—except with a baseball bat. *You* control your inner states of feeling." And frequently I cite Eleanor Roosevelt's maxim.

I do, of course, go on to explain that I am not in the least denying their *feelings* of humiliation. I am simply showing them that when they acted "idiotically," and other people mocked them for doing so, they had a *choice* of feeling the *healthy* negative feelings of sorrow, regret, and annoyance or the *unhealthy* feelings of shame, embarrassment, and humiliation. In making the latter choice, they told themselves, once they noticed (or imagined) their "wrong" behavior and others' disapproval, (1) "I am behaving wrongly, stupidly, or badly and being judged by others for doing so," and (2), "that makes me a shameful, idiotic, and inadequate person!"

Many clients are able to see this fairly quickly and begin to get it into their heads and hearts. At least, they see it lightly—i.e., *acknowledge* that they are doing so. But it usually takes them awhile to start to really undo their feelings of shame by regularly zeroing in on and disputing their self-denigrating musts.

When I show my clients this REBT theory of self-shaming, they usually see it and work a bit on it. But many of them, particularly the most resisting ones, strongly condemn themselves for their social disabilities and have an extremely difficult time refraining from doing so. This is because they have been biologically predisposed, socially taught, and have practiced self-blaming and its correlative self-shaming for a good many years, and often have had trouble giving it up. I therefore explain to them the rationale of the shame-attacking exercise and try to induce them to do at least one of them as a homework assignment. I say something like the following:

"Shaming is the essence of a great deal of human disturbing. It largely consists of first doing some foolish or incompetent behaving and noticing that you do it; second, realizing that others may be condemning you for it; and third, agreeing with others' (real or imagined) condemnation. Fourth, you are putting yourself down severely by telling yourself, "Because I acted foolishly, I am a totally stupid, silly, incompetent person. In other words, you may be rightly downing your behavior, but you are wrongly downing your total self, your being, your essence for doing that behaving. I want you to be able to see this very clearly and one of the ways to see it is to do a shame-attacking exercise.

"If you do the following exercise, you will clearly see your own tendency to defame yourself and will, I hope, be encouraged to stop rating yourself globally. So think of something that you would consider very shameful and humiliating. some of the most frequently-used shame attacks are getting on the bus and yelling out the stops at the top of your lungs (and staying on the bus and trying to not feel ashamed). Or you can go to a department store and loudly shout out the time: "Ten thirty three and all's well!" Or you can go to a hotel lobby or some popular meeting place, stop a stranger and say, "I just got out of the loony bin. What month is it?" Or you can walk a banana on a red leash and feed it with another banana.

"So try one of these actions, or try one that you yourself would feel particularly ashamed of if you did it. Don't do it as a joke and for amusement, but really pick something that you would feel quite embarrassed to do and do it in public where other people can see you and stare or laugh at you. This may not change your whole life, but I can almost guarantee that if you keep doing these exercises several times, you will begin to see that you are the shamer of yourself and that nobody else can make you feel humiliated. You have the choice of feeling sorry and regretful if people look askance at you, or feeling anxious and depressed. You are probably habituated to feeling shame and anxiety instead of regret or concern; I would like to see you break out of this pattern. How do you feel about doing this important exercise?"

My clients are often quite amused at the idea of doing a shame-attacking exercise, yet also very anxious. They lightly see that it may well do them a lot of good and help them counter-attack their self-downing. But that hardly makes them do it. A few of them actually go out and do one or more shame-attacking exercises immediately. But they are usually the ones who somehow throw some humor into it and do it partly as a lark. Most of them, if I keep after them, are able to do a number of shame-attacking exercises and almost always benefit somewhat doing it; many wind up making remarkable progress in reducing shame and self-consciousness.

I usually give shame-attacking exercise to my four therapy groups at least once a year. Each member picks her or his own particular exercise to do, commits to doing it within the next week, and reports back to the group on it. Many of the members—especially those who have been in REBT for awhile and already done some—fairly readily agree. Other members are very recalcitrant and may outrightly refuse, but older group members encourage them to try one exercise during the week and report back on it.

Some time ago, I had in group a very shy 25-year-old male who avoided all social engagements and particularly ones where he might meet a woman to whom he was attracted. As a result, his social life was practically nil. When I gave his group the shame-attack homework, he refused, especially to agreeing to do something that would be socially disapproved. But I and the group finally convinced him to do one of our favorite ones.

To get the agony over with, he went out onto 65th Street, right outside our Institute, and approached a very well-dressed man from an expensive apartment house across the street. "I just got out of the mental hospital," he said to this man. "What month is it?" The man looked at him in shock and obviously thinking that he was completely crazy, scooted quickly away from him. But he saw that he was able to do this exercise, and that it was easier than he had thought, he felt exhilarated. He wound up doing about twenty more shame-attacks with different people, particularly ones who looked snooty or affluent, and had the best week, socially, of his entire life. He was so successful in sabotaging his self-sabotaging limitations that within the next few weeks he began to regularly make social overtures to attractive women.

Everything, of course, does not turn out that well. I had another client who stopped somebody in the subway and said, "I just got out the loony bin. What month is it?" And the individual he stopped angered himself so much that he actually lightly pushed my client. I warn clients, however, not to impose too much on others, and certainly not to really frighten or harm them in any way, such as by poking them in the back. I also warn them not to do anything (such as taking off their clothes in the street) that will get them in trouble with the police or other authorities. Although I have heard about thousands of people doing shame-attacking exercises, I have yet to hear about anyone who has gotten into any serious trouble.

Clients often have strong biological as well as social learning foundations. Consequently, you show them with REBT and CBT methods that they are partly responsible for their own disturbances: that feeling ashamed is a natural human tendency and that they can learn to change it by insight and hard work.

In other words, you can, teach your clients that while they construct a good deal of their disturbed behaviors, they can also see how destructive this behavior is and implement changes. The ability to change one's dysfunctional thoughts, feelings, and behaviors, even when one has helped create them for many years, is one of the essences of being human. As a therapist, even though you are showing your clients that they have a good deal of responsibility for choosing—or not choosing—to be distinctly bollixed up about adversities, you are helping instill in them an optimistic, self-accepting, and creative outlook.

THE USE OF ENCOURAGEMENT

Along with Adlerian individual psychology, REBT endorses acts of encouragement of clients, particularly those who resist therapy (Ellis, 1999, 2000; Ellis & Velten, 1992, 1998). As a therapist, you had better believe that resistors can change even though they have great difficulty doing so. If you keep after them long enough and they keep after themselves, they can sometimes make remarkable changes. Coaching and teaching clients to change are regular parts of REBT and, as you might guess, they are particularly useful with some difficult individuals.

With the 35-year-old drug addict that I mentioned previously in this chapter, I was very encouraging, even though he kept falling back to drugging and other destructive behaving. While almost everyone in his community kept telling him what a hopeless failure he was, I showed him that it was very hard for him to change but that he could still do it and could raise himself by his bootstraps, which he finally did. He was very appreciative that I never lost faith in his ability to change and that I kept vigorously encouraging him to do so.

Of course, this won't work in all cases. One of the hallmarks of resisting individuals is that despite encouragement by their friends, relatives, and therapists, they still won't move their butts and change their thinking, feeling, and behaving. So encouragement is a good form of diagnosis in that if you do it without angering yourself, and it still doesn't work, it may well be that some clients are suffering from a severe personality disordering and or are having certain specific reasons for resisting. If so, your encouragement can continue, along with some of the other forceful and vigorous techniques that I describe in this and other chapters of this book.

USING STRONG LANGUAGE

Although I am known for my use of strong language, the use of four-letter words is really not an integral part of REBT. I used vivid colloquialisms when I was an analyst back in the 1940's and early 1950's, and found it to be helpful in connecting with many clients, even though I was not practicing very forceful methods at that time.

By the time I began using REBT in January, 1955, I therefore had no difficulty using strong language and kept doing so. But by no means do all REBT practitioners employ the kind of language that I use, particularly my four-letter words.

Strong and sometimes so-called "obscene" language can be particularly useful with some individuals, such as those who keep acting delinquently and psychopathically. When you employ such language with them, your clients may see that you are not a rigid authority figure, as are practically all the other people they deal with, that you are not especially conventional, and that you are not likely to damn them for their difficult behaving. I have found that conduct-disordered adolescents particularly take to my strong language: as soon as they see that I am definitely non-authoritarian, they frequently open up in ways they would not normally do with a therapist.

Most clients, including many non-resisting ones, speak to themselves very powerfully, even though they may not publicly use that kind of language, and can often be reached when a therapist employs the kind of vigorous self-talk that they use. Strong language, however, is to be used discriminatingly, since it will help turn some people off and therefore add to their resisting. I often take the risk of using it, however, and it rarely seems to turn out badly, but that is partly because of my own ease in using strong language. Other REBT and CBT practitioners by no means have to imitate me (although some try to do so) and would be better off using their own language style.

I also include some strong and unconventional language in my rational humorous songs, such as, "Maybe I'll Move My Ass," sung to the tune of Charles K. Harris' famous old song, "After the Ball." It goes as follows:

After you make things easy
And you provide the gas,
After you squeeze and please me,
Maybe I'll move my ass!
Just make life soft and breezy,
Fill it with sassafras!
Then possibly, if things are easy, I'll move my ass!

An even more unconventional and so-called "obscene" song that I sometimes use with some of my resisting clients—especially those who childishly insist that others must give them everything they want—is "I Am Just A Fucking Baby!" sung to the tune of Kerry Mills' "Meet Me in St. Louis, Louis." It goes:

I am just a fucking baby,
Drooling everywhere!
How can my poor life okay be
If you do not care?
If you tell me no or maybe
You will quarter me and slay me!
For I am just a fucking baby—
Please take care, take care!

It is important that these be used selectively with people you think will find them useful. Using them with people of a highly rigid or conventional nature probably won't work!

THE USE OF GROUP METHODS WITH RESISTING CLIENTS

Group therapy and many public workshops such as my Friday Night Workshops in New York, are particularly effective with many resisting clients, because when they are in a group they may have their childish and rigid ideas disputed by several other group members, and not merely by one therapist. As their peers keep disputing their nutty ideas, the other members of the group are more likely to see how silly they are and to give them up. They may surrender their IBs for the wrong reasons, because other people seem to disapprove of them for holding them, and they can't stand such disapproval. But they also may dispute them because they see how ineffective they are.

Participants are able to observe other group members effectively using various vigorous and forceful REBT methods and consequently are encouraged to use them themselves. When members of a group collaborates with each other to create their own homework assignments, they are also more likely to perform them than if they are assigned by the therapist.

One of the most difficult clients I have ever had was a 42-year-old male suffering from manic depression. He had been in therapy continuously since the age of 20 and had been hospitalized four times. A brilliant professor of physics, he had never been reached by his previous therapists and still kept enraging and depressing himself almost every day about what other people would have considered trivial frustrations, such as his students coming late to class or not turning in homework assignments on time.

I reached this client more than all his previous therapists had by using very vigorous REBT disputing of his demands that everything must always go well and by showing him that he would be far better off accepting Murphy's Law: "Anything that can be screwed up, will be!" Although humorously stated, this "law" describes reality to a considerable degree and implies very strongly that one had better expect people to foul themselves up and to act badly with others, because that seems to be an essential part of the human condition.

The above client, Bill, edited out many of my arguments by insisting that I was only a therapist paid to help him and that therefore I would naturally try to argue against his Irrational Believing-emoting-behaving. I finally induced him to overcome his reluctance to join one of my regular therapy groups. He participated in three of these groups—his teaching schedule kept changing—and after he saw that other group members argued just as vigorously against his nonsense as I did, he was able to accept some of the principles of REBT and to surrender a good deal of his raging and his depressing and the dysfunctional convictions and the behaviors accompanied these feelings. Bill would probably have eventually benefitted from individual REBT sessions, but being in a few of my therapy groups helped him more profoundly realize how self-defeating some of his beliefs were and to fight them.

Large groups—such as some of the public REBT workshops given at the Albert Ellis Institute and elsewhere—can be particularly effective venues for teaching people to dispute their dysfunctional dogmas. At these workshops, after the leader talks to volunteer clients for about 20–30 minutes and shows them how they are needlessly defeating themselves, ten or twenty members of the audience may raise their hand and give their own ideas about the volunteer's dysfunctional dogmas. This is sometimes very effective, because people from all different walks of life actively dispute the IB's of the volunteer, and we sometimes record the demonstration and give the volunteer the tape to listen to later. No matter the size of the workshop—10 or 150 people—participants are invited to join the professional leader of the workshop in arguing against other members' IB's. This again proves exceptionally helpful with workshop participants who at first don't seem particularly convinced, but who, after hearing several people vigorously dispute their IB's, begin to reassess some of their self-defeating views.

THE USE OF PLEASURABLE PURSUITS

Many resisting clients, as Paul Meehl pointed out many years ago, and as I repeated in the first edition of *Reason and Emotion in Psychotherapy* (1994), are anhedonic. They have difficulty enjoying themselves in normal ways and may in some instances be biologically "allergic" to doing so. These clients usually have a number of Irrational Beliefs and can be shown how to Dispute them. This works to some degree, but would preferably be combined with encouraging such clients to find constructive pleasures in the realm of sports, massage, acting, music, work, or other activities. *A Guide to Personal Happiness,* which I co-authored with Irving Becker (1982) contains an extensive list of we give a long list of potential pleasures which people can use to enhance their hedonic enjoyment.

In the first edition of *A Guide to Rational Living* in 1962, Robert Harper and I showed that if people will acquire a vital absorbing interest and commit themselves strongly to it for a number of years, it won't exactly cure them of all their troubles, but it will distinctly help them distract themselves from their IB's. This "vital absorbing interest" can be devotion to a social or political cause, writing a book, becoming a peer therapist, or practically anything that the individual really enjoys on a long-term basis. Mihaly Csiksmentmihaly (1990) has, since the 1980's, been researching the fact that people, including some severely disturbing people, can get absorbed in what they consider serious pursuits and while they are doing so, they *flow* with the pursuit, interrupt their worrying, and help themselves considerably.

Self-help groups, religious organizations, and other groups that help commit their members to some cause or ideal are often particularly useful in this respect, providing their members not only with an engaging activity, but also giving them a philosophizing outlook that helps change some of their fundamental disturbed thinking.

Sometimes, as in the case of some serious addicts, attending A.A., SMART Recovery, or one of the other anti-addiction groups provides considerable assistance in helping them give up their addictive behaving. Many other people just naturally devote themselves to some cause or ideal, which averts their falling into drinking, drugging, gambling, or other habits. On their own, or with your help, many clients can be encouraged to take up vital absorbing interests which prevent them from becoming equally absorbed in dysfunctional doings.

THE USE OF EMOTIVE CONFRONTING
AND DISPUTING OF IRRATIONAL BELIEFS

With certain clients, your vigorously confronting them with and
Disputing their Irrational *Beliefs* works better than almost any of the
other techniques that you may use. For example, one of the main
things that self-angering people do is to deny that it is what they tell
themselves about others' so-called horrible behavior that is incensing
them, and stoutly contend that it is the "terrible" external events that
are setting them off. Sometimes, they are partly correct, because if
other people didn't act as abominably as the disturbed people think
they act, they would not enrage themselves. But most of the time you
can show your clients that however "badly" other people behave, *they
themselves* add their negative philosophizing to this "bad" behavior
and thereby make themselves exceptionally angry.

When clients stubbornly continue to deny that their self-statements
largely cause their raging, you can confront them vigorously and show
them that in all probability this is incorrect. For example, with a client
who denies saying anything to herself when angering herself at her
lover, you may sometimes say things like, "Baloney! I never heard of
anyone as angry as you who is not commanding and demanding that
her lover absolutely *should* not act the way he does. Now let's be honest. When you threw that plate against the wall, were you not telling
yourself something like, 'You lousy bastard! You shouldn't be lying to
me like that'? Weren't you strongly insisting, in your mind, that he
ought to tell you the truth and absolutely *should not* be lying?"

By confronting resisting clients in this manner, you sometimes
smoke out their Irrational *Beliefs*—but be alert to not giving them
beliefs they don't actually have. You may be so powerfully convincing
that you may wrongly get them to agree with you. But if you are willing
to retract your own vigorous confrontation when it doesn't seem to
work, then you can risk this kind of forceful Disputing.

I particularly confront some people strongly when they deny that
their convictions lead to their dysfunctional feelings, as they often do
in my therapy groups. And as soon as I strongly insist to them that
they do have destructive Irrational *Beliefs,* several other members of
the group quickly join in with me, and this kind of solid confronting
by several people is very effective. Even when during a given session
we fail to reach angry clients, they frequently think it over and tell us
during the next session that our interventions finally sunk in and
acknowledged the fact that indeed they were mainly creating their
own rage.

USING RATIONAL EMOTIVE IMAGERY

As I have mentioned before, using imagery is largely a form of cognizing, but it also has a highly emotional and dramatic quality and has been advocated by a number of therapists (Lazarus, 1997). Maxie Maultsby, Jr. (1971), who studied with me in the late 1960's, originated rational emotive imagery, which I and many other REBT practitioners have been using ever since that time. It is a technique that uses cognizing, feeling, and behaving and combines them quite successfully. I frequently use it at my workshops, and many of the volunteers with whom I do therapy demonstrations report back to me that they have subsequently used the imagery, and that it helped them considerably to get in touch with—and change—their strong dysfunctional feelings.

Rational emotive imagery helps people vividly experience one of the fundamental concepts of REBT: that when people are faced with Adversity, negative emotions are almost always healthy and appropriate when they consist of feelings of sorrow, disappointment, frustration, annoyance, and displeasure. It would actually be aberrant for a person to feel happy or neutral when these events occurred. Having certain negative emotions is fundamental in helping people to deal with unpleasant reality and motivate themselves to try to change it. The problem is that practically the whole human race very often transmutes the healthy negative feelings of disappointment and regret into disturbed feelings like anxietizing, depressing, raging, and self-pitying. These are legitimate emotions in the sense that all emotions are legitimate; however, they usually sabotage rather than help people.

Therefore, it is preferable that in using rational emotive imagery, you encourage your clients to think of something that they see as very unpleasant and to strongly feel the kinds of unhealthy negative feelings that they frequently experience. They then get in touch with these feelings, feel them strongly, then work on changing it to a healthy negative feeling about the same unfortunate situation. When they have changed their feeling to a healthy negative one, they are then to keep practicing, preferably at least once a day, for the next thirty days, until they train themselves to automatically or unconsciously experience the healthy negative feeling whenever they imagine this Adversity or when it actually happens. They usually can manage to bring on their healthy negative feelings within two or three minutes, and within a few weeks, they are usually able to automatically bring them on.

I used rational emotive imagery with a volunteer client with whom I demonstrated at a workshop in England before an audience of 100 counselors and therapists. The volunteer had been angering himself at his mother for 20 years because she hadn't taken care of him as a child as she, of course, *should have* done, and had criticized him severely all his life for little things which she, of course, *shouldn't have done*. She was nasty and mean to others, except to his younger sister, to whom she was consistently nice. People agreed with him, including his own father, that his mother had treated him badly, so he was sure that (1) she was definitely wrong, (2) his anger was justified at her, and (3) her wrongdoing directly created his anger and probably would for the rest of his life. On the other hand, he knew that his anger was disabling, especially since his physician had told him that it wasn't doing his nervous system and his cardiac functioning any good; and his wife kept complaining to him about his making himself so angry and said that he was neglecting her because of it. So he had some incentives to change.

I showed this client that he was in all probability creating his anger by demanding that his mother not be the way she now was and was probably going to continue to be until her dying day. He agreed with this lightly but argued that because he had such great evidence of how wrong his mother was, how much she harmed himself and others, he was justified in remaining enraged at her. Oddly enough, I pointed out, he seemed to believe that she *could* change her behavior, while he couldn't change his angering himself at her until she behaved differently.

So I used rational emotive imagery with him, beginning with having him close his eyes. "Now imagine the worst—that you are going to meet your mother and father as you usually do for Christmas, and that she is going to act just as badly as she always does. She's going to accuse you of everything including, practically, murder and say that you are no good, and that if you don't change your ways, you're going to get in trouble forever. And she particularly picks some minor infringement of yours and harps and harps and harps and harps on it very negatively. Can you vividly imagine that?"

My client immediately replied, "I certainly can! That's typically her." So I said, "All right. Now strongly keep focusing on her ranting and railing against you . . . Stay with the experience. How do you feel?" When he responded, "Homicidal," I said, "Good. Get in touch with that and let yourself feel it, feel it strongly. Let yourself feel very angry, very horrified, very homicidal—as enraged as you can be. Really get in touch with it; really feel it."

My client said, "Oh, I do. I do." And I said, "But really thoroughly feel it. Make yourself feel as angry as you possibly can and stay in touch with your rage, feeling it in your gut and in your heart." And he said, "I'm feeling it quite strongly—as if she were in the room."

So I said, "Okay. Now that you really feel it, experience it, and know what it feels like once again, try to make yourself—right now—feel exceptionally sorry and regretful that your mother acts this way, but not feel enraged against her. Sorry, disappointed, and regretful, but not, not, not enraged." He said, "I'm having a very hard time doing this." And I said, "Understandably so, since you practiced so many years feeling enraging when you think of this kind of thing or when it actually happens. But now make yourself feel very sorry, disappointed, regretful—which you are able to do."

My client was silent for a couple of minutes. As with other of my demonstratees, I hadn't met him previously and we had no unusual rapport. But as with others, I had told him before I gave him the rational emotive imagery to do that he creates his own anger, and that he can definitely change it if he changes the musts, shoulds, and oughts that create and maintain it.

So my client finally said, "Well I am still feeling pretty sorry and regretful, but right now I'm feeling a lot less anger." So I said, "Fine. How did you get there? What did you do to change your feeling from the unhealthy feeling of rage to the healthy feeling disappointment and regret?"

Maxie Maultsby, who invented this technique, usually asks the client at this point what Rational Beliefs he used to change his feelings until he solidly does so. But since I want the client to be able to see on his own how he reduced his rage, I never ask him, "What did you say to yourself?"—because that would give the solutions to his problem away; or he might give me the "right answer" that he really didn't believe. My goal is to enable him to change his unhealthy negative emotion by himself, to see that he is really in charge of his feelings. Rather than tell him what to say to produce healthy negative feelings, I merely say, "What did you do to change?" This particular client said, "Well, I told myself that she's really a very disturbed person, she's always been that way, and that although it's very sad and very disappointing, there's no reason why she *shouldn't* be that way—and in fact, there are many reasons why she should be."

I said, "That was very good, and I think you'll be able to use this process effectively: To strengthen your skill, I want you to do exactly what we just did for the next thirty days. That is, vividly imagine that your mother is going after you and beating you over the head verbally. Let yourself feel your feelings—including the rageful ones—and then change your extreme anger the way you just did, using the coping statements that worked for you."

The client asked, "What kind of coping statements?" I replied, "you have a choice of several: 'Isn't it too bad that she behaves that way, but alas she does and it seems to be her nature.' Or, 'I'll never like her putting me down and calling me all kinds of names, but I definitely can stand it—it won't kill me. I can still lead a happy life in spite of it. I just don't like it, but I have the power to feel only sorry and regretful, rather than horrified and terrified.'" The client said, "Oh, I see." And I said, "Fine. Will you commit to doing this once a day? Just now, it took you only a couple of minutes, and after a while it will even take you less time."

He agreed to this thirty-day plan. I said, "Okay. Just to make sure—or to make almost sure—that you do it, let's give you a reinforcement for doing it." "What do you mean?" "Well, what do you like to do that you do almost every single day of the year—some pleasure?" He said, "Golfing." So I said, "Fine. That's very good. Only allow yourself to play golf *after* you've done the rational emotive imagery and changed your feeling. Make your golfing contingent on it; then, once you do it, you can golf all day if you want to, especially if it's a weekend. Now what do you hate to do that you normally avoid because it's such a pain in the ass?"

The client gave the same response as many clients: "Cleaning and straightening up the house."

I then counseled him, "If bedtime arrives on any one of the next thirty days and you haven't done the Rational Emotive Imagery, you are to stay up for an hour cleaning the house. And if your house gets too clean, you can put your neighbor's house in order."

"Fine."

"Now will you really do that?"

"Yes."

The client actually wrote me a letter from England two months later and said that he had been practicing Rational Emotive Imagery, and after about 15 days he had begun to almost automatically feel disappointed and sorry about his mother's behavior, but not enraged at her.

Rational Emotive Imagery can be done in various ways, but I usually do it this way because I want to emphasize its emotive-evocative-experiential elements. I also want my clients to continue to be able to do it on their own, and not because I instructed them to change their feeling by revising the self-statements they use to create their unhealthy feelings.

Usually Rational Emotive Imagery is done together with several other REBT techniques, so there are only a couple of studies where the researchers specifically did it and to see if it was effective. But I have clinically observed that many people who strongly use it to de-anger themselves or de-depress themselves tend to get excellent results. They still may fall back—especially if they have a severe personality disorder. But it does help them to significantly decrease their dysfunctional feelings of rage, depression, guilt, or anxiety.

USING FORCEFUL SELF-DIALOGUES

When clients engage in the process of Disputing their Irrational *Beliefs,* they frequently come up with the "right" answers. That is, they are able to tell themselves—and temporarily believe—that people *should* act very badly when they *do;* that they themselves are fallible and thus will inevitably fail at some important tasks and have no chance of being perfect; and that rotten conditions *have* to be as bad as they are and may never improve. So clients often agree that if they can't change aversive people or conditions, they can live with them and not make themselves totally miserable. But although they give lip service to agreeing with these Effective New Philosophies (E's) that they arrived at after Disputing their dysfunctional *Beliefs,* they often tend to believe their new Rational Beliefs only lightly and temporarily.

I particularly noticed this a number of years ago when one of my very bright clients, who frequently disputed effectively with other members of his therapy group, became incensed because early that morning, when he was jammed up against a young boy in the subway train, the boy kept cracking bubble gum in his ear until he almost went crazy. Twelve hours later that same day; in the group, he was still raging. We helped him to Dispute his dysfunctional conviction that the boy *absolutely should* know better, *shouldn't* do such a terrible thing, and was an irredeemable jerk. But although he reluctantly gave the more functional answers, it was obvious to the group that he was still enraging himself. So we gave him the homework assignment of recording on tape his Irrational *Beliefs* that "the goddamned boy" shouldn't be the way he was, and then disputing these *Beliefs* very vigorously. I emphasized that only by his strongly Disputing them and really feeling E, an Effective New Philosophizing about this incident, would he likely surrender his anger.

The client carried out his assignment and brought us in a recording of his doing his Disputing. The tape was certainly very vigorous and scared the hell out of some of the members of the group, because it was so vehement that his raging was still obvious. Part of his recording went as follows:

IRRATIONAL VOICE: "That goddamned boy who kept cracking bubble gum in my ears in this jam-packed subway—is a thorough bastard! I hope he drops dead!"

RATIONAL DISPUTING: "Don't you think that's a little too harsh? After all, he probably didn't even know he was bothering you. Can't you forgive him?"

IRRATIONAL VOICE: "No! That kind of thoughtless and irritating behavior is absolutely unforgivable."

RATIONAL VOICE: "Really? Isn't that an extreme punishment for such a mild crime?"

IRRATIONAL VOICE: "No! Nothing is bad enough for such scum of the earth!"

As you can see, my client was enraging himself more than ever—a whole week after the incident. (Actually it was two weeks later, because the first week he came in with some very mild disputing which was right on the ball. It said that the boy should be the way he is and that even if he realized that he was cracking the gum loudly, he had the right to do so.) But the mild Disputing didn't work. The second week he did the homework assignment of supposedly doing very vigorous disputing, and even that didn't work; if anything, his self-dialogue may have incensed him a lot more.

When I had this client Dispute his Irrational Beliefs a third time, this time he was to concentrate on making his rational voice much stronger. After a clear battle between his irrational and rational voices, he was finally able to powerfully conclude on the tape, "I don't care how inconsiderate this gum-chewing boy is! He's still a very fallible human and he has a perfect right to his god-damned fallibility! His behavior *stinks,* but he is still a worthwhile *person!* And if I keep hating him (and people like him)—rather than his bad *act* then I'm going to continue to have very serious problems!" Subsequently, he was able to become much less angry toward people he perceived to be acting badly, including other members of his therapy group. It was over twenty years ago that I came up with this technique of forcefully Disputing Irrational *Beliefs* on a tape recorder and then presenting it to the therapist or therapy group. Since that time, I often get my resisting clients to make recorded self-dialogues in which they very strongly try to talk themselves out of their disturbed views and feelings (Ellis, 2000, 2001a, 2001b).

Firestone (1998) has developed a special form of people's discovering and Disputing their unhealthy negative *Beliefs* which he calls *voice therapy.* To encourage your clients to use this method, help them to discover their self-critical, self-destructive thoughts and to forcefully accuse themselves just as another person would accuse them. For example, they address themselves in another's voice, "You're really no damned good! Almost no one likes you. You might as well give up trying to improve yourself and win others' approval. You're hopeless!"

Using REBT or other forms of Disputing, your resistant clients can then vigorously and persistently overcome this other's voice—which is really, of course, their own.

USING ROLE-PLAYING

Role-playing began to be used as an effective therapy technique by J. L. Moreno (1990) in the 1920's and has been employed by many other therapists, such as Raymond Corsini (1999), since that time. It is *dramatic*, because one takes on a role somewhat as an actor does. It is quite *behavioral*, since it involves acting out that role. And it is also *emotive*, because it deals with subjects about which the participants have strong feelings.

We have always used role-playing in REBT, especially to help clients practice doing tasks that they are very afraid of failing at. For example, if Mary has trouble undertaking a job interview, or approaching a potential sex/love partner, we have her role–play this anxiety-provoking situation. Or Mary will encounter her job interviewer, as played by a friend, a therapist, or a group member, and try to present herself in an effective and an unanxious manner. Then observers witness her role-play, give her feedback on what she has done well and what she has done poorly, and help her to replay the role again until she becomes more effective in her job interviewing.

However, in REBT we strongly emphasize not just the verbal presentation, but the emotional blocks that interfere with effective communication. If, in the course of her role-played interview, Mary is clearly starting to become anxious, we may stop the role-play for a while and say to her, "You appear to be experiencing an increase in anxiety right now, and you're probably creating your anxietizing by telling yourself something. Now what do you think it is?"

Mary and the observers then try to come up with several rational and irrational ideas that Mary may be telling herself. They focus in particular on the irrational ones, then try to help her Dispute and change them so that she can then focus on the practical aspects of the role-play. Thus the main emphasis on the role-play is to zero in on Mary's Irrational *Beliefs* and to Dispute them right then and there and change them to Rational *Beliefs* that will give her a better emotional grounding, so that she will be more effective in her current role-play as well as in future situations.

Many variations on this role-playing technique can be used. For example, if Mary is having trouble giving up her notion that the person who is playing the job interviewer *absolutely must* be favorably impressed by her and give her the job, not only Mary herself—but the person playing the interviewer and other observers—can help Mary vigorously Dispute her irrational convictions.

REVERSE ROLE-PLAYING

One method of employing role-playing, and particularly using it to vigorously Dispute any IB's that the client holds, is to have the client tell his role-playing partner what his problem is and allow both of them to figure out what main Irrational *Beliefs* are making him anxious, depressed, or enraged. Suppose, for example, that Jimmy's main angering *Belief* is that the person who is interviewing him should be kind and considerate and should help him in every possible way instead of giving him hard time in the interview. Once he and his partner figure this out, then his role-playing partner takes on Jimmy's irrational conviction and begins to voice it aloud very strongly and rigidly. Jimmy himself then tries to talk his partner out of this belief—which is really Jim's own belief—but the partner refuses to give it up. In this way, Jim gets a good deal of practice in strongly disputing his own Irrational *Belief* instead of using the previous weak ways in which he may be disputing it by himself.

A variation on this approach is for two or more people to take Jim's dysfunctional convictions and rigidly keep holding them while he has to keep talking them all out of them. He thereby gets even more practice disputing several variations of his own IB's, and is thus better able to talk the role-players (and subsequently, himself) out of these notions.

Raymond Corsini (1979) especially recommends the use of the "You Be the Therapist" method with resistant clients. He says to the client, "I am going out of the room for about ten seconds. When I return, you will be me and I will be you. We will meet for the first time, and I will tell you my problem and you will be the counselor" (1979, p. 55). Using this method, you can help the client make therapeutic suggestions that may work well.

REBT and CBT use a similar method when clients stick to a self-defeating thought, feeling, or behavior and indicate that they can't change it. I often ask them, "If you have a friend or relative who holds this same self-sabotaging *Belief* and won't give it up, what would you advise him or her to do about it?" Frequently, my clients come right up with a good answer and see that they can use it themselves. Or if they insist that they have to excoriate themselves for certain ideas, emotions, and actions, I ask, "If your daughter or a friend behaved this way, would you encourage them to denounce themselves as *people* for doing so?" My clients often give a suitable answer that they can then use with their own resistance.

JOINING FORCES AGAINST A COMMON ENEMY

Howard Young (1974), who worked brilliantly with difficult teenagers, devised a method of joining forces with them against a common enemy. He writes:

> It has been my experience that counseling teenagers is difficult. Counseling teenagers who are downright opposed to counseling borders on awful!
>
> Usually, adolescents who are the most resistant to counseling are those who have been referred by someone other than themselves: their parents, teachers, probation officers, or friends. Although they may suffer genuine psychological conflicts and could benefit from therapy, they often refuse to admit to having any problems. Especially when forced to attend counseling sessions, they may offer intense and persistent opposition. Every effort must therefore be made to engage the reluctant client in some kind of problem-facing and problem-solving venture as quickly as possible.
>
> I have found that a problem-focused alliance can often be attained by using a tactic I call "joining forces against a common enemy." Essentially, this maneuver involves identifying some obstacle to the client's happiness (usually a person) and then offering assistance in coping with that problem. Often this can mean agreeing to work on a problem area that is quite unrelated to what the referral agent views as the issue requiring therapy.
>
> An example will demonstrate how this approach is put into action. The following excerpt is from an initial interview with a seventeen-year-old who was referred by his parents because of poor school attendance.

> THERAPIST: What brings you to see a counselor?
>
> CLIENT: (sarcastically) My car.
>
> T: Clever! You mean you have a car problem? If so, you're in the wrong place. You need a mechanic, not a headshrinker. I help people with mental and emotional problems.
>
> C: (even more sarcastically) Then I don't belong here because I'm not mental. I'm not crazy.
>
> T: I agree. You certainly don't seem crazy to me. Who told you to come here for help?
>
> C: My asshole parents!
>
> T: What did they tell you was the reason you had to see a counselor?

C: I don't know. Why don't you ask them?

T: I can't. They're not here now. But I think I know what your problem is.

C: (very defiantly) What?

T: You've got problem parents. You've got parents that think they know everything. They plan your life for you, and if you don't like it, they figure there's something wrong with you, not them!

C: You're Goddam right! My parents are fucked up! They're all over my case.

T: Then you're in the right place.

C: What do you mean?

T: I specialize in problem parents. I can help you learn to manage your parents better.

C: I don't need your help!

T: Sure you do! You're getting nowhere doing things your way. In fact, that's what got you in here. Isn't it? Do you like being in here?

C: No.

T: I'll bet coming in here and seeing a counselor isn't the only hassle you've had to endure because of your parents.

C: Yeah, . . . They won't allow me to drive the car and no one's allowed to come over to the house.

T: The more you fight them, the worse it gets. And you're telling me you don't need help with your parents.

C: What kind of help could you give me?

T: First, help in controlling your temper. I've talked to you for just a little while, but it seems that your temper is a problem. Second, I can show you how to talk to your parents so you don't always end up in trouble.

Having thus gained his agreement that there existed a problem worthy of his consideration, I then explained the relationship between cognitions and emotions, pointed out why his thinking was irrational, and showed him how to challenge and correct such thinking. In addition, I suggested some verbal strategies he could begin using with his parents (i.e., fogging and negative assertion). He was quite receptive to REBT philosophy; he stayed in therapy, worked on a number of issues in addition to his problem parents, and obtained very good results (including improved school attendance).

STRESSING POSITIVE GOALS, PURPOSES, AND PHILOSOPHIES

Clients, when they resist therapy, obviously have somewhat conflicting goals. They very much want to improve and fulfill themselves, but for a number of reasons lose sight of these goals and/or choose contradictory goals—e.g., they engage in short range hedonism, avoid effort, demand immediate change, insist that it's impossible for them to change, demand that others change first, etc.

Using a cost-benefit analysis, as I have shown in chapter 5, can help many clients see that the pains of *not* changing are considerably worse than the pains of modifying their self-defeating thinking, feeling, and behaving. By all means keep stressing this kind of cost-benefit analysis, and as I often do, emphasize to your clients the frightful cost of sticking to their resisting by inflicting many years of extreme deprivations, handicaps, inconveniences, and "horrors" on themselves.

At the same time, you can realistically highlight the positive side of achieving inner peace, creativity, and self-fulfillment—as the self-actualization writers have done for many years (Seligman & Cziksentmihali, 2000). Thus, you can help your clients remember their previous successes, creatively imagine new goals and vital absorbing interests, encourage them to go for progress rather than utopian perfection, actually plan with them enjoyable pursuits that they can bring about, explore new possibilities in the fields of art, science, education, work, and sports. Help them see that they are almost always capable of *expanding* their horizons and *experimenting* with new pursuits—provided that they work to alleviate their energy-consuming destructive beliefs, feelings, and behaviors (Ellis, 2000, 2001a, 2001b; Ellis & Becker, 1983; Leahy, 2001; Schneider, 2001).

POSITIVE STORIES AND POSITIVE COMMUNITY IMAGES

Allen Ivey (1998) has advocated for many years that you help your clients develop visual, auditory, and written stories with positive contents. He recommends that these positive representations be self-directed and foster community goals. Thinking about and visualizing social as well as individual positive goals may include an I-thou spiritual element that will tend to spur potential resisters to community values and enhance their motivation for change.

WHAT TO DO WHEN YOU AND YOUR CLIENT ARE STUCK IN THERAPY AND COUNSELING

Lee Williams gave some serious thought about what to do when family therapists and other therapists are stuck with particular clients, and asked a number of other therapists what they found best to get themselves unstuck. Here are some of his suggestions together with some of my own:

1. Identify the clients' negative consequences with which they are struggling to change.
2. Clearly assess the clients' goals and whether they see you as helping them work on these goals.
3. Discover whether your clients see therapy (and you) as credible and useful.
4. Find out if you have identified key therapeutic themes or are focusing on too many irrelevant themes—do the clients have biological limitations and/or environmental restrictions that you have ignored?
5. Shall you honestly discuss with your clients the fact that you are stuck or do you think that such a discussion would do more harm than good?
6. Consider expanding the therapy to include your clients' associates—such as mates, children, teachers, parole officers, psychiatrists, etc.
7. Try to encourage the disclosure of secrets that your clients are not discussing.
8. Counsel with professional colleagues about your stuckness.
9. Take a break from what you are doing to consider quite different tactics you might use.

REACHING FOR NEW
ENJOYABLE EXPERIENCES

REBT usually first tackles clients' grim experiences and reactions, and then helps them—with problem-solving and skill-training—to achieve happier, self-actualizing heights. Self-fulfilling experiences can also be used, however, to jolt clients out of their disturbed stuckness, to enable them to see what healthy behavior is like, and to motivate them to minimize their overwhelming anxiety, rage, and depression.

Alvin Mahrer (1998) encourages clients to hurl themselves into acting—and being—a qualitatively new person. He has them crash themselves into the feelings of playful unreality, hilarity, fantasy, comedy, and even unrestrained madness and silliness. This may not be your manic-depressive clients' cup of tea, but with more restrained clients it may jolt them out of their overly staid ways and stimulate new ideas for future enjoyments. Some clients, of course, may go from unrealistic extremes of depression to unrealistic extremes of elation. Let them spontaneously hurl themselves into "mad" experiences; but monitor their possible running them into the ground.

R.C. Nelson (1998) suggests a more modest approach by encouraging clients to take a few moments to focus on their assets and write them down on a brightly headed page. They begin with simple actions and skills and keep adding simple and more complex assets to the list. They then help themselves realize what useful and enjoyable things they are able to do, interrupting their anxious and depressed moods, and see that they are not all of their lives.

Barbara Fredrickson (2001) reviewed the psychological literature and found much empirical support for the hypothesis that "the capacity to experience positive emotions may be a fundamental human strength central to the study of human flourishing" (p. 218). Even resistant clients hear *some* positive emotions. Find them, emphasize them, and use them to their and your advantage. They may well prove helpful!

USING FAITH, RELIGION, AND SPIRITUALITY

Jerome Frank (1994) has for many years insisted that clients' faith in the therapist, the therapist's theory and technique, and in themselves are key elements in making therapy effective. This kind of faith may, however, have its hazards, because profound faith in anything is prejudiced—and may be factually misleading. Nonetheless, I have been convinced, over the years, that even clients' misleading faith—such as their devotion to cultist beliefs and practices—may have some good effects. Why? Because when they are (unrealistically) sure that they will benefit from their faith—they sometimes will! Oddly enough, the more difficult they are and the more they are first convinced that they can't change, the more their devotion to some cause—"sensible" or "crazy"—may help them (Nielsen, Johnson & Ellis, 2001; Richards & Bergin, 2000).

This leaves you with something of a dilemma. If you, as I am, are skeptical and follow scientific principles, you may find that some of your clients benefit from following unrealistic, illogical, and unscientific dogmas, and you may see these as probably "false." But suppose, for these particular clients, they work? Hmm!

If the profound faith of some of your clients is largely harmless— e.g., faith that a kindly God or fairy godmother is personally on their side and helps them—you may go along with it, despite your own firm disbelief. If, however, it seems to be harmful—e.g., that the Devil is on their side and will reward them if they help him harm other people— you had better refer them to another therapist!

I and some of my REBT colleagues have found that profound faith in God —especially in a kindly, forgiving God—or in other religious and spiritual ideas that I personally disbelieve, can definitely help some clients. Faith of this sort endows people with such *Beliefs* with emotional allegiance, encouragement, and strong action tendencies—all of which may be therapeutic. Stevan Nielsen, W. Brad Johnson, and I point this out in our book, *Counseling and Psychotherapy with Religious Persons: A Rational Emotive Behavior Approach* (Nielsen, Johnson, & Ellis, 2001). Give this matter some serious thought and decide for yourself whether or not you will go along with some of the religious faith of your clients which you personally may not hold.

As for spiritual faith, this may be quite different from religious faith, since it may consist of faith not only in oneself but in "higher" social realms, such as helping others, promoting national and international peace, and building a better community. This kind of "spirituality" has distinct personal and social value and may help your clients to achieve a quite "rational" spiritual involvement (Ellis, 2001c; Robb, 2001).

Force and Energy in Overcoming Resistance   8

As can be seen from some of the material I am presenting in this book, REBT makes a special issue of force and energy in influencing thinking, feeling, and behaving change. This is because what we usually call emoting largely consists of strong, vehemently held cognizing and behaving while so-called dispassionate thinking or light thinking less frequently lead to what we call disordered feelings.

A key theory of REBT also hypothesizes that when people weakly desire something and moderately wish to fulfill it, they relatively rarely upset themselves about the desired goal not being achieved. They almost always feel healthfully sorry, disappointed, and regretful and thus emote about their failure to get what they want. On the other hand, as soon as they very powerfully and strongly desire something, then they frequently insist that they absolutely must have it or must not experience something that they strongly dislike—and then they lead themselves to unhealthy negative feelings, such as depressing, angering, and pitying themselves.

Pierre Janet noted this tendency of people to powerfully insist on the pursuing of their strong desires and making themselves upset when they did not achieve what they strongly wanted, and in the 20th century, Robert Abelson (1963) distinguished between cool cognitions and hot cognitions. REBT also adds, warm cognitions. Thus, "This is a table" is a cool cognition since it merely describes a table. "I like this table" or "I dislike this table" is a warm cognition. Finally, "This is the worst table that ever existed and I hope it blows up!" or "This is the best table that ever existed and I can't live without it!" are hot cognitions.

Why do we have cool, warm, and hot cognitions? Probably because they help us survive better in that they enable us to get more of what we want and less of what we don't want. Moreover, there is nothing wrong with a fairly hot cognition, such as "I like this table very much and I'm going to buy it and keep it in good shape!" or "I hate this table very much and I'm going to give it away!"

133

As long as you do not put in the shoulds, oughts, and musts and say absolutistically, "This *has* to be a good table or a good chair!" Or: "I *must* be satisfied with it!" Or: "This is a totally rotten chair and I can't be satisfied with it at all!" you do not get into trouble.

On the other hand, as soon as you put in the *musts,* you take your likes and dislikes to extremes and therefore often cannot cope with them. If this table *is* bad and it *must not* be, you then are in trouble. And if you view the table as good, if you absolutely *must* have it, and you can't have it, then again you will upset yourself.

Extreme views, therefore, often ignore the Aristotelian mean between the extremes and tend to lead to self-distressing. This has partly been recognized by therapists for at least 100 years. Many therapies therefore emphasize being forceful or what I call *emotional,* since musturbatory statements are quite forceful and therefore lead to unhealthy negative feelings when the universe does not afford you what it supposedly must.

Some therapies, such as Rogerian therapy and the Gestalt therapy of Fritz Perls, consciously employ emotional methods with their clients, but they rarely talk about the *vigor* of people's convictions that lead them to disturbed feelings. REBT makes an important issue out of force and vigor in at least two major ways: One, it shows that forceful human ideas are very important in the creation of disturbance. Two, it says that often, though not always, therapists had better be forceful in order to encourage the client's positive thinking, feeling, and behaving.

Some persuasion psychologists, such as Hovland and Janis (1959), have given a good deal of attention to the issue of forceful arguments. Also, of course, in the realm of salesmanship and advertising, putting across a product in a forceful and dramatic manner is often taken for granted. Therapists can learn from persuasive methods and can sometimes use them with their resistant clients.

REBT, as has been mentioned, distinctly differentiates so-called intellectual insight from so-called emotional insight. It contends that what we usually call emotional insight into one's serious problems includes the following points:

1. Clients have some degree of intellectual insight—that is, admit that they are partly disturbing themselves. Without this kind of "intellectual" acknowledgement, they will probably not arrive at emotional or "fuller" insight.

2. Clients usually realize that their present behavior has some antecedent causes and does not magically spring from nowhere or just from the adversities that occur in their lives. It follows, sometimes immediately, from these Adversities, but there is a great deal of evidence that the same difficulties hardly lead to disturbing in all individuals.

3. Clients tend to acknowledge to some degree the ABC model of REBT and recognize that their *Belief* system (B), which includes their believing-emoting-behavings, is highly instrumental in creating their disturbing Consequences at point C.

4. Clients realize that their Irrational *Beliefs* may have been partly acquired during their early childhood by the indoctrinations of their parents and culture, but that right now they still consciously or unconsciously actively reaffirm and keep holding them.

5. Clients clearly and strongly see or acknowledge that they can now do something to change their IB's and therefore to change the habitual disturbing feelings and disordered behavings that tend to spring from their IB's. They see that their dysfunctional convictions are in effect much or most of the time and that they hold them strongly and are sometimes quite reluctant to give them up.

6. Clients feel determined to work at changing their IB's—to accept their own part in their dysfunctioning, to see that many of their devout convictions do not accord with social reality, to see their illogical or contradictory aspects, and to keep striving to give them up and fight against their recurrence.

7. Clients not only keep determining to work at challenging their Irrational *Beliefs* but actually do this kind of work and do it often and vigorously. Thus, if a woman has a phobia of swimming, she had better keep convincing herself, many times over again, that swimming is *not* terribly dangerous and also repeatedly swim until she significantly sees and feels safe doing so.

8. Clients keep realizing that their emotional disturbances are considerably under their own control, and they can continue to act, think, and feel their way out of them when they occur.

9. Along with their thinking and feeling along the above lines, clients keep actually forcefully, vigorously, and persistently *acting* against their dysfunctional feelings and behavings.

People who have intellectual insight instead of emotional insight may follow some of the above procedures but usually follow them weakly and intermittently, and also often think, feel, and act against them. Clients with emotional insight follow the principles of willpower that I have previously enumerated in chapter 6 and concertedly and steadily act according to their decision and determination to create the *power* in willpower.

To emphasize the importance of force and vigor in using REBT with resisting clients, let me take a quite common Irrational *Belief* that many resistors hold and refuse to surrender. This is the conviction, "I *absolutely must* perform well in important tasks and *have* to win the approval of significant other people by doing so. If I significantly fail in these respects, it is *awful,* I *cannot stand* it, and I am a *rotten person!*" Let us assume that one of your resistant clients has this profound dysfunctional philosophy and that it leads him to anxietize and depress himself and to function far below his goals. How would you instruct him to give up his self-defeating philosophizing and inactivity? You might teach the following points:

1. "You had better fully realize that, in large part, your insistent notions that you *absolutely must* perform well and be approved by significant others are among the main factors encouraging you to disturb yourself.

2. "You can use REBT to keep disputing these convictions and asking yourself, 'Where is the evidence that I *must* perform adequately well in this task? Why do I *have* to win the approval of others by doing so? What proof exists that it is *awful,* and not merely inconvenient, if I fail in these respects? Where is it written that I *cannot stand* failure and rejection? Does it follow that I am a truly rotten person instead of a person who may have acted ineffectively on this occasion?

3. "There is a real difference between your intellectually and lightly answering these questions and your thoroughgoing emotional answers to them. You may well give correct answers to your Disputing questions and may see that you absolutely do not have to perform a task well and be approved by others for doing so, but you may not believe this 100% of the time. You may *partly* believe it; but if you forcefully and vigorously believe it, and see that your similar convictions get you into frequent trouble, you will tend to believe your IB's only occasionally and lightly. Therefore, you had better strongly dispute and surrender these dysfunctional convictions quite often.

4. "Your Irrational *Beliefs* tend to be totalistic. You devoutly and fully hang on to them when you make yourself depressing and anxietizing. You probably will never get rid of them totally or 100%, but to basically erode them you had better keep working at holding them in a less totalistic and less prevailing manner.

5. "Your self-sabotaging *Beliefs* are frequently held intensely rather than lightly and weakly. Both thinking and feeling can be done half-heartedly or forcefully. But oddly enough a great many of your dysfunctional convictions are held dogmatically and with great intensity.

6. "You can therefore actually Dispute your Rational *Beliefs* when you hold them half-heartedly or lightly. When you conclude that it is not terrible but merely highly inconvenient to fail and to be rejected by significant others, you can ask yourself, 'Why is it not terrible? Prove that others cannot truly affect me if I don't always heed them. Where is

the evidence that performing an important task well is not attached to my worth as a person, even though it is good in its own right?' You can therefore dispute your weak Rational *Beliefs* until you tend to affirm them much more solidly.

7. "You are a quite fallible human. Therefore, even when you think, feel, and behave adequately on your own or with the help of therapy, you frequently tend to fall back into dysfunctional behaviors. Accept that you most probably will return at times to your silly ideas and self-defeating actions—and that is *too bad* but *not horrible*. You are not a lesser person for falling back. When you do fall back, focus on your behaving and how to change it instead of your you-ness and the condemnation of your whole being.

8. "Accept that no matter how many times you fall back to dysfunctional ways of thinking, emoting, and behaving, you can give them up again and return to more satisfying ways. You are naturally a constructivist and therefore able to problem-solve and to problem-solve again and again. You can work at strongly determining that you will diminish your self-defeating and other-defeating. Determine, determine, determine to keep rehabituating yourself to more efficient and more satisfying ways of living and, of course, working, working, working to back up that determination."

To help your clients use more forceful ways of Disputing their Irrational *Beliefs* and subscribe to more self-helping preferences, review some of the emotional-evocative techniques that are described in chapter 7.

ARRANGING CRISES TO FORCE CLIENTS TO CHANGE

Rian McMullin raises a very important point in *The New Handbook of Cognitive Therapy Techniques* by noting that "most clients change only in small painful steps if they change at all" (2000, p. 104). He also says that no matter what techniques their therapists use with them "many clients will continue to suffer through their problem until some crisis forces them to make a choice" (p. 104). My many years of experience as a therapist tell me that Rian is correct about this.

What to do then? Arrange a crisis that will force clients to change? Quite dangerous and doubtful. What I fairly often do, and sometimes at the start of therapy, is to forcefully tell certain clients, "Look! You have been this destructive way so long, and may have such strong biological tendencies to be and remain that way, that you will endlessly suffer from anxiety and/or depression for the next 40 years or so (depending on the age of the client) unless you work very hard at changing. Yes, suffer all the rest of your life! So you have a choice of suffering—or of working very hard to change. But you can—definitely can—change if you work at it. And, in addition to ridding yourself of much suffering, you can—yes you can—enjoy many pleasures. If you work at changing yourself!"

By showing clients that they most probably will have crises and suffering, and also that they can have a good many pleasures, if they change, I often motivate them to do so without actually arranging any crises for them. If this prediction of later crisis does not work, I tell them, "Okay, we'll see if a crisis occurs to urge you to change. Let's wait and see!"

This tack, too, of course has its dangers. But so far, I find that it does much more good than harm. Again, you have a somewhat risky choice. In any event, as I and Rian McMullin have found, teaching clients to counterattack their strong dysfunctional beliefs, feelings, and behaviors often involves having them do so with intense emotion and a high state of arousal.

The Value of Efficiency in Helping Resisting Clients　9

The value of efficiency is quite important in practically all psychotherapy, but is often neglected. Many outcome studies are done, but the vast majority of them, as I keep emphasizing in this book, are performed to see whether the clients feels better at the end of therapy than at the beginning and sometimes, whether he or she maintains this improved feeling (Ellis, 1999, 2001a, 2001b). The problem of whether the client actually gets better in the sense I have described it in chapter 3, is frequently ignored. But actually there is very little efficiency if the client only feels better for awhile but doesn't get to the philosophic, emotional, and behavioral underpinnings of her or his disturbance. Feeling better has a great advantage, but it is limited in many respects.

Also, of course, a great deal of trouble has been undertaken by therapists to decrease the time that they spend with various clients. It is assumed, and probably correctly, that if similar clients can take the time, trouble, and expense of going to therapy for a shorter period of time and be equally helped, it will definitely be more efficient for them than if they take a significantly greater period of time to do this. But both these problems, of taking less time to help clients with therapy and at the same time helping them to get better and not merely feel better are probably part and parcel of each other. Both had better be served simultaneously (Ellis, 1996).

REBT particularly faces the issue of brief therapy, because one of the main reasons I broke off from psychoanalysis in 1953 and started REBT in 1955 was that I wanted to accomplish better results of therapy in a shorter period of time. My six years of experience doing psychoanalysis proved to me that a great deal of the time spent, though not all of it of course, in practicing it with clients was wasted. This was largely because I assumed that the clients' early childhood experiences caused their dysfunctioning, that if they fully got in touch with these and had insight into what happened in their childhood, then they would stop repressing gruesome experiences that had happened to them in the past and almost automatically be improved. I saw by my trying psychoanalytic therapy that these hypotheses seemed to be quite misleading.

First of all, I realized more and more that, although early childhood experiences, as well as later experiences, significantly contributed to people's malfunctioning, they were only rarely the crucial influences. Their biological tendencies to disturb themselves were exceptionally important and frequently, if they were born with what could be called good tendencies, they refused to disturb themselves too much even in the face of a fairly disastrous upbringing. Secondly, even assuming that the early childhood disturbances led to greater disturbances, having insight into this was relatively useless. They had also better have insight into exactly what they told themselves about their early grim experiences, learn precisely how this self-indoctrination and attitudinizing largely led to their disturbances, and most importantly, work hard to change their basic philosophies in drastic ways *today.*

I found, in my early experimentation with forms of REBT, that all this could sometimes be done in a relatively brief period of time. At least clients could be shown what they were telling themselves as both children and adults, how this contributed to their dysfunctioning, and how they could change it and change their grandiose demands into reasonable preferences and thereby significantly improved themselves. They could understand this in a relatively few sessions of psychotherapy, if their therapists were not distracting them with needless details of their childhood experiencing. Not all of them, of course, would quickly see and Dispute their IB's, but a significant number were able to do this and would do so if properly instructed by their therapists. They would look at what they were doing and reconstruct their demands back into desires and stop upsetting themselves. Again, they were most likely not to do this completely at first, but after a few sessions of starting to use REBT, they would be well on their way to feeling better and getting better.

Of course, I risk turning a few of my clients off by emphasizing that they largely upset themselves and that they can definitely stop doing it, and by not hearing at great length their gruesome stories which they usually like to tell me. But I also risk turning other clients off if I delay what I usually do, instead of quickly helping them to see and Dispute their IBs.

When my clients don't get the REBT theory, or get it and don't use it, then I first go over the same basic material several times and give them time to digest it and especially to do their homework assignments.

From the first session onward, I normally give them at least one cognitive, emotive or behavioral assignment and see whether they quickly do it. If they do it between the first and second session, then that is a good sign that they can be helped in a relatively short length of time. Again, the REBT philosophy says that people can change relatively quickly if they do their homework between the sessions. The sessions themselves are importantly instructive, but clients had better do their therapeutic homework, just as students in school had better do so in order to learn their material thoroughly and convincingly.

Therefore, as you can probably see, resisting clients, along with your regular not-too-resisting clients, had better be motivated to do cognitive, emotional, and behavioral homework. It is your job to convince them that the therapy that they do during the session, although it may be exceptionally valuable, is often relatively unimportant to that which is done in between sessions. For it is there where the resistant clients particularly are oppositional. They may listen carefully and even discuss sensibly what you are showing them and how you are explaining what to do about their disturbances; but then they resist doing the homework. So it is important, especially with resisting clients, to motivate them to work in between sessions.

To summarize some of the points I have been making on efficiency in psychotherapy, you may consider these possible procedures.

1. Let your therapy explanations be brief and clear. Aim to get across some of your main points in the first few sessions, but don't insist on doing so with all clients.

2. No matter how effective your therapy is and how well you teach it to your clients, the efforts they make to use it in between sessions is what really counts and therefore, they had preferably better be motivated to work and to do their homework.

3. Clients, no matter how intelligent and educated they are, frequently interfere with their effectiveness by anxietizing, depressing themselves, and raging. Be as clear as you can be in your explanations, your describing of your methods, and your outlining of homework procedures. Check your clients' *understanding* of what you are presenting. Get them to repeat it in their own words. Don't just assume that they understand you.

4. Try to discover your clients' basic disturbed feelings, attitudes, and behaviors and not merely their presenting ones. If they have a phobia of public speaking or of job interviews, question them as to whether they have a general fear of rejection. If they are anxietizing about sports or test taking, do they have a general horror of failing? What feelings or ideas do they have that are included in several symptoms? Reveal and tackle these wide-ranging issues.

5. Look for secondary symptoms. When the clients have primary symptoms such as procrastinating, they frequently blame themselves for having these "stupid" symptoms. Thus, they procrastinate because they will put themselves if they write a poor term paper—and then put themselves down for procrastinating. A double form of self-damnation! Discover their thinking-emoting-behaving that tends to create their symptoms and also their Irrational *Beliefs* about having these symptoms; and help them see and deal with their disturbing on both levels.

6. Deal with future disturbability. Clients are prone to feel panicky, depressing, and raging when they come to therapy, and you can effectively show them what they did to upset themselves and how to think, feel, and act differently to decrease their dysfunctioning. But for efficient therapy, you will try to show them how to cope with future Adversities and become less disturbable. Thus, if they are self-damning about behaving incompetently at work, you can show them how to criticize their poor behaving without defaming their entire being, their personhood, for behaving that poorly. But you can also help them see that self-damning is generally dysfunctional and will lead to poor results, including increased incompetency. You can thereby help them see that, prophylactically, they had better monitor and work against all forms of self-downing, to make themselves considerably less disturb*able*.

7. Rethink and revise your techniques. Use what generally works for you and your clients, but not rigidly and dogmatically. Think, experiment, and revise. Keep in mind Paul's (1967, p. 111) question: "What treatment by whom, is most effective for this individual with that specific problem and under which set of circumstances?" This can be a truly efficiency-oriented question!

Let me repeat that efficiency includes depth-centeredness in psychotherapy. Unfortunately, the concept of depth-centeredness has been preempted by the psychoanalytic theorists and practitioners who believe, probably correctly, that there is an underlying cause to people's disturbing themselves and that this has to be thoroughly understood and worked through over a period of time before it can really be resolved and dealt with. In existential and philosophic therapies, it is also assumed that a symptom has depth-centered roots. In REBT, it is assumed that people's disturbing themselves largely consists of their having a basic absolutistic or musturbatory philosophy. That is, "I must not suffer any form of severe discomfort of failure, and it is terrible when I do!" Unless this kind of philosophy is seen and counterattacked, as I have been showing in this book, clients may temporarily feel better, but it is unlikely that they will get and remain better.

In REBT, an existential view of depth-centeredness in psychotherapy has various advantages over less depth-centered views. For example:

1. People's underlying philosophizing, especially their demands and their musts, if they are brought to the surface and consciously revealed, can not only help them see the source of their current disturbingness, but preferably will also help reveal prior and later distressing.

2. Clients may, in addition to eliminating their negative symptoms, show themselves how to lead a more joyous, creative, and fulfilled existence. So the second main goal of therapy, self-actualization and self-fulfillment, may be more readily obtained than in other kinds of therapy.

3. Depth-centered psychotherapy, which gets at the root of people's self-disturbing philosophizing, may promote a general understanding of so-called human nature that may be relevant to many aspects of living, including their social and political relations and even their sports and artistic pursuits. This kind of basic understanding of human disturbability and how to minimize it can have important national and international influences.

Ironically enough, because of the simplicity and the clarity of some of its formulations and techniques, REBT is often accused of being superficial. Actually, it tries to be depth-centered by determining and modifying central philosophies that help create disturbance. It assumes that the most serious resistors are little aware of their key irrationalities and/or rigidly hold to them. It encourages therapists to work hard at revealing, clarifying, and disputing these fundamental believings-emotings-behavings. By taking this kind of a piercing, deep approach, REBT tries to reach many resistors who otherwise would be less receptive to therapeutic change.

PERVASIVENESS IN PSYCHOTHERAPY

Pervasiveness in psychotherapy may be defined as a therapist helping his or her clients to deal with many of their problems, and in a sense their whole lives, rather than with a few presenting symptoms. Thus, a psychoanalyst who sees a woman who has poor sex with her husband will try to zero in not merely on that particular issue, but also on her general relationships with her mate and with other significant people. And a rational emotive behavior therapist may first show this woman that she has a real fear of failing sexually with her husband—because of her absolutistic philosophizing, "I have to do well sexually and must win his approval"—but also shows her how her dire "need" for success and love are interfering with her other marital and nonmarital functions.

Like depth-centeredness, the value of pervasiveness in therapy has distinct benefits:

1. It shows clients that they can easily create several symptoms from the same underlying attitudinizing and philosophizing and how, by changing their core attitudinizing, they can deal with or eliminate more than one or two present symptoms. They can also deal with related or even unrelated symptoms.

2. It helps them to understand and relate better to other people. They understand how others upset themselves and can possibly unupset themselves, how naturally and frequently this is accomplished, and they tend to be more forgiving than they otherwise would be to these others who act badly. They therefore have a better degree of unconditional other–acceptance (UOA).

3. Pervasiveness in psychotherapy may enable people, especially if they learn by REBT and CBT how to reduce their own disturbances, also can see how to deal therapeutically with their close relatives and associates. Sometimes they are pretty well stuck with these people and cannot very well leave them and had better accept what they cannot change. But if they realize that they carry on their dysfunctional philosophizing and emoting into practically all relationships, especially those that they may not like and be stuck with, then they can better handle this unfortunate situation.

EXTENSIVENESS IN PSYCHOTHERAPY

Extensiveness in psychotherapy means that clients can be helped not only to minimize their disturbing negative feelings—for example, anxietizing, depressing, and raging—but also to maximize their potential for happy living—that is, to be more productive, creative, and enjoying. Intensive therapy, as noted above, explores any number of disturbing symptoms that the client holds and not merely the presenting one. But it also deals with exploring and augmenting pleasurable aspects of life, such as sensuality, sexuality, laughter, and creativity. Efficient psychotherapy, therefore, includes intensive as well as extensive treatment, providing for self-actualizing as well as minimizing the inhibiting aspects of people's lives.

Actually, as I shall show a little later in more detail, REBT accepts the fact that some individuals have severe personality disorders and are not just "nice neurotics." Therefore, they have biological tendencies to disturb themselves more than other people and also may have strong tendencies to depress and anger themselves even though there are few unfortunate events in their lives. People with severe personality disorders can sometimes only be helped in a limited way, and therefore REBT attempts to help them more thoroughly; but when it looks like this isn't likely, it teaches them to act better with their limitations, to distract themselves with a number of relaxation and other methods, and to engage in pursuits that they find enjoyable. Once again, try to help them acquire a vital absorbing interest, which will keep them pleasurably occupied and preoccupied, perhaps for a number of years.

THE USE OF MULTIMODAL METHODS

Although one or a few main methods of psychotherapy may significantly help people change their dysfunctioning and even to some degree get better as well as feel better, this beneficial outcome is more likely to be achieved when you have at your disposal a good many cognitive, emotive, and behavioral methods. As I keep emphasizing, thinking, emoting, and behaving are processes that hardly exist in any pure state, but significantly overlap and interact with each other. Therefore, what is usually called emotional disturbance has cognitive and behaving aspects as well. As Arnold Lazarus (1997) has particularly shown, if you have a large number of techniques, you will be able to explore, in individual cases, to see which of these work better than others and which are likely to lead to more profound results. The more comprehensive your armamentarium of techniques is, the more likely will you be able to find suitable procedures for your especially difficult clients.

With resisting clients in particular, REBT uses a wide variety of methods. It assumes that if the usual techniques do not work, some unusual ones may be productive. It also assumes that if one method, such as vigorous disputing of Irrational *Beliefs,* does not seem to be effective, a different emphasis, such as a more laid back and cautious kind of disputing, may work. Like several other forms of therapy, REBT tries to be creative and wide-ranging in its selection of methods that may be suitable for regular clients and, especially, for resisting ones.

THE DANGERS OF USING PALLIATIVE METHODS

As I emphasize in this book and particularly stress in my books, *Feeling Better, Getting Better, and Staying Better* (Ellis, 2001a) and *Overcoming Destructive Thoughts, Feelings, and Beliefs* (Ellis, 2001b), innumerable techniques work to help clients palliate their disturbances.

Relaxation methods in, particular, interrupt their worrying, their depressing, and their obsessing and therefore give them a chance for pleasanter activities that sometimes make them feel great. Resisting clients avoid some of the more difficult and prolonged methods of getting better and opt, consciously or unconsciously, for the palliative ones. They do this for several reasons: (1) They feel so relieved by the temporary or partial removal of a painful feeling like depression that they do not get the core of it. (2) They often have serious low frustration toleration (LFT) and therefore will welcome palliative procedures, such as tranquilizers or meditation, to quickly alleviate the worst feelings they have, rather than working at more elegant philosophic changes that will help them more permanently. (3) Many clients are so desperate to "cure" a painful feeling, such as panic, that they quickly try to alleviate it by some palliative method and then stick to this technique even though their panic returns, and sometimes returns in a worse form, later.

Efficiency in therapy, particularly with resisting clients, therefore consists of convincing them thoroughly that they'd better go for a more elegant, rather than a less elegant, change. It doesn't discourage their using palliative techniques but encourages their using them along with more curative ones. It warns resisting clients that they are quite likely to fall back to the old disturbance, even when they have temporarily relieved it, and therefore will be more improved if they get a basically new frame of reference that does not interfere with their truly getting and staying better. Because it stresses unconditional self-acceptance (USA), REBT shows clients that even when they fall back to old Irrational *Beliefs* and thereby redisturb themselves, they are okay as *persons* and do not have to put themselves down. Therefore, they can go back to the fray and diminish their self-disturbing again, and also go on to make its relief more profound and more permanent.

THE USE OF PREVENTIVE METHODS

Actually, the main goal of therapy could be said to be, though this is usually not faced by many therapists, both the minimizing of present disturbingness and the prevention of future disturbingness. This is because, once again, REBT hypothesizes that the tendency to seriously disturb oneself about things that may not be very serious in their own right, is very common to humans all over the world. Therefore, showing your clients palliative techniques of minimizing their current disturbingness, or even helping them to permanently undisturb themselves about, let us say, failing at test-taking or at participating in sports, won't necessarily prevent them from needlessly upsetting themselves in the future. Consequently, REBT—especially with resisting type clients—specializes in preventive psychotherapy. It does this in several ways:

1. It is highly educational and tries to teach resistors and other clients that they do not merely get upset or become upset but also unduly upset themselves, and that they do not have to do so.
2. It shows them that if they actively and forcefully keep disputing their Irrational *Beliefs* after they feel disturbed, they will tend to automatically learn how to stick with their RB's before they disturb themselves and will therefore ward off much, though hardly all, maladjusting.
3. It teaches them several emotional and behaving methods, such as rational emotive imagery, through which they can imagine dire happenings in advance of their actually occurring and can train themselves to react healthily rather than unhealthily if these events actually occur.
4. It uses a considerable amount of in vivo desensitization and active, forceful homework assignments, including relapse prevention, that help train resistors to rehabituate themselves so that they not only overcome current anxietizing but lessen the possibility of their falling prey to new kinds of disturbing.
5. It particularly works with the resistors who have secondary symptoms, such as anxietizing about anxietizing and depressing about depressing. As these clients come to see how they needlessly horrify themselves about their primary disturbing and how they can stop doing this, they often prevent themselves from developing new distress to which they can then attach secondary symptoms.

ILLUSTRATIVE CASE PRESENTATION

Let me be much more concrete in regard to helping clients more efficiently attack their problemizing by giving a concrete example. Calvin, a forty-year-old physician, was exceptionally depressed when he came for REBT. He damned himself for his medical errors and for his failings as a husband and father. He was extremely hostile toward his wife whenever she disagreed with him about important matters, and he fumed and frothed about even the smallest unniceities of his life, such as a leaky roof or a hole in his socks.

Calvin resisted when he first came to therapy, because he had started it only because his sister had benefited from REBT and kept insisting that he just had to go and try it. He was not psychologically oriented, preferring to believe that his depressing only resulted from physical factors, and thought that if therapy helped at all it had to be psychoanalytic therapy that intensively explored his past and the part his parents played in making him disturbed. In other words, Calvin did everything to deny the REBT view that people's believing-emoting-behavings (B) largely gave them disturbed consequences, such as depressing themselves at point C. He rigidly held the contrary view—that adversities (A), including biological factors—caused his severe depressing.

I tried to use the main efficiency factors in REBT with Calvin and treated him along the following lines: Calvin's treatment was brief. He was seen for four months on a once-a-week basis, first for one hour and during the last two months for half-hour sessions. His therapy made little inroads into his very busy medical schedule.

In regard to depth-centeredness, Calvin was helped to zero in on his three basis musts or absolutistic philosophies, which permeated almost his entire life and largely led to his depressing.

1. "I must do outstandingly well in my work and be approved of by all my patients."
2. "My wife must never disagree with me about important matters and has to do things my way!"
3. "Conditions under which I live must be easy and unhassled and practically never frustrate me too badly."

Although Calvin was at first convinced that his depressing was purely biological and endogenous—even though several self-prescribed antidepressants had not in the least lifted it—I was able to show him that every time he was feeling very low, he was invariably demanding and not merely wishing that he do well and was castigating himself when he did not perform outstandingly. Also, he was frequently commanding that things be much better than they were, particularly that his performance be outstandingly good. He soon acknowledged that his musturbatory philosophizing underlay much of his depressing and his angering himself, and that with his god-like attitude, he was helping to make himself distressing.

In the area of pervasiveness, although Calvin first only wanted to discuss his horror of failing at work, and occasionally his anger at his wife, he was shown that his self-downing and his low frustration tolerance were invading other areas of his life as well—including his sexual activities and his social relations. In fact, he responded better at first in his sexual and social areas than he did about giving up his perfectionistic tendencies at work, and he was partly able to reduce his work demands by first reducing his sexual and social demands.

Regarding extensiveness, Calvin was not only taught how to work against his presenting depression and anger but to add interest and pleasure to his days—such as music and running. These enhanced his existence, distracted him somewhat from his incessant worrying, and gave him two vital absorbing interests that made life more enjoyable.

As for multiple methods, Calvin was not only treated by me with highly cognitive techniques of REBT, but given a number of emotive exercises and in vivo activity homework assignments as well. Thus, he especially seemed to benefit himself from shame-attacking exercises, rational emotive imagery, and deliberately staying in some painful situations—such as visiting his boring in-laws and showing himself that he could stand, if not like, the pain and trouble of these situations.

Best of all, Calvin seemed remarkably able to maintain his therapeutic progress and to do preventive psychotherapy on his own and thereby increase his helping himself. He first, after four months of therapy, stopped depressing himself, went back to a full schedule of work, and started getting along remarkably well with his wife and family in spite of some difficulties that they presented. This seemed surprising, considering the brevity of his therapy. But even more surprising was what he reported when he returned to see me two years later to talk about his wife, who was severely panicking herself about driving a car. She had previously driven one without troubling herself for twelve years, but now she panicked at even the thought of driving, and was going through a period of severely depersonalizing herself. Calvin was handling this situation with her remarkably well in spite of the immense transportation difficulties it was causing his entire family.

To make matters worse, Calvin had become afflicted, for the past six months, with a rheumatic condition that handicapped him seriously in his practice. One of his sons turned out to be dyslexic and was behaving in a highly troublesome manner. In addition, both Calvin's parents were dying of cancer, and his economic situation, because of some of his poor investments, was deteriorating. In spite of all these adversities, his spirits were unusually high. He refused to anger or pity himself in the face of these frustrations. He did not put himself down for his economic blunders. He was also doing a reasonably good job of using some of the REBT principles he had learned to help his wife, his children, and his parents cope with their serious emotional troubles.

This is the kind of "elegant" therapeutic result that I particularly strive for and like to help effect. Calvin not only overcame his presenting symptoms and maintained this change, but he also improved significantly after therapy had ended. He reached a stage, two years after the end of therapy, where he wouldn't allow virtually any kind of setbacks to disturb him too seriously—that is, to make him depressing, panicking, angering, or self-pitying.

OTHER KINDS OF EFFICIENCY IN THERAPY

In addition to the ways I have just outlined, some other kinds of efficiency in psychotherapy may be obtained as follows:

1. Efficient therapy tends to be stated in clear and simple terms, so that you have your clients easily understand it. Abstruse or esoteric methods of therapy may have desirable qualities, but they tend to have a limited appeal to your clients and especially to resisting ones.

2. You can learn efficient therapy fairly easily and it does not require you to undergo years of training and apprenticeship. Nor does it require that you have years of personal psychotherapy yourself. Training and personal psychotherapy may at times be highly desirable, but they sometimes take long periods of time and considerable effort that may even interfere with the efficiency that the therapist is going to try to achieve with his or her clients. In our three-day training practica we give our trainees some brief, and often highly effective, personal REBT sessions.

3. Efficient therapy is often intrinsically interesting to both you and your clients and motivates them to stay with it. Since resisting clients frequently have to work at changing themselves for a considerable length of time, they had better not be uninterested and bored with the therapy itself. However, making therapy interesting and dramatic may have its boomerang effects, because some of the most questionable and potentially harmful forms of psychological treatment, such as fanatical devotion to the cult of therapy itself, may actually misdirect people and lead to some harm.

4. Efficient psychotherapy helps your clients in many instances to achieve maximum good with minimum harm to themselves and others. Some therapies, including some of the most esoteric and bizarre ones like primal therapy, still help bring about healthy or beneficial results for certain clients. But it also has been shown that some forms of treatment have fairly clear harmful results (Garfield & Bergen, 1994; Zilbergeld, 1983).

5. Efficient psychotherapy favors flexibility, lack of dogma, and provision and encouragement for its own change. It not only tends to

help your clients be less absolutistic, rigid, unscientific, and devout in their own right, but it also endorses scientific falsifiability. That is, it sets up theories so that they are ultimately falsifiable and views them skeptically and tentatively and constantly strives to check on their errors and harmfulness. In this manner, efficient therapy not only tries to achieve, but does its best to maintain, effectiveness.

My work with many clients, and especially those who keep resisting, leads me to hypothesize that even when psychotherapy is shown, by controlled studies, to be effective, it may still be inefficient. Unless it includes some of the elements discussed in this chapter, it may remain so.

Methods of Overcoming Resistance that Emphasize Behavioral Techniques

10

Just as REBT invariably uses a variety of cognitive and emotive methods, so is it just about always highly behavioral. Resisting individuals, especially, often require active, directive, and usually a good deal of in vivo homework assignments. Let me say again that one of the main reasons I abandoned psychoanalysis and created REBT in 1955 was because one of my attractive, highly intelligent female clients refused to meet eligible males, even though she was highly desirous of forming a permanent relationship. I helped her gain all kinds of insight into why she was inhibiting herself, yet she still refused to act on her desires. I finally gave her the ultimatum of returning to see me for therapy only after she had made some real attempts to encounter some eligible males. Three months later, after acting on this assignment, she returned to therapy and from that time onward, she began to overcome her problems of shyness.

Noting this, and successfully trying similar methods with several other inhibited and withdrawn clients, helped me to reject much of psychoanalytic theory and practice and to begin developing REBT.

I still saw people somewhat psychodynamically, in the sense that they were unaware of a good deal of their motives and often attributed them to reasons which were not very legitimate. But from the start of my using REBT with clients, I included active-directive behavioral methods (Ellis, 1962). Some of the most useful of these include the following methods which you can selectively consider and with which you can experiment.

FACILITATING HOMEWORK ASSIGNMENTS

Homework assignments are given regularly in REBT and CBT. Don't forget the third main insight of REBT: There is usually no way but work and practice—yes, steady work and practice—to implement the other insights of Rational Emotive Behavior Therapy.

Several research studies and reviews of the literature have shown that homework is a valuable part of therapy (Burns, 1980/1999). These have led to the devising of methods to enhance the likelihood of clients actually doing the homework that they agree to do. These studies indicate, enhancing clients' carrying out their homework assignments may be done in three main ways: (1) focusing on the characteristics of the homework tasks; (2) focusing on client characteristics; (3) focusing on therapist characteristics. Let us consider some of these ways you can help improve client compliance with homework under these headings.

Enhancing the Characteristics of the Homework Tasks. You can clearly define the homework tasks and can write them out and give the client a memo of them. You can start out with small assignments and build up to more demanding ones. You can arrange assignments that best fit the client's main therapeutic goals. You can give specific pleasure-seeking assignments, such as suggesting that depressed clients do enjoyable things. You can make homework assignments brief, so that they do not consume too much of your client's time and energy.

Enhancing the Clients' Characteristics that Make Them More Amenable to Homework. You can emphasize the importance of homework for achieving your clients' main therapeutic goals and help motivate them to do relevant projects. You can give your clients considerable choice in selecting their homework. You can find assignments that your clients find easy and enjoyable; you can help create assignments that your clients find challenging and rewarding. You can roleplay with your clients, take their role and let them take the therapist role and suggest homework and persuade you (roleplaying them) to carry it out. You can discuss with your clients the pros and cons of their completing the homework. You can arrange for reinforcements (such as personal pleasures) when clients do their homework and for penalties when they fail to do it (Urdang, 2000).

Enhancing the Characteristics of the Therapist that May Facilitate Homework. You can show understanding and empathy for your clients' difficulties in doing the homework; and you can show positive feelings and encouragement when your clients carry out their homework. You can discover which of your own characteristics and therapeutic tactics that your clients most likely object to, and you can make some efforts to change them. You can change your language with some of your resistant clients who may object to your "too rough" or "too gentle" language. You can correct some of your therapeutic behaviors—such as coming late to sessions, canceling sessions, taking too few or too many notes—when they are viewed as "irresponsible" or "too indulgent."

Arnold Lazarus (1997) suggests that you don't use words like homework, because some clients have a history of hating school homework and may be turned off by your language. You can follow the REBT rule of trying to actively persuade clients that it is to their real benefit for them to carry out their agreed-upon homework. Among other writers, Kahneman and Tuersky (2000) have recommended therapists framing homework goals for more in terms of showing clients the *gains* they may get than the disbenefits they may get from *not* doing it.

There are several ways of encouraging hesitant clients to do their agreed-upon homework assignments, including these:

1. Clearly define the assignments so that your clients understand them.
2. Begin with simple and easy assignments and build up to more complicated and difficult ones.
3. Give your clients specific written assignments.
4. Collaborate with the clients on suggested assignments. Give them some alternative choices of what homework to take.
5. Try to enhance your clients' commitment to therapy.
6. Be persuasive and enthusiastic about the value of assignments.
7. Have your clients involve their family and friends in doing their assignments.
8. Roleplay your clients and have them persuade you to do their homework.
9. Give clients a self-help handout showing how valuable carrying out their assignments may be.
10. Socratically question your clients as to how valuable they think the homework will be.
11. Stress the benefits of following the homework rather than the pains of not following it.
12. Give your clients tasks that they can perform may increase their sense of self-efficacy.
13. Praise your clients for doing their homework, and especially for doing difficult tasks.
14. Actually do some assignment with clients or have them get a friend to do it with them. Thus, I have found that more clients will do REBT shame-attacking exercises if a friend accompanies them than if they do it alone. However, clients who do assignments by themselves may benefit more than if they do so without a friend or therapist to help them.

INDUCING CLIENTS TO TOLERATE DISCOMFORT

Resistors frequently are afflicted with low frustration tolerance (LFT) and therefore will not follow the maxim that there is rarely any gain without pain. Consequently, it is sometimes wise to forcefully bring their LFT to their attention and to show them that unless they consciously and deliberately court various kinds of discomfort, they have little chance of changing.

As an example of this, I had a 50-year-old client, an accountant who had always worked below his level of competency and started therapy because he wanted to go into selling but found it "too difficult" to keep up with other salesmen in his company. I said to him, "You want to know what is the 'inner sickness' that keeps you from being satisfied at work? Well, I'll tell you what a great part of it is: It's called two-year-old-ism—your demand that the world treat you like a two-year-old and do everything for you. Technically it's called low frustration tolerating. But it's really two-year-oldism—that is childish demandingness. As long as you have this LFT and keep cultivating it, you'll whine and scream, as you are now doing. But when you admit that that's the real diagnosis—two-year-oldism—you'll then presumably stop your whining and push your ass to do the best you can at selling.

"I would predict that you'll actually do very well on your present job because you are bright and competent enough to do so. But not at first. At first, you'll be very uncomfortable—because it's hard selling and competing with others. But it also would be 'too hard' if you started a new job. If you push and push yourself, as you would have to do if you wanted to play a sport very well, you'll finally tend to find it easy and enjoyable. Not at first—but finally.

"So I would advise you to make yourself do the work you dislike, force yourself to do it and do it. Deliberately push yourself to be uncomfortable—yes, uncomfortable—until you finally find the work easy and comfortable. Then, as I said, you also may well find it enjoyable. By courting discomfort and by that hard route alone, you'll most likely become comfortable. Not right away, but later."

Although this client fought me for most of this session and often talked over me so loudly that he couldn't hear anything I said, I strongly persisted and at last got through to him. He admitted that his "fear" of his new job was mainly discomfort anxiety or low frustration tolerance and not ego-anxiety, as he had previously loudly claimed. He accepted the homework assignment of forcing himself to work hard at his new job until it finally became more comfortable. Within several weeks, he proved that my prediction came true and that he actually did find the new job easy and enjoyable—and had also lost his fear of not being able to do it well.

So if you keep after resisting clients many times, and sometimes quite forcibly, until they do what they are irrationally afraid to do or what their low frustration tolerating stops them from attempting, you may help them see that many situations are not "horrible" or "terrible" but only inconvenient—and even ultimately enjoyable.

A considerable amount of resistance is tied up with unhealthy procrastination. Bill Knaus and I wrote a best-selling book, *Overcoming Procrastination,* in 1977 and it is still popular in college bookstores. It stresses the two main causes of needless delay—low frustration tolerance and perfectionism—and gives many cognitive, emotive, and behavioral methods of overcoming them. Bill Knaus (2000) and Michael Bernard (2000) have brought up to date and summarized some of the main Irrational *Beliefs* that may lead your resistant clients to delay their working at therapy—sometimes indefinitely! And they have also summarized some of the main methods you can use to help your clients use to overcome their procrastinating. These include:

- Begin now, don't wait for the moment of inspiration.
- Find your Irrational *Beliefs* leading you to procrastinate and actively and energetically Dispute them.
- Write yourself reminders, such as "Doing your REBT homework gets you healthy; not doing it gets you nowhere."
- Learn to expect—and not tolerate—backsliding.
- Blame your delaying your therapy efforts but never blame *yourself* for this delay.
- Do your harder therapeutic tasks quickly, to get their hassle out of the way.
- Break your homework into small, manageable parts and give yourself a time limit for doing each step.
- Work a minimum of five minutes on onerous homework. Then you can go on for another 5 minutes—and more!
- Do almost anything at all on the large task you wish to accomplish. Gradually eat holes or chunks in it.
- Penalize yourself for *not* doing a "too hard" therapy task.
- Do a cost-benefit analysis and show all the benefits of doing your therapeutic homework and the disbenefits of *not* doing it.

Show your clients that these are not sure-fire ways of overcoming their procrastinating on their therapy efforts. But they can help considerably!

Subtle followers of the practice of neurolinguistic programming, recommends that you go out of your way to foster the value of delayed gratification or high frustration tolerance in resistant clients. You encourage them to focus on images, sounds, words, feelings, smells, and tastes that are connected with good homework outcomes—on the pleasures and satisfactions they will achieve if they delay some of their harmful satisfactions and bring about future gains. This cognitive and kinesthetic focus on the pleasures of the future instead of their "need" for immediate gratification may significantly help them to do today those behaviors that will benefit them tomorrow.

It probably cannot be too strongly repeated that practically all clients resist changing themselves and that unless you yourself persist at persuading them to commit to therapy and persist at change, they will frequently avoid doing so. As is emphasized in this book, you can do so in several ways: (1) Actively-directively persuade them of the value and near necessity of commitment to work and practice. (2) Keep showing them the cost-benefit aspects of refusal to change. (3) Encourage their constructivism and their positive values of reconstructing their lives. (4) Show them that their goal-directed implementation intentions often lead to *automatic* beneficial responses. (5) Show them that you personally have faith in their strength and ability to change (Robin & Balter, 1995).

USING IN VIVO DESENSITIZATION

As I frequently tell my workshop audiences, and as I have related in my writings, I originally got over my "terrible" phobia of speaking in public and also of approaching datable women. I got this idea from John B. Watson's experiments (1919) and several of his other associates. They put a child at the end of a long table and a feared animal—such as a rabbit or a mouse—at the other end. The child was at first terrified, but as they gradually talked to him and moved the animal closer, he became desensitized, and within about twenty minutes was often petting the animal and enjoying it. So I used this technique of in vivo desensitization, plus the ideas I learned from reading the ancient philosophers and the modern philosophers who showed that it's not the things that happen, but people's catastrophizing and awfulizing ideas about them, that create anxiety.

When I first started using REBT at the beginning of 1955, I used in vivo desensitization much more that I used imaginal desensitization which Joseph Wolpe was promoting at that time. This is not to discourage you from using Wolpe's imaginal desensitization, because if you can induce your clients to imagine some fearful event happening at a distance from them, and get them to use Jacobsen's (1938) Progressive Relaxation Technique to interrupt their anxiety, they will frequently make themselves less anxietizing as they imagine the same event closer and closer.

The trouble with this technique is that, first, it has to be eventually proven in action, because a client can say that she is not afraid of a snake any longer, now that she has faced it many times in her imagination. But to prove that she really is not afraid, she will have to actually risk facing it—yes, alive.

Second, I and a good many clinical demonstrations and experiments as well have shown that exposure, or in vivo desensitization, is probably the quickest and most thorough going way for most individuals who severely anxietize, to overcome their problem. Thus, Edna Foa and her associates (Foa & Olasov, 1998) have pioneered in applying various forms of exposure to extremely anxietizing individuals.

I have personally found that resistors will not change in many instances unless you encourage them to stay in unpleasant situations until they became comfortable and even enjoying. Also, they will not be helped to give up their self-defeating catastrophizing unless they are induced to keep repeating, in vivo, acts that they irrationally fear—such as dancing or talking in public. By all means, then, use your best persuasive methods to push your resisting clients, especially those who are awfulizing about undangerous things, to get them actually to try these so-called dangers and find in their own experience that they can well survive them.

As a case in point, I saw a 38-year-old male who had never even petted with a woman, even though he was obsessed with heterosexual fantasies and had masturbated daily, using these fantasies, for 25 years. It took me six months of active-directive REBT to induce him to make a single date and another four months to persuade him to make any sexual overtures to the woman he began dating. After giving him literally scores of homework assignments about talking to, dating, and making advances to women, and after getting him to burn $800 in penalties for not carrying out these assignments, he finally began making passes at his partners in his eleventh month of treatment. Within a year, he was so unfearful of dating and petting that he had intercourse with five different women!

Although at first it took quite a while for my client to begin to have sex, he then kept looking eagerly for new women to date. I finally had to work with him on his obsessive-compulsive dating and convince him that there are other things in life besides sex! Without my strongly encouraging him to do in vivo desensitization, it is most doubtful, as we both agreed, that he would have ever overcome his extreme fear of sexual rejection.

Similarly, I saw a 30-year-old woman who washed her hands at least 20 times on every occasion that she urinated or defecated, for fear that even if minute amounts of urine or feces remains on her hands, she would be hopelessly contaminated. I persistently showed her that she had virtually no chance of giving up her lifelong feelings of overwhelming anxietizing unless she forced herself, however painfully, to refrain from her hand washing. I helped her decrease it by 10% every week and she was able, at the end of ten weeks, to wash her hands only once every time she went to the bathroom. For the first several weeks, she anxietized severely every time she left the bathroom. But her panicking decreased as she kept vehemently telling herself, "I don't need absolute safety. If I get contaminated, tough, I'll still live and be happy!"

Eleven years of previous psychoanalytic therapy had hardly affected this woman and may have been iatrogenic. But in ten weeks of REBT-oriented in vivo response prevention, she improved remarkably. As her hand-washing and her anxietizing decreased, she also became much less shy and more active and began to have a fuller social life, whereas she had for many years been a recluse. In her case, as in that of many people I induce to do in vivo desensitization and response prevention, my convincing her that unless she deliberately courted and lived through her current anxietizing, she would probably have to suffer with it forever, significantly helped her to deliberately take on present discomfort to achieve future gain.

USING IMPLOSIVE DESENSITIZATION

Although gradual desensitization exercises to decrease irrational anxietizing have been favored by behavior therapists for many years, they have their disadvantages and limitations. This is especially true with some resisting clients. They can build up renewed fears in the intervals between the gradual desensitizing procedures. Perhaps more importantly, these clients often have abysmal low frustration tolerance (LFT) and if they are encouraged to surrender their self-defeating behaviors *easily* and *gradually* this procedure implies that they *have to* avoid pain and in some ways it may sustain or even increase their LFT philosophy.

Consequently, you may often find it advantageous to have your resistant clients desensitize themselves implosively with massed instead of gradual practice. To illustrate, I frequently tell the story of a 45-year-old accountant who had suffered from an elevator phobia for more than 30 years and who went to great lengths (sometimes walking up and down more than 20 flights of stairs) to avoid riding in them. He refused to do the gradual desensitization homework assignments which I and his therapy group gave him, even though three other members of the group gradually went in elevators and overcame their long-standing phobias of doing so. He came to me one day for a special session of individual therapy and said, "I'm getting desperate. I could get several better jobs than the one I have but all of them are on the upper floors of tall buildings and I would have to get over my elevator fears to take them. What shall I do? How can I overcome my phobias?"

Knowing this man's great resistance to gradual homework, I said to myself, "I may never persuade him from working through his anxiety of riding in elevators, but what have I got to lose? I think I'll be very strong and see what happens." So I said to him, very powerfully and with all the sincerity I could muster, "Well, seeing what your record of resistance has been so far, not only to REBT but to the 15 years of therapy you had before I saw you, I would say that you only have two good possibilities to overcoming your self-indulged fear of elevators."

"What are those two possibilities?" he anxiously asked. His voice was quavering and his hands were waving around in a distraught manner.

"One," I said, "get in those damned elevators for at least twenty times a day every single day for the next 30 days. Yes! At least 20 times a day for the next 30 days, or"—I deliberately paused dramatically, knowing what my next highly significant sentence was going to be. "Or what?" he asked.

"Or suffer enormously for the rest of your life! Yes, s u f f e r, suffer! Forever! Which of these two would you choose?"

My client's face blanched and his lips compulsively clamped. I thought he would have a fit, but he grimly and silently held his facial muscles in check. A few minutes later he left my office, and I was convinced that he would still do nothing about getting into elevators.

Well, I was wrong. As he reported to the next group session five days later, that very afternoon he forced himself to ride in 22 elevators. The next day he took 21 rides, the third day 24 rides, and the fourth day 23 elevator rides. By the eighth day of his implosive in vivo therapy, he had overcome over 80% of his fears of elevators. On the tenth day, he forced himself to ride an elevator in the Empire State Building, one of the highest buildings in the world, on a day so windy that the building was shaking somewhat, as tall buildings sometimes do, and when the workmen were fixing some of the elevators. Nonetheless, he took the express elevator to the top floor and experienced little anxiety.

This does not mean that if you use implosive therapy with your resisting clients it will always work? Definitely not! Frequently they won't carry it out—or they'll do it only briefly, then stop. But if you keep after them and strongly convince them that no matter how hard it is to do, implosive in vivo assignments frequently work much better, and especially more quickly, to overcome their irrational fears, you will sometimes help resistors to use this kind of therapy. In the case of my accountant client, once he overcame his elevator phobicizing, he clearly saw that several of his other aspects of catastrophizing, especially his horror of talking to strange women and of going on job interviews, were quite unfounded, and he began to talk to women, to go on interviews, and to do several other things that he had been paralyzing himself about doing previously. But, once again, this does not mean that implosive therapy always or even usually works. When used discriminately in selected cases, and vigorously pushed, it can induce some resistors to overcome their emotional and behavioral difficultizing that they otherwise might never conquer.

Avoidance is one of the main reasons why clients resist surrendering their "terrible" feelings of anxietizing and depressing, no matter how painful these feelings may be. Perversely enough, just because they are painful many clients immediately want to escape from them and therefore, both consciously and unconsciously, invent a whole variety of ways of camouflaging their feelings. Thus, they refuse to keep in touch with them, deny having them, distract themselves from experiencing their full blasts, drink or drug to dull them, and use other methods to cover up their painful feelings. As I keep showing in this book, these distracting methods may work very well—temporarily! But they fail to get at the Believing-Emoting-Behaving sources of clients' disordering feelings; and in some cases they preoccupy them and decrease their incentives for revealing and undermining these sources.

As I note in this chapter, in vivo desensitization or exposure to dreaded activities has a good record in minimizing dysfunctional avoidances. By all means use it. Rian McMullin (2000), however, has experimented with methods of cognitive flooding that are effective in blocking clients' natural tendency to avoid painful feelings and thereby harmfully contribute to perpetuating them. Here are some of his suggestions:

1. Image flooding. Encourage clients to imagine, in vivid detail, a "terrifying" experience (e.g., being stuck in a stalled elevator or train) and their Irrational *Beliefs* that accompanies it (e.g., "This is going to last forever! I'll die if I don't get out of here immediately!"

2. Let the clients keep feeling their painful emotion until they get sick of feeling it; and let them keep thinking the same awfulizing thoughts until they get tired of them and change them for *preferences* that they avoid feeling discomfort instead of *demands* that it quickly vanish.

3. This imaginal flooding can be supplemented by in vivo flooding when the clients experience actual "terrifying" situations and the "horrible" emotions they bring on about these "terrors."

4. Verbal flooding. Encourage your clients to discuss in great detail and for long periods of time a past "traumatizing" experience or several of them. Listen to every "trauma" many times until they are tired of talking about them.
5. Practicing negative IB's. Encourage your clients to repeat some of their Irrational Believes(IB's) repeatedly until they get fed up with repeating them and refuse to think about them any longer.

Note that these and similar modes of verbal flooding are indeed cognitive and imaginative, but they also include intense feeling. They involve clients getting in touch with clients' avoided emotions and instead experiencing them and seeing that they are not "horrible." So these "verbal" methods are actually cognitive-emotive-behavioral.

USING REINFORCEMENT METHODS

REBT often uses both reinforcers and penalties to help some clients change (Ellis & MacLaren, 1998; Ellis & Dryden, 1997; Ellis & Velten, 1992, 1998). With many recalcitrant clients, you can encourage them to give themselves highly satisfying reinforcers—such as special foods or the pleasure of masturbating—only *after* they have done the therapeutic homework that they have promised to do but have kept avoiding.

The problem with resistors, of course, is that they promise to do their homework and then frequently do it irregularly or meagerly, or else not do it at all. REBT has some special methods to encourage them to follow through with the actual doing of their therapeutic homework.

1. When clients fail to do the homework they have agreed to do, as noted above, they allow themselves pleasurable reinforcers only after they have done it. They use operant conditioning to make for their enjoying these pleasures contingent upon their doing the onerous homework.

2. When clients still avoid homework and nonetheless indulge in stipulated pleasures—for example, eat their favorite foods when they have not engaged in the activities they have promised to do—you can ask them, "When you didn't do the homework, what did you tell yourself to make you avoid doing it?" The usual answer is, "It was hard to do it, and I told myself it was too hard. It *shouldn't* be that hard! How *awful* that it's as hard as it is! I *can't stand* doing it!" You then show these clients how to dispute these Irrational *Beliefs* and how to come up with rational self-statements or effective new philosophies, such as, "Yes, it's hard doing this homework, but it's not *too* hard. It's harder, in the long run, for me *not* to do it. No matter how hard it is, it should be that hard—because that's the way it is. It's not awful, but only damned

inconvenient to do it—and more inconvenient if I don't do it! Although I may never like doing this homework, I definitely can stand it—and had better bear it if I want to change!"

3. When resisting clients engage in pleasurable pursuits, even though they have promised not to do so if they don't do their homework, you can again help them see their Irrational *Beliefs* that drive them to self-sabotaging pleasures, such as: "I *need* this enjoyable food even though I have not done my homework to earn it. I *can't bear* giving it up. I *should* be able to enjoy it and not have to forego it when I don't do my homework!" If you can help these resisting clients to clearly see the philosophic, emoting, and behaving underpinnings of their low frustration tolerance and then to have them actively Dispute and surrender their Irrational *Beliefs* that create their LFT, they will have an easier time using the principles of reinforcement to help them do their homework.

4. If some people still resist, they can be given a monitor—such as a mate or a close friend with whom they live—who will check their homework assignments and see if they actually implement them. Thus, if Joe says that he will only listen to music after he has exercised for twenty minutes, his mate or roommate can watch to see if he actually does exercise before he allows himself to listen to music, and can report to him and to his therapist when he does so.

5. You, as a therapist, can monitor clients who create difficulties, by checking their reinforcing, checking to see how they use it, and sometimes warning them when they don't do their homework and when they let themselves have the pleasure they promised not to have if they avoided it. Thus, if a client agrees to go on a vacation only after she has dieted for two months, you can hold the money she is going to send to the travel agency and not give it to her until she has shown that she has actually dieted.

Clients can condition themselves to fear something harmless—e.g., riding in the subway—by linking it with something harmful—e.g., smelling smoke when riding a subway. Thereafter, they are afraid of *all* subway rides and have a phobia. By steadily imagining themselves riding in a subway train and *not* sensing any smoke, they can decondition themselves to the subway *without* the smoke and can overcome their anxiety and their phobia about subway riding.

USING PENALTIES

For many years, as a result of my own experience with what I call the DC's (difficult customers), I have used penalties as well as reinforcers to encourage people to do their homework assignments. As I frequently tell my lecture and workshop audiences throughout the world, many of the experiments that back up B.F. Skinner's theory of operant conditioning and that presumably prove that reinforcement is better than penalizing to help people change their behaviors are untrustworthy. These experiments are often done with children as subjects, and children will do almost anything for M&M's and at the same time, they will deliberately not do something if they are going to be penalized for doing it. But adults, and particularly difficult customers, often won't act in this manner. To help difficult adult clients change, REBT may be used with stiff penalties in addition to, but not necessarily instead of, reinforcing procedures.

To this end, you can have your resisting clients agree to penalize themselves severely every time they promise to perform some homework assignment and then refuse to carry out that assignment. But what kind of penalties are effective? Many kinds, depending on what your individual client finds penalizing—such as burning a $50 bill, contributing to a cause she or he loathes, cleaning the toilet for an hour, visiting a boring friend or relative, or doing unpleasant paperwork.

For example, one of my women clients agreed to stop smoking but kept smoking two whole packs of cigarettes a day, no matter how many times her therapy group showed her what she was telling herself to continue her smoking, and no matter what reinforcements she employed, such as food and music, to help her stop. She finally agreed to kiss one of her male suitors whom she considered ugly and unsexy every time she smoked more than five cigarettes a day. From that time onward, her cigarette smoking dropped to two or three a day and only went back to a pack or two when she temporarily withdrew this penalty, wrongly believing that she could easily reduce her smoking without it.

In the case of difficult clients, you can encourage them to give themselves stiff penalties whenever they fail to carry out their promised homework assignments. Don't make the mistake here of confusing penalties with punishments. REBT teaches people never to punish themselves—meaning to castigate, to down, or to damn—themselves when they do badly. It always encourages rating one's *performances* but not rating one's *self* globally. But it encourages clients to penalize without damning themselves when immediate penalties would probably help them to do suitable homework assignments. So try to see that your clients who use penalties, use them *without,* at the same time, damning themselves.

In the case of penalties, just as in using reinforcements, if your difficult clients say that they will use penalties and then actually cop out, you can monitor them as follows:

1. Help them to see and to dispute the Irrational *Beliefs* they use to make themselves cop out of their homework.
2. Arrange for some person close to them to monitor them and to see that they actually really use the penalties that they say they will use if they avoid doing their homework.
3. You yourself can act as a monitor and can burn their $50 bills or mail them to a cause your clients consider obnoxious when they fail to enact this agreed-upon penalty. It would be preferable if they reinforced and penalized themselves, but for a while you could do it until they acquire this self-helping habit.

One form of penalizing that clients can use to fight against their Irrational *Beliefs* (IB's) in addition to penalizing their dysfunctional actions is to use similar penalizings to fight against their IB's. Rian McMullin (2000) calls this technique cognitive aversive conditioning.

Thus, I worked with a woman, Ronnetta, who continued smoking although she had severe emphysema and was, according to her physician, in real danger of dying. Giving herself reinforcements, such as delicious cheesecake every time she refused to smoke, didn't particularly help her to stop. The pleasure of smoking far outweighed her pleasure of eating cheesecake.

At my suggestion, Ronnetta tried penalizing herself by lighting every cigarette she smoked with a $20 bill. This led her to smoke fewer cigarettes, but not to stop smoking. She also gave up this form of penalizing when it proved too expensive.

My third suggestion to Ronnetta was to take her main Irrational *Belief* that drove her to smoke and to penalize it. Her main IB was, "I can't stand the idea of not smoking when I really have the overwhelming urge to do so. I *must* relieve this urge—or suffer incredibly." She deliberately kept repeating this IB—and penalized herself with the forceful self-statement, "Hitler and Stalin did great deeds by murdering millions of people!" That worked. She nauseated herself so much every time she forcefully expressed this Irrational Belief that to stop making it she stopped smoking. Her penalizing her IB's was quite effective.

USING MODELING

Modeling oneself after the good behaving of other people, or after their avoiding poor behavior, has been shown by Albert Bandura (1997) and other psychologists to be one of the most common methods that children can use to help themselves. Perhaps it is used somewhat less by adults, but it can be used very effectively in REBT and CBT. First of all, you yourself, the therapist, can be active-directive, reliable, hard-working, and display other characteristics that serve as good models for your clients to follow. As usual, this method may sometimes produce poor results, because clients may get so discouraged about your good behavior that they think they could not possibly live up to it, and therefore give up trying. So you have to experiment and see whether it really works.

Resistant clients, in particular, may benefit from your being an unusually active role-model. Thus, if you are distinctly active during therapy sessions, if you do your homework and prepare properly for these sessions, if you indicate that in your personal life you rarely procrastinate and you concertedly work at things you promise yourself to do, you may be a helpful model to your resisting clients that will encourage them to take some healthy actions to change themselves.

You can also encourage them, of course, to use other people as good models of thinking, feeling, and behaving. They can use their friends and relatives, or they can read about or hear about people who, in spite of their unusual handicaps, still lead happy lives and still often accomplish unusual achievements. Again, you can warn your resisting clients that they don't have to completely follow the favorable behavior of other people, but that it can show them some methods of doing so and help them in reducing their dysfunctional behaving. To remind yourself that the techniques of therapy that are used by you and other therapists include cognitive, emotional, and behavioral elements, you can easily see that this is true of modeling. When clients model themselves after someone else who behaves well, they first of all are using their cognizing to notice the difference between them and others and to determine to follow some aspects of these others. Second, they may do this in a forceful, vigorous, determined manner, which gives it an emotional context and which makes it much more likely that they will do efficient modeling. Thirdly, of course, modeling means acting as other people do, and this means, your clients have to force themselves to act differently. So modeling has important cognitive, emotional, and behaving aspects. All these aspects can be pointed out to clients to encourage them to do efficient modeling.

SKILL TRAINING

REBT and CBT use a considerable amount of skill training with clients who do not have certain skills and with those with cognitive, emotional, and behavioral deficiencies. This includes clients with severe personality disorders, who are considered in the following chapter.

Resistant clients—who frequently are unskilled in useful skills—can frequently be helped by skill training. They may require assertion training, communication training, relationship training, sex training, and other kinds of skills that REBT and CBT teach many clients. You may provide these skills yourself in individual or group therapy, recommend outside educators (such as voice teachers), or recommend special classes (such as dancing classes) for regular or resistant clients who you think may benefit from various kinds of skill training (D'Zurilla & Nezu, 1999; Ellis, 1962; Lange & Jakubowski, 1976; McMullin, 2000; Wolfe, 1992).

As a case illustration, I saw a 59-year-old woman who had suffered from painful intercourse with her husband of 30 years and with four previous lovers. All the men in her life had been blue collar workers who saw sex mainly as intercourse and who had only tried to satisfy her with penile-vaginal copulation. She had unassertively let them do as they would and had consequently only had painful sex and highly incomplete intromission. Yet a recent gynecological examination had shown that there was nothing wrong with her vaginally or sexually.

I had a hard time at first trying to help this woman see that sex was not shameful and that she had a perfect right to talk to her impatient husband about her sex problems and try to induce him to arouse her fully before intercourse and to satisfy her noncoitally if she didn't experience orgasm during intercourse. Being anxious for her husband's approval and ashamed of sexual discussion, this woman at first resisted sex therapy and also refused to bring her husband in for conjoint therapy so that I could educate him as well to some of the sexual facts of life.

Seeing that I was not getting very far with this client, I used REBT assertion training with her. I showed her, in social and business affairs, how to be much more assertive without being aggressive. I also had her read several sex manuals, including *The Art and Science of Love* (Ellis, 1960), *Sex and the Liberated Man* (Ellis, 1976b), and *The Intelligent Woman's Guide to Manhunting* (Ellis, 1963).

As this client acquired assertive and sex skills, she became more confident of her own abilities for the first time, saw that she could enjoy herself sexually, forced herself to speak up to her husband after thirty years of verbal shilly-shallying, and overcame her shame and guilt about going after what she really wanted in bed. The shame-attacking and self-accepting philosophies that REBT teaches helped her significantly. But without the assertion training skills and the sex information that were also provided to her in the course of therapy, the Disputing of her Irrational *Beliefs* may not have taken hold and been effective.

REBT, therefore, often includes information giving, role-playing, and other elements of active skill training. If you use REBT-oriented assertion training, communication training, sex training, and other types of skill training with your difficult customers, you may help them considerably.

Najavits (2001) has developed a special kind of integrated skill training program, which she calls *seeking safety,* for clients with a dual diagnosis and posttraumatic stress disorder. Her treatment manual addresses 25 topics that are designed to offset the destructiveness of these patients and other people with severe personality disorders.

Her program teaches them honesty, compassion, creating meaning and other cognitive, behavioral, and self management skills and has shown some degree of success.

USING BEHAVIOR REHEARSAL

I discussed role-playing in chapter 7, and pointed out that it was largely an emotional technique. But, of course, it is also distinctly behavioral. Thus, a number of resisting clients may avoid doing their activity homework, and they cannot easily be monitored by you, their mates, their relatives, or their friends to see that they do it. With some of these clients, behavioral rehearsal in the form of role-playing within individual or group REBT sessions will serve as a substitute for activity homework and may induce these clients, ultimately, to start doing their homework.

For example, I had a 40-year-old teacher in one of my therapy groups for a year and a half, and she would still not stand up to her pupils, her fellow teachers, and her principals, as the group kept encouraging her to do. Her overweening horror of others' disapproval always interfered with her being more assertive and prevented her from carrying out her homework assignments. Finally, I started to use role-playing regularly with this particular client.

Every week, for a period of about 10 weeks, I convinced this teacher, Janie, to play herself while one of the group members played someone in school with whom she was having difficulty asserting herself—for example, a surly pupil or an intimidating supervisor. In doing this kind of role-playing, we quickly brought out Janie's feelings of anxietizing and self-downing and were able to show her what she was telling herself to create these feelings. Thus, she kept insisting that she *couldn't stand* others' raised voices; and we helped her see that she *could* stand them and did not have to put herself down when she heard them. By behavioral rehearsal in role-playing with other members of the group, moreover, we were able to help Janie acquire a repertoire of adequate verbal and motor responses to her "persecutors" at school.

As she rehearsed these responses, she became more able to use them in practice and to start doing her homework assignments that we had previously given her in vain.

Behavior rehearsal through role-playing can often be used to soften people up, as it were, for actually doing difficult homework assignments. They can learn what to do during a role-play and then have confidence that they are able to do it, and anxietize less about doing it in their outside life. Then they can actually try it and increase their skill training.

A brief behavioral activation treatment for depression and other disturbances has been developed by Lejuez, O. Hopko, LePaqe, S. Hopko, and McNeil (2001) at West Virginia University. It is called Behavioral Activation Treatment for Depression (BATD) and teaches clients with low levels of activity and high levels of undesirable activity to use behavioral interventions that directly influence unfortunate environmental variables. As clients behaviorally, as well as cognitively and emotionally, work at changing these environmental Adversities, they reduce their allowing themselves to be defeatingly influenced by them. So this form of treatment works on the A's (Adversities), the B's (Belief Systems), and the C's (Consequences of human disturbance).

USING COGNITIVE HOMEWORK

As noted at the end of chapter 3, REBT has always specialized in the use of cognitive homework, especially in using various kinds of rational self-help forms, to encourage clients to Dispute their Irrational *Beliefs* (IB's) until they change them. Then they can create strong Rational *Beliefs* (RBs) and an Effective New Philosophy (E) of life.

Resisting clients particularly may require cognitive homework because: (1) They tend to hold their IB's very rigidly. (2) They often do not see that they hold them, even after the therapist has pointed them out several times. (3) They tend to insist that their Irrational *Beliefs* are really rational. (4) They temporarily surrender their IB's—but then often go back to strongly believing them again. (5) When urged by their therapist to look for and dispute their unrealistic and absolutistic IB's, they fail to do so, or they do so sporadically and sloppily when they had better do so consistently. It is therefore often desirable to encourage specific cognitive homework, including the filling out of REBT Self-Help Forms—to help the resistors keep working at doing them, to bring them in for discussing, to learn how to correct them, and then to get in the habit of using them.

At the Albert Ellis Institute in New York, we have experimented over the years with different kinds of self-help forms and have found that just about all of them can be highly useful. But we have found some of them to be complicated and require too much work by our clients. We recently have been using the form devised by Windy Dryden and Jane Walker and revised by me, and find that it is simple and comprehensive enough so that it is regularly filled out. This form is included in chapter 6.

Another self-help form that we have found useful with many clients, and again, particularly with resistant ones, is Disputing Irrational Beliefs (DIB's) (Ellis, 1994). In using DIB's, you encourage your resisting clients to write down one of their main Irrational *Beliefs* and then to ask themselves a series of questions about it and to write their answers until they change that *Belief* and tend to keep it changed.

For example, one of my borderline clients, a 32-year-old male who devoutly believed that he must never make any kind of a serious mistake at his job of being a claims adjuster, filled out DIB's as follows:

WHAT IRRATIONAL BELIEVING-EMOTING-BEHAVINGS DO I WANT TO SURRENDER? "I must never make a serious mistake at work!"

IS THIS BELIEF CORRECT? "No. It is incorrect. It has distinct false elements."

WHY IS THIS BELIEF INCORRECT? "Because, first, if I must not under any conditions make a serious mistake at work, then that would be a law of the universe and I could not possibly make one. But obviously I can and do make mistakes, so that the law does not exist. Second, I definitely have made many serious mistakes at work, and I am still around to make more of them, nothing terrible has happened and my firm is still in business. Third, everyone else I know who works for my company, including several of my superiors, keep making serious mistakes, and they do not get fired and manage to survive reasonably happily."

IS THERE ANY EVIDENCE THAT MY BELIEF IS CORRECT OR USEFUL? "No. There doesn't seem to be any. It is true that if I make serious mistakes at work, it will be unfortunate and I may be penalized. I may lose my salary increases. This shows that it is highly desirable that I not make serious mistakes at work. But because it is highly *desirable* hardly proves that it is *necessary* that I don't make mistakes. And it doesn't prove that I absolutely must not make them. No matter how desirable any of my actions is, there doesn't seem to be any proof that I therefore *must* act that way. It is good and proper that I act desirably, but hardly *necessary.*"

WHAT ARE THE WORST THINGS THAT COULD ACTUALLY HAPPEN TO ME IF I KEEP MAKING SERIOUS MISTAKES AT WORK? "First, I could get criticized by my superiors. Second, I could lose raises and promotions. Third, I could possibly be fired. Fourth, if I were fired, I might find it difficult to get a job that is equally good. Fifth, at the very worst, I might not be able to get any other job and might have to go on welfare. But even if any or all of these worst things came to pass, it would only mean that I would be highly inconvenienced and not that I would starve to death and die. Even if I never got another job as good as this one, I could still be reasonably happy at a lesser one—or for that matter, if I were on welfare. I wouldn't like any of these things to happen, but there is no reason why, if worst came to worst, that I could not have a fairly happy existence.

WHAT GOOD THINGS COULD HAPPEN OR COULD I MAKE HAPPEN IF I KEEP MAKING SERIOUS MISTAKES AT WORK? "I could learn from my mistakes and therefore do better in the future. I could give myself unconditional acceptance in spite of my errors, accept myself as a fallible human who will always make some blunders just because I am human. I could discover that some people with whom I work, including some of my supervisors, actually like my making mistakes— because it makes them feel better about their own fallibility. Even if some people in my office begin to dislike me for making serious mistakes, I do not *need* their approval, though it would be very nice to have it. I could still be a happy person without their liking me. By continuing to make serious mistakes in my job—and in other parts of my life—I can accept the challenge of seeing myself as an okay individual even if I am criticized, even if I make less money, and even if my job never turns out too well. If I keep making some serious mistakes after I have calmed myself down and have stopped castigating myself for making them, I may discover that this is really not the right job for me and I might be able to find another kind of work where I make fewer errors and get along better."

After this client had filled out DIB's in this manner, and after he had filled out a number of other DIB's sheets on doing poorly in his social life, he anxietizied less about his work and about his social relations. He then began to perform better in these areas. With the help of DIB's sheets, and by using the REBT self-help form, he began to accept himself with his failings for the first time in his life. Although he did not solve all his emotional problems, he felt that he had significantly improved. I still see him from time to time at one of my Friday Night Workshops in Problems Of Everyday Living, and he tells me that he is doing much better but that he continues to successfully use the REBT Self-Help Form and DIB's, whenever he temporarily falls back into anxietizing or depressing.

USE OF MASSAGE THERAPY AND OTHER BODY TECHNIQUES

Tiffany Field (1998) has reviewed the effect of massage therapy involving deep tissue manipulation with pronounced stimulation of pressure receptors. This has been one of the oldest forms of treatment for pain reduction and physical ailments, for alleviating stress, depression, and anxiety. She finds considerable research evidence for its effectiveness, but concludes, "Regarding the question of lasting effects, there is no reason to believe that massage effects would continue after the end of the treatment any more than drugs, diet, or exercise would be expected to exist" (1998, p. 1279). For various reasons, you may suggest that your resistant (and other) clients, use physical methods of therapy, including massage. These may often be largely palliative and short lasting, but they have their legitimate uses. In my self-help book, *Feeling Better, Getting Better, and Staying Better* (Ellis, 2001a), I indicate their usefulness.

There are a large number of sensory and body methods that sometimes work for regular and resistant clients. Wilhelm Reich (1960) went to extremes in this respect and advocate attacking resistance through attacking the somatic muscular armor. This has distinct dangers, such as the use of Reich's Orgone therapy, and is to be used very carefully— if at all.

In less extreme form, Eugene Gendlin (1999) has developed focusing therapy that emphasizes clients' getting deeply in touch with their bodily sensations and experiential feelings. It may help them experience an entire problem globally and get in touch with thoughts and feelings that they usually are not aware of. Although Gendlin claims that it marvelously breaks through defensive resistance, this has yet to be empirically validated.

MONITORING CLIENTS' SELF-DEFEATING BEHAVIORS

As a therapist, you naturally will monitor your client's self-defeating beliefs, feelings, and behaviors. But of course, you had better carefully watch the manner in which you point them out to your clients. Many of them—especially those prone to resisting therapy—may destructively use your pointing out their self-sabotaging. They may conclude: "See, I told you. I can't change!" "You're proving to me that changing is too hard, and therefore not worth the effort." "If I am failing so much to use the helpful things you are telling me, I really must be a total loser. What's the use of my trying not to be?"

Practically every time, therefore, that you show clients their self-defeating behaviors, also indicate optimism and hopefulness:

- They *constructed* their self-sabotaging and therefore can *recon*struct it.
- Like other self-saboteurs, they *can* change.
- Their efforts to improve can be *long-lasting* and are well worth it.
- They can enjoy the fascinating *challenge* of changing.
- Their changing will help their family members, other relatives, friends, and other people.
- They can enjoy providing a good example for and helping other people, and even their community to change.

USING RELAPSE PREVENTION

Relapse prevention is an integral part of REBT and CBT. As the following section of this chapter indicates, helping resistant clients to strengthen and maintain their therapeutic gains is one of REBT's main goals. But because they frequently fall back to their former disturbances once they have minimized them, REBT and CBT have developed methods of preventing their relapsing (Ellis, 1999, 2001a, 2001b; Irwin, Bowers, Dunn, & Wong, 1999; Marlatt & Gordon, 1989).

Be aware, of course, of the great likelihood of your resistive clients—and of your other clients, too—relapsing. Humans often *do* slide back to prior and old habits—and, especially, personality disordered people slide easily and frequently! Here are some of the steps you can take to monitor and reduce their relapsing. Help your clients to:

- Identify high risk situations of falling back to addictions and other unhealthy behaviors. Show them how to spot temptations, easy access to addictive substances and actions, 'helpful' friends, and excuses.
- Stay away from risky conditions, situations, and other 'triggers'!
- Have realistic expectations about slipping. Monitor their tendencies to relapse.

- Strongly realize that they need not give into their strong urges to slide back.
- See that they have Irrational *Beliefs* that encourage them to slip. Especially, "I *need* to give in to my urges! It's *too hard* to resist! I can't resist!" Help then to see that their *urges* are not *shoulds.*
- See that they often put themselves down for relapsing and thus make it *more* likely to happen. "I'm no good for relapsing—so how can a no-goodnik like me prevent further relapses!"
- Actively and forcefully Dispute their IB's that encourage their relapsing. Use an REBT Self-Help Forms to help their Disputing.
- Again and again, force themselves back to the drawing board.
- Come up with coping statements that will help them relapse less. "I *can* stand being frustrated!" "I'm never worthless, no matter how foolishly I behave!" "I refuse to berate myself for relapsing! I'll only deplore the *fact* that I slipped."
- Stave off relapsing by using relaxation techniques—thereby giving themselves time to Dispute their relapsing beliefs, feelings, and actions.
- Watch their dysfunctional feelings that lead to relapsing—such as anxiety, depression, and rage—and look for and Dispute the IB's behind them.
- Change their dysfunctional negative feelings to healthy feelings by using rational emotive imagery or other emotive techniques.
- Use positive-enhancing imagery—such as imagining themselves resisting real temptations to relapse.
- Use cost-benefit analysis to review the distinct advantages of not slipping and the distinct disadvantages of slipping.
- Use reinforcements when they resist slipping and possible penalties when they allow themselves to relapse.
- Figure out alternate pleasures to the pleasures they get from relapsing.
- Contract with a mate, relative, friend, therapist or group member to receive some distinct pleasure or advantage *after* they avoid relapsing and perhaps to receive some deprivation when they relapse.
- Rehearse in advance what to think, feel, and do when they slip.
- Devise constructive long-range goals and vital absorbing interests.
- Proselytize by helping to talk to other people out of relapsing. Example: Alcoholics Anonymous encourages members to talk others out of drinking.
- Accept the great and difficult *challenge* of permanently changing themselves and rarely falling back to prior dysfunctioning.

If you help your resistant clients to do some of these things to avoid their relapsing and to propel themselves into going back to changing themselves, you will see that they include many aspects of REBT and CBT that will promote their changing in the first place.

HELPING RESISTANT CLIENTS TO STRENGTHEN AND MAINTAIN THEIR THERAPEUTIC GAINS

As noted in the previous section of this chapter, virtually all psychotherapy clients and particularly resisting ones, tend to fall back temporarily or permanently after they have made significant progress in changing themselves. According to REBT theory, this largely stems from their human condition: the propensity of men and women to work at doing better, and then to fairly easily fall back to their old lazy habits of thinking, feeling, and behavioral disturbingness. Must you and your client, then, feel hopeless about achieving and maintaining therapeutic change? Not quite! REBT faces this challenge by stressing, among other things, its behavioral insight number 3: that there is normally no way but work and practice—yes, work and practice—for people to make themselves and keep themselves functioning better.

We find helpful in this respect one of the pamphlets published by the Albert Ellis Institute in New York and given to all clients, and particularly emphasized with resisting ones. This pamphlet, "How To Use REBT to Maintain and Enhance Your Therapeutic Gains," is included as an appendix at the end of this book. Go over it yourself to see whether you agree with it and consider giving it as a handout to your clients and from time to time checking to see if they understand and use it.

Of course, if you have some problems of your own, you can use some of the ideas in the pamphlet to work on them too!

Overcoming Resistance with Clients Who Have Severe Personality Disorders

11

REBT can be used, as this book has been showing, with individuals who are seriously "neurotic"—a diagnosis no longer recognized in the DSM II, but that I still use with some of my clients who for one reason or another, resist psychotherapy. In this chapter, I shall discuss clients who have severe personality disorders (PDO's). I shall barely mention clients who have psychotic afflictions, since they are often different from those who neuroticize themselves and those who have severe personality disorders. In this chapter, I shall deal mainly with clients with personality disorders (PDO's) and with techniques that tend to work with them. Additional material on treating individuals with severe personality disorders and with addicts is included in the second part of my book, *Overcoming Destructive Beliefs, Feelings, and Behaviors* (Ellis, 2001b).

Individuals with severe personality disorders, according to the most recent psychological and neurological findings, frequently had an abysmal childhood that included verbal, physical, and sexual abuse. But that hardly seems to be the whole story. Most of them probably inherit or acquire in their early childhood physiological and neurological defects—that is, deficiencies and handicaps that have an important biological aspect. In this respect, they are much more prone to emotional disturbance than less disturbed individuals and frequently had better be treated with several psychological techniques and also, often, with psychotropic medication.

People who have severe personality disorders (PDO's) usually suffer with several main kinds of diagnoses—and even though they have one outstanding kind, they frequently have elements of the others. There are many possibilities, such as those who are suffering from borderline, schizoid, narcissistic, dependant, avoidant, obsessive-compulsive, histrionic, and psychopathic conditions. They also may be biologically and socially prone to pronounced anxiety sensitivity (Reiss & McNally, 1985). I have seen a great number of these individuals over the years; and since 1962, I have found that a large percentage of them seem to have biological underpinnings to their behavior. This has been confirmed in the psychiatric literature, particularly in recent brain studies, and has been amply described. Any therapist who is likely to treat these kinds of individuals had better be quite aware of the literature in the field (Cloninger, 2000; Harvard Mental Health Letter, 2000; Paris, 1999; Persons, Davidson & Thompkins, 2001; Zuckerman, 1999).

My own experience with clients with personality disorders leads me to believe that they almost always have three basic kinds of deficits, deficiencies, or handicaps that are partly innate. Then, as I shall soon state, they have Irrational *Beliefs* on top of their physiological deficiencies, and they are most often treated badly by their family members, their teachers, their peers, and other individuals. So they are indeed triply handicapped! They often have several cognitive deficiencies, such as attention deficit disorder, hyperactivity, rigid thinking, impulsive thinking, forgetfulness, definite learning disabilities, perceptual difficulties, severe self-downing, purposelessness, and deficient semantic decoding. Because of these cognitive deficits, as well as their dysfunctional *Beliefs,* they have a great deal of trouble in thinking straight about common life problems.

Second, individuals with severe personality disorders almost always have some kinds of emotional deficits or handicaps. They tend to be easily depressive, dysthymic, enraged, over-excitable, high-strung, emotionally unreceptive, panicking, and they often think, feel, and behave in a histrionic or over-dramatic manner.

Third, clients with severe personality disordering almost always have a number of behavioral deficits. These include proneness to being hyperactive, hyper-vigilant, impulsive, obstreperous, interruptive, restless, temper-ridden, anti-social, suicidal, addictive, over-dependent, phobic, hypochondriacal, and inert.

It really doesn't matter whether these dysfunctional tendencies of people with severe personality disordering are partly or largely biologically induced because if stem from social learning, they still lead to exceptional distress. Their cognitive, emotional, and behavioral tendencies all interact with each other, supporting the REBT theory that thinking, feeling, and acting all include and strongly influence each other (Ellis, 1962, 1994). The interaction of these deficits with clients who have personality disorders frequently adds to their deficiencies.

Personality disordered individuals often know or sense their deficiencies and seriously denigrate themselves for having them. They have

Irrational *Beliefs* or cognitive distortions about them, just as the "nice neurotics" do about their (lesser) deficiencies. Especially in our competitive culture they often defame *themselves,* their *personhood,* as well as their handicapping traits: "I *am* an inferior *person* for having an undesirable trait!" Some of them, such as the schizoid individuals, seem to be both naturally *and* socially prone to severe self-denigration.

Personality disordered individuals also frequently have low frustration tolerance about their handicaps. Like "nice neurotics," but perhaps more so, they also often tell themselves, "It's *more than* inconvenient to be *so* handicapped. It's *awful!* I can't stand it!" As a result of their LFT and their self-downing, their initial inefficiencies generally worsen. Then they are doubly handicapped—and, of course, easily damn themselves for their increased ineptness.

Personality disordered people are frequently rejected and put down by other individuals—by their own family, by their peers, by their teachers and others; and since, like most humans, they think they *need* the approval and acceptance of these others, they often denigrate themselves more and awfulize more about not having it—and then make themselves still more dysfunctional.

As a result of this self-defeating process, people with severe personality disorders are often *triply* handicapped, function still worse, are criticized by others more, and then defame themselves and indulge in low frustration tolerance still more. A pretty picture!—and in some instances, even less pretty. With all these difficulties—far more than the rest of us "nice neurotics" have—it is hardly strange that they develop more self-damning and low frustration tolerance than the "normally" disturbed clients that you see. Unusual frustration doesn't *have* to lead to low frustration tolerance; but you can safely bet that it often will!

Assuming that what I have said in the last several paragraphs is largely factual, I think that it simply shows the PDO's are more severely disturbed than most ordinarily disturbed humans and that you may well have a hard time handling them. So be it. To deal well with them, perhaps you'd better look at your own possible disturbances. Do you *have to* always do therapy well and do you denigrate yourself if you don't? Do you awfulize about doing therapy when things get really hard? Watch it! Tend to your own garden first! Use the REBT (and other) techniques on yourself that you use to help your clients. To thine own self be true!

Okay. So you think you have your own neediness and demandingness under control. What next? You next use what you think are the most suitable cognitive, emotional, and behavioral techniques that you have used successfully, before you select from the new techniques that you may have learned from the rest of this book. But in using them, you take into consideration the fact that you *are* dealing with a person with PDO—and one who may well react badly or indifferently to the same methods that frequently help others. Experiment *cautiously*. Watch for idiosyncratic and harmful results. At times, don't hesitate to back up! Consult other therapists or supervisors. Acknowledge but refuse to damn yourself for your mistakes. If nothing else works, try some unusual tracks—but, again, be ready to stop them and return to more tried and true pathways.

There are too many different kinds of PDO's to try to tell you what works best in each specific disorder—such as OCD. As I noted above, you can find more details on how to treat PDO's in the second part of my recent book, *Overcoming Destructive Beliefs, Feelings, and Behaviors.*

Many clinical and research reports have been published showing how REBT and CBT can be effectively used to treat PDO's (Beck, Freeman, & Associates, 1990; Clark, 2000; Cloninger, 2000; Ellis, 2001b; Falsetti & Resnick, 2000; Kuehlwein & Rosen, 1993). Progress in this respect, I am reasonably sure, will continue to be made. REBT and CBT are also being increasingly used in the treatment of people with psychotic disorders (Shelley, Battaglia, & Associates, 2001).

However, the problems of people with severe personality disorders go on and on! Many of them get in some kind of therapy, particularly if they are raised in middle class families, and they have unusual difficulty in the course of it. No matter how effective this therapy usually is, it is less effective with people with personality disorders, and may actually create troubles in its own right. Consequently, these sadly put-upon individuals often disturb themselves about their therapy. If their therapy includes medication, and the medication has some poor side-effects, they then often upset themselves because of these hindrances and sometimes make themselves feel utterly hopeless about therapy.

For all these reasons, people with severe personality disorders may well be difficult to reach, to help them see what they can do to help themselves, and to encourage them to follow therapeutic instructions. You had better be realistic about this if you are a therapist! Some of the realistic ideas you can have about treating them are the following:

1. Expect limited gain and less than you would normally expect to get with disturbed neuroticizing individuals. In some instances they will achieve remarkable gains, but even then less than you may prefer. You are not a miracle-maker and in all probability never will be!

2. Because clients with personality disorders are likely to be more afflicted than your regular client during therapy, you'd better give unconditional other acceptance (UOA) and to see that they

achieve unconditional self-acceptance (USA). Especially since most of them live in competitive societies, like the United States, and will probably achieve less than many other people in their culture, they'd better learn to accept themselves with their deficiencies, handicaps, and disabilities and not to condemn themselves for having unusual troubles.

3. At the same time, again because they are severely criticized by many others, and are unfairly dealt with in their communities, give them maximum unconditional other acceptance (UOA) so that they will not additionally anger themselves against you.

4. Face the fact that they probably will have a great many more frustrations than other people, and try to help them achieve high frustration tolerance (HFT) or unconditional life-acceptance (ULA) and antiawfulizing. Use several of the HFT and ULA methods that I keep describing in this book.

5. Use a number of cognitive, emotive, and behavioral techniques with them, because the usual techniques may not exactly work well and some unusual ones may work much better.

6. Since many of them seem to have real cognitive, emotive, and behavioral deficits, these can sometimes be made up by intensive and extensive training. Thus, people who are born with muscular weakness, or who develop it as a result of some illness during their life, may be able to exercise more than others and build up muscle. Some of them even become proficient swimmers, runners, or other athletes. Similarly, clients with severe personality disorders can often take one of their disabilities, such as a learning disability that results in poor reading, and work on it until they largely make it up. They then will be closer to the norm of people in their culture and will in all probability have more self-efficacy and be happier.

7. As noted above, consider, experimentally, referring people with severe personality disorders to psychopharmacologists, to determine whether it is likely that any kind of medication will work without having debilitating side-effects. Try to help the clients themselves take an experimental and positive attitude toward medication, to see whether it will work and what disadvantages it may possibly have.

8. In extreme cases, where nothing else seems to be working, in consultation with physicians and psychopharmacologists, consider unusual procedures, such as electric convulsive therapy, neurological surgery, or some other possible remedial procedure. Naturally, extreme caution had better be taken in regard to these kinds of procedures.

ILLUSTRATIVE CASE ILLUSTRATION

Let me give as an example a case illustration. A number of years ago I saw Rona, a 25-year-old attractive bookkeeper who was severely depressed and had been depressing herself, she said, ever since the age of 5. She thought that she was on one side of the human race and everybody else was on the other side. She had practically no social relations, though men were attracted to her and tried to date her. She was extremely shy and inhibited, had made suicide attempts at 16 and 21, both times after she had had some therapy and it hadn't worked. So she concluded that she was absolutely hopeless and there was no use in going on miserably. She thought that that was a rational decision. She had tried various kinds of medication, and none of them worked, so she now refused to try any more. She felt bored and empty and spent the time when she was not working sleeping and looking at T.V. One high school boyfriend, John, kept after her, in spite of her negativism and her not treating him well, and kept seeing her every month or two if she would allow it. She did not permit him to have any sex with her and was quite hostile to him. But if he disappeared for awhile, she became needy and felt she got along a lot worse without him.

She concluded that she was completely hopeless and that no therapist could help her even though I was doing my best. She resented the fact that I went out of town to give workshops and talks and even managed to discover the hotels where I was staying and sometimes called me there. Not for extra sessions, which I would sometimes arrange over the phone, but just to ask me a question or prove that I really cared for her.

I saw Rona for three years and generally had a difficult time with her. But I persisted at showing her how to achieve unconditional self-acceptance (USA), despite her disturbances and despite her continual failings. Largely with the use of some of my books, I helped her to see what REBT really was and to devote herself to it. When she got the concept of USA, she then became devoted to it and started using it with other people. She had several acquaintances with severe personality disorders whom she had met at some of her stays in the hospital. She had been hospitalized for a few weeks three times, especially in regard to her suicidal attempts; and she realized that some of the friends she had met there were as severely disturbed as she was, and hated themselves and hated others. She became adept at trying to get them to see REBT and to acquire USA. Her working with them helped her work with herself, and after about nine months of doing this continually, she really did solidly achieve USA.

We also used assertion training and enabled Rona to ask people for things she wanted and not to feel horrified and needy when her assertiveness didn't please them. She let herself finally realize that John had his failings, since he was not as bright or adept as she would have liked him to be; but he was consistently devoted to her as no one else, including her parents, had been. They favored her two sisters, probably because her sisters were less difficult individuals and succeeded more in life. The parents had conditional self-acceptance for themselves and were very proud of the fact that both her sisters became attorneys, while Rona remained an unaccomplished bookkeeper.

I would not say that Rona ever became completely cured, because I see her occasionally at my Friday Night Workshops, and she still has her difficulties. She also has not achieved a high-level career, which she would be intellectually capable of achieving. But her relationship with John continues, and it looks like one of these days they may marry. I have convinced her to give herself unconditional self acceptance, which has made her stop damning herself and see that she is a worthy individual who deserves whatever pleasures she can get. So I view my therapy with her as a success, but I do not fool myself into believing that she is cured and that she is now merely a "normal" person rather than one with a personality disorder. She, however, is quite satisfied with her improvement and looks upon her therapy very favorably.

OTHER EFFECTIVE METHODS TO USE WITH CLIENTS WHO HAVE SEVERE PERSONALITY DISORDERS

As I have said previously, almost any method, including some unusual ones, can work with people with severe personality disorders. But some of the techniques that I have used more successfully than other techniques are the following:

1. *Forceful Disputing.* Because people with severe personality disorders vigorously and forcefully hold on to their irrational beliefs about their deficits, I have frequently found that forceful disputing is effective (see chapter 6). Although they complain of the pains of suffering because of their deficiencies, I show them that they will continue to suffer mightily with them unless they fully accept themselves and fully accept others and achieve high frustration tolerance. And I graphically bring their prolonged suffering to their attention, in case they remain exactly the way they are.

2. *Proselytizing.* In the case of Rona, I found that helping her to vigorously and forcefully Dispute others' Irrational *Beliefs,* particularly

her *Beliefs* that she was worthless when she failed, was quite effective. She actually helped some people with personality disorders but she particularly helped herself. They would argue against the concept of unconditional self-accepting, and then she would have to try to prove to them that it could be achieved. So that helped her considerably.

3. *Forceful confronting of low frustration tolerance.* Most of my clients with personality disorders have abysmal low frustration tolerance. As I said before, they have distinctly more frustrations than other individuals, and therefore, perhaps, they develop LFT. But they frequently have it, and I show them that it is very hard for them to change but it's much harder for them not to. So I forcefully indicate that they can't get away with their goofing off, that in the long run it will definitely do them in, though in the short run it may give them pleasure and help them avoid pain. There are many abysmal consequences to having low frustration tolerating, and I go over and over with them Benjamin Franklin's original statement, "There are no gains without pains."

4. *Activity homework.* Practically all disturbed clients have to do activity homework to convince themselves that they can change and that they can get real comfort after awhile by changing. Individuals with severe personality disorders, especially, can be monitored to do their cognitive and activity homework, and to do it steadily. So I keep monitoring them, checking them, unangrily and with, I hope, high frustration tolerance of my own. Homework is not absolutely required, and my clients are not the scum of the earth if they don't do it. But it is a requisite for change in most instances; and again, they had better court discomfort in order to get eventual comfort.

5. *Appeal to the clients' intelligence.* With my clients, and especially with my brighter clients, I show them that they are stupidly upsetting themselves and indulging in their own severe personality disorder, instead of fighting it tooth and nail. So I appeal to them as intelligent individuals to fight, fight, fight against their disturbance.

6. *Role-playing.* With severe personality disordered individuals, I use a good deal of practical role-playing to show them how to do things better and get helpfully criticized when they are doing it. But I also show them how they easily upset themselves during the role-play, what they tell themselves to upset themselves, and how they can interrupt and dispute that self-upsetting. I also use reverse role-play, where I or a member of group or a friend will hold to the client's dysfunctional ideas very forcefully, and they have to dispute them and give them up. But these are really their own ideas that they're disputing, so they get practice at it (see chapter 6).

7. *Encouragement.* I particularly encourage practically all my clients to act differently, think differently, and feel differently, but especially

those with personality disorders seem to require firm and extra encouragement. Because discouraging themselves is one of the things they very easily do, I and their therapy group keep pushing them and pushing them in an encouraging manner, as did Alfred Adler, to try to change themselves and to benefit themselves with pleasurable pursuits.

8. *Reinforcing and penalizing.* I use a great deal of reinforcing and sometimes of penalizing with clients who have personality disorders. They easily fall back to their disruptive behaving and frequently have little motivation, especially when they are depressing themselves, to change it. So we figure out some truly enjoyable things for them that they can do contingent upon their doing onerous things they'd better do to help themselves.

In some instances, although B. F. Skinner did not encourage this, I give them stiff penalties if they keep promising and promising to work at changing and then don't do so. If they contribute $100 to an obnoxious cause, or do something extremely distasteful, such as continuing to date a boring individual, then they may use that as a penalty for not changing. As usual, this does not always work and may have a boomerang effect, but frequently if they penalize themselves if they do not institute some of the changes they say they will make, they will not refuse to try to make these changes. So the penalties may help them. See also chapter 9.

9. *Dealing with historical Irrational Beliefs.* Many people suffering with severe personality disorders are hung up on past Irrational *Beliefs* and continue them into the present. They seem to be stuck with them. Therefore, some amount of time, though not an inordinate amount, is spent by me going over with them exactly what the IB's were, what results they led to, and how they are continuing with them today. Especially if they believe that their parents or peers persecuted them in the past and that therefore they rightly should anger themselves against these parents or peers today, I show them that this is not wise, because they had some distinct dysfunctional convictions about what these parents or peers did and are continuing them. If we track down their Irrational *Beliefs* about the past, we can help them to surrender them and replace them with rational preferences. Although "normally" disturbed clients frequently do not have to do this kind of past exploration and Disputing, and may even be allergic to it, the severe personality disordering individuals often benefit from it, as Jeffrey Young (1990) has shown. However, you can easily overdo this and sidetrack clients with focusing on their past.

10. *Explaining others' Irrational Beliefs and the consequences.* When people with personality disorders keep blaming past or present individuals for their behaviors, I often stop and show them that they

may well be assessing this conduct of others accurately, but that that is not upsetting. And I show them that they upset themselves about it in the past—and in the present. But I also show them in many instances what these other people dysfunctionally probably irrationally believed to *make* themselves act very badly. Thus, when Deirdre, a woman with a borderline personality disorder, kept blaming her mother for criticizing her for practically everything she did as a child, I accepted her description of her mother's behaving and showed her that she was still upsetting herself about it during her childhood and up to the present. But I also showed her that her mother was probably irrationally convincing herself, "My daughter has the ability to act well and is deliberately not doing that. Therefore, she is a thoroughly rotten person who *should* behave differently to get along well with me and other individuals." Her mother probably didn't realize that she was telling herself these dysfunctional *Beliefs,* but nonetheless she may have been and therefore she unfairly kept criticizing Deirdre. When Deirdre realized this and saw how self-disturbing her mother was, she overcame much of her hostility toward her mother.

These are some of the techniques that I have found effective with personality disordered individuals. They all tend to have a pronounced, forceful cognitive, emotive, and behavioral quality, and I think that it is the combination and interaction of these qualities that makes them effective. But, once again, I often find that it is a specific method that works when others don't, and that this method works well with this particular individual, but not necessarily with others who have a similar form of personality disorder. Since I use a large number of techniques, cognitive, emotive, and behavioral ones, and I can try them out until I find which ones will work best, I have a better chance of helping different clients than I do if I favor only a few techniques and keep rigidly sticking to them.

11. *Encouraging a vital absorbing interest.* Let me repeat again that clients who are encouraged to acquire a vital absorbing interest, and get devoted to some cause, idea, activity, or even sport, for a long period of time, help distract themselves from their disturbances. At the same time, they acquire central meaning or purpose in life that adds considerably to their existence (Ellis & Harper, 1997). This is important perhaps for practically all self-disturbing individuals, but it is even more important if it can be achieved by those with personality disorders. They are so put-upon by their handicaps, and often so anxietizing and depressing, that anything that will thoroughly distract them will work temporarily and even on a long-term basis. So I encourage practically all my clients with personality disorders to try to come up with a constructive goal, purpose, or vital absorption that will unusually

preoccupy them for preferably years to come. Even if they never eliminate their severe anxietizing and depressing, they distract themselves so well from it that at times it doesn't bother them very severely.

TREATING CLIENTS WITH INTENSE ANGER

One form of personality disorder that is frequently neglected is that of clients who are intensely and frequently angry. Clients with intense, frequent, and persistent anger often do not see themselves as having an emotional problem, do not come to therapy unless almost forced to do so, and resist the best efforts of their therapists to help them reduce their raging. Why? Probably because anger has evolutionary roots in self-protection; and it provides considerable pleasure to its "sufferers"—unlike feelings of intense anxiety and deep depression. Angry people are sure that they are "right" and the people they are angry at are indubitably "wrong" and "unfair." So they feel justified and even noble in their raging. They rise on the see-saw of "self-esteem," while their "oppressors" descend to hell. Moreover, humans make the common mistake of believing and feeling that when other people are *really unfair,* they deserve to be completely damned *as persons* instead of their *behaviors* being seen as abominable.

What can you do to help clients who are obsessively-compulsively eating themselves up with anger, who are escalating their blood pressure and creating psychosomatic problems, and who are ruining, perhaps, their family, marital, friendly, and work relationships? REBT, partly following Seneca and Epictetus, has from its beginnings shown people how they largely anger themselves and can *choose* not to do so. My writings—such as *How to Live With a Neurotic* (Ellis, 1957), *Reason and Emotion in Psychotherapy* (Ellis, 1962), and *How to Control Your Anger Before It Controls You* (Ellis & Tafrate, 1998) have helped thousands of people with their anger problems. Several leading practitioners of REBT and CBT have followed my lead in developing effective anti-anger methods—for example, Albert Bandura (1997), Michael Bernard (2000), Jerry Deffenbacher (1999), Raymond DiGiuseppe (2000), Marsha Linehan (1992), and Jerry Wilde. Because of their clinical and experimental work with angry people, cognitive-behavioral methods of helping individuals and groups overcome anger have become prominent.

What are some of the specific things you can do to induce your "justifiably" angry and resistant clients to surrender their intense and persistent rage? To briefly summarize some of the work that has been done in this area:

- You can show them what Epictetus showed his students two thousand years ago: They largely *construct* their anger out of people and events that treat them "badly." They also may construct the "badness" of these events.
- Their *desires* to be treated "well" and "fairly" are useful and sensible—but not so their *insistences* and *demands* that they *always, under all conditions* be "justly" treated (Bernard, 2000; Hauck, 1974).
- Show angry clients how to achieve unconditional self-acceptance (USA) and thereby to stop taking others' criticisms and rejections *too* seriously, thus often encouraging them to scorn and damn these others.
- Especially show them the value of unconditional other–acceptance (UOA)—how it greatly adds to their own life and leads them to make themselves angry at other people's *misbehaviors* but not totally damn the *person* of those whose behaviors they deplore.
- Help them achieve high frustration tolerance (HFT) or unconditional life acceptance (ULA), so that they minimally enrage themselves about Adversities that they can't presently change.
- Show your clients, and help them consciously acknowledge, the enormous price that rage entails—on their own minds, feelings, and bodies, and on their relationships with the victims of their fury.
- Try to help them take the *challenge* of controlling their own deadly feelings of anger even when they are unduly put upon by people and circumstances. As I note in one of my books, *How To Stubbornly Refuse To Make Yourself Miserable About Anything—Yes, Anything,* they can adopt this self-protective plan—and sometimes even change some of the worst conditions for the better. What have they got to lose?
- Watch your own potential anger at your impossibly angry clients! Work determinedly on your own UOA. You can damned well use it! And if you still fail with intolerably angry clients, see that you are a fallible human who can always give yourself USA!

TREATING PSYCHOPATHS, SOCIOPATHS, AND CLIENTS WHO ARE NOT MOTIVATED TO CHANGE

Some of the people with the most severe personality disorders are termed psychopaths or sociopaths. This means that, for the present, and usually for a good deal of their past life, they perform antisocially and either think that they *can* get away with this kind of behavior or that it doesn't make any difference if they get caught and convicted for their crimes. REBT has in some respects specialized in the treatment of these kinds of individuals (Ellis, 1962; Ellis & Gullo, 1972), and several other CBT practitioners, such Yochelson & Samenow (1977), have also specialized in trying to treat these individuals.

Because people who are consistently psychopathic have personality disorder, the techniques I have been describing for use with other personality disordered people are often useful. More specifically, my own experience in treating a good many sociopathic behaving persons has led to the following treatment recommendations:

1. Whatever their criminal and heinous behaving has been, you can still unconditionally accept *them* while pointing out the immorality and irrationality of their behavior. They are highly fallible, messed up humans who often can be and always deserve to be helped just because they are human. You can therefore be critical of their *acts* without trying to demean them.

2. It is often best to speak to them honestly and directly, in down to earth and sometimes "obscene" language, to show them that you are not a moralistic, very conventional, individual who does not really understand nor can comfortably relate to them. Don't insist, of course, on strong language with moralistic clients who object to it.

3. Try to show psychopaths the real risks and dangers of their antisocial behaviors, which they frequently put out of mind. Show them that if they want to risk these dangers, they can of course choose to do so—as long as they are willing to pay the consequences. Stress what the consequences would usually be.

4. Try to show them that they cannot in the long run get away with their antisocial behaving; that almost inevitably they will have to "pay the piper"; and that the penalties for their acts are rarely worth it. Keep forcefully but undamningly bringing them back to social reality.

5. Show them the alternative nonself-defeating activities that they can take. They are capable of leading constructive, social, enjoyable lives. They have the ability to change and do better—if they will choose to use it and work hard at doing so.

6. Show them that their hostility to others is largely *self*-induced. It stems from the unrealistic demands and commands that other people absolutely *must not* act the way they indubitably do often act. Lean over backwards to agree with them that others' *behaving* is often poor and rotten, but that this does not make them *bad people*.

7. Try to help them see the pains and troubles of others and to become more emphatic. Dramatize what some of these victims go through and how pained they may feel. Show the psychopathic-acting

individuals some of the social ramifications of their acts—how they lead to widening rings of human suffering.

8. With some of the brighter and more receptive psychopathic-behaving individuals, explain to them what kind of personality disorder they probably have, how it includes crooked thinking, feeling and behaving, and how it is supported by low frustration tolerance. Then show them how it can be changed and how it would be useful for it to be changed. Teach them how to look at their thinking and fantasizing that leads to their often impulsive acting out and show them how to change it (Ellis, 1962; Ellis & Gullo, 1972; Yochelson & Samenow, 1977). Try to get them to use a cost-benefit way of thinking that will help them conclude that in the long run their "clever" behavior is not worth the results it brings.

9. In some cases you may be able to show psychopathic-behaving individuals how autistic they are and how their lack of empathy and social interest is handicapping to them. You may teach them the values of social involvement and the joys of helping others and may possibly even influence them to engage in some cooperative and altruistic behavior. They can sometimes be persuaded to help other criminals as they do in organizations like the Fortune Society.

10. You can teach psychopathic-behaving individuals that they frequently do what they do in order to prove how "strong" they are. Actually, they behave weakly, since they feel that they have to be "strong" and exceptionally forceful in order to compensate for their underlying feelings of weakness.

11. Show these psychopathic-behaving individuals that you are just about always on their side and believe that they can do better and get more rewards for less hassles in life. You can indicate how to enhance their problem-solving skills and skill training better and get distinctly more out of their existence without engaging in antisocial behaving.

12. If the psychopathic-acting individuals you see are in prison, or on parole or probation, you may be able to show them how to act better to remove the limitations that they are presently placed under. You can also show them how to have higher frustration tolerance about their poor environment. This kind of training may help them to adjust better to later life situations that are also restricting.

13. By teaching these individuals how to accept themselves unconditionally and fully with whatever inadequacies they have, you may be able to divert them from trying to overly compensate for these inadequacies by acting antisocially. If they look at their feelings of inadequacy directly, acknowledge that they are weaknesses rather than strengths, they may be able to surrender their antisocial behavior and engage in more normal activities.

THE TREATMENT OF ALCOHOLICS, DRUG ABUSERS, AND OTHER ADDICTING INDIVIDUALS

REBT sees most people who engage in serious addicting behaving as having either one or two serious problems. First, they may have abysmal low frustration tolerance and think that they absolutely need what they want—such as they absolutely need alcohol, drugs, gambling, smoking, compulsive sex activities, and other behaviors to which they addict themselves. Obviously, they do not need and will not die without these addictions, but they practically think that they will, or that they will suffer so much from not engaging in it that their life will hardly be worth living at all.

REBT shows the individuals who behave in an addictive fashion that they have unusual low tolerating of frustration, and it tries to get them to ameliorate and develop much higher frustration tolerance. These are often difficult customers to treat, because they really do not want to give up their addictive behaving and they may be biologically prone to develop it. Alcoholism, for example, may run in families and be biologically predisposed. Exceptionally low frustration tolerance may also be partially innate and therefore difficult to alleviate. Obsessive-compulsive behavior in general may stem from physiological deficiencies in people's neurotransmitters and enable them to fail to check their compulsions, even when they know they are self-defeating and they theoretically want to give them up. Nonetheless, revealing to your addicted clients and inducing them to work against their low frustration tolerance can be very effective.

In fact, the statistics show that most people who give up serious addictions, such as drinking, smoking, drugging, and gambling, do it on their own. They somehow convince themselves that the cost-benefit ratio of their addictions is not worth it, that it does them much more harm than good, and that the pleasure it entails may be great but not worth the ultimate pain that they experience. LFT, low frustration tolerance, which leads to a great deal of self-defeating behavior, is low in addicts cost-benefit analysis. If you can help your clients to see this, to reflect on the disbenefits of their particular addictions, they may go a long way toward making themselves much less addictive.

However, with the great majority of addicts who continue their self-sabotaging in spite of recognizing that it is exceptionally harmful, things are more complicated. I think that they all have to some degree the LFT, but it is integrally mixed in with their general disturbance. They do not merely addict themselves to alcohol, drugs, gambling, and other self-defeating behaviors, but they do so to sedate their other disturbances.

Disturbed addicts first have distinct believing-emoting-behaving problems, such as anxietizing or depressing. They develop these problems because they usually afflict themselves with the ABC's of disturbingness that have been described in this book. Thus, they think they *need* to perform some important projects well and they actually perform them poorly, so they tell themselves that they are pretty worthless individuals. At the same time, they tell themselves that they *can't stand* the *awful* difficulties they encounter. Consequently, again, they disturb themselves.

Once they actually feel and behave badly, they frequently have low frustration tolerating and self-downing *about* their disturbances. Thus, they tell themselves that they are *no good* for having disturbed feelings, and that those same feelings are *too much* to bear. So they conclude that they rapidly *have to* get rid of their feelings or tone them down with amazing rapidity. Either by accident or design, they discover that some addictions tend to distract and insensitize them to their exceptionally anxietizing and depressing. So they, let us say, take to alcohol, and while under the influence of it, they "feel no pain." You might say that *temporarily* they are happy with the pleasure of their addiction.

When their addictive behavior becomes serious—that is, when they start getting into various kinds of trouble with it—they frequently defensively lie to themselves and others about the extent of it. Thus, they tell themselves, "I'm not really an alcoholic. I can get away with a good deal of drinking and not suffer bad results. My nature is to drink, and I can't stop it. It's the only pleasure I have. I can't be effective without it." Excuses, excuses!

Finally, addicts may acknowledge that they really have a serious drinking problem and then they often create self-downing and low frustration tolerating about their acknowledged problems. Self-deprecatingly, they insist to themselves that they're *no good* for drinking; that they *must not* be addicted as badly as they are; that they're *too weak* to stop; and that they *cannot stop* because of their inadequacy. With their intolerance of frustration, they tell themselves that it's *too hard* and not merely *hard* to stop; that they *need* the gratification of the alcohol; that they *must* have help to stop; and they show other aspects of LFT.

Frequently, alcoholics stop drinking or cut it down considerably for awhile, but then they very often relapse. In order to relapse, they tell themselves things like, "I can't *keep* stopping! It's *too boring* to stay stopped! I *have to have* the pleasures I had while I was addicted. One slip shows that I'm hopeless and cannot stop. I'll go crazy if I stay stopped!" These are all low frustration tolerating attitudes. Then they may put themselves down severely and say, "I'm *no good* for relapsing. Other people stay stopped, and I'm *unable* to do it. I'm a *hopeless* drunk." And so on.

The main point of all this is that most serious cases of alcoholism, drug addiction, gambling addictive behavior, and other addictive compulsion include first, serious disturbances about work, school, relationships, sports, or something else. Then the addicts tend to interrupt or decrease these disturbed feelings by resorting to addictions. They tell themselves they *can't stand* the anxietizing, the depressing, the raging, and other miserable feelings that their disturbances bring on, so they sedate themselves with an addiction.

If you use REBT or CBT with people who are compulsively addicting, you ultimately work on their severe low frustration tolerance, because that is almost always involved on some level in the addictive process. But you also try to get at their main disturbances or personality disorders that produce dismal feelings that practically drive them to their addictions. Most cases are complicated, and each case is somewhat different. But you use the techniques that you would employ with emotional disturbance and also the special techniques we have been discussing in this book that you would employ with resisting individuals.

The goal, then, is basically to help addicts become less disturbing. Frequently, their behavior is so destructive, as in the case of severe alcoholism, that the first goal is to help them stop the addiction. In some cases, they may even be institutionalized to temporarily achieve nonaddiction. But once their addictive behavior is somewhat under control, then the emphasis is on helping them to be much less disturbed *and* much less addictive. Unless they make inroads against their disturbing themselves, they will very likely become addictive again. So to help them to become unaddictive as well as undisturbing is the essence of REBT and CBT treatment of serious addiction.

With addicts, you keep using the clients' constructive ability to assess and keep assessing the cost-benefit ratio of their addictions, as well as the cost-benefit ratio of their creating general self-disturbing, as they usually do.

As usual, REBT and CBT treatment of addiction includes a wide variety of cognitive, emotional, and behavioral methods of therapy and strives for the elegant solution—that is, showing clients how to be less disturbing *and* less disturbable in the future. The second part is particularly important in the case of addicts because they are very likely to fall back again, even though they have once considerably diminished their addiction. For both biological and social learning reasons, they are not to be trusted with *merely* stopping their addictions nor with *merely* reducing basic disturbances. Unless they use elegant REBT they tend to fall back to their old dysfunctional thinking, feeling, and behaving (Ellis, 2001b). I include details on the REBT and CBT treatment of seriously addicted individuals in my books, *Rational Emotive Therapy With Alcoholics and Substance Abusers* (Ellis, McInerney, and DiGiuseppe, 1988), *When AA Doesn't Work For You* (Ellis & Velten, 1992) and *Overcoming Destructive Beliefs, Feelings, and Behaviors* (Ellis, 2001b).

Rational Emotive Behavior Therapy and Multicultural Counseling

12

People keep asking me, "What position does Rational Emotive Behavior Therapy (REBT) takes on multicultural psychotherapy and counseling?" And I am rather surprised at the question. The basic theory of REBT says that its practitioners never dispute or argue with clients' strong preferences, desires, and goals—all of which are considered "rational" in REBT. Instead, therapists only question and dispute clients' absolutistic *demands and musts* about their preferences and goals—many of which are considered to be "irrational" or "self-defeating." *Also,* they only question cultural demands if their clients want to change the results they are getting—that is, want to change their anxiety or self-downing.

Thus, if clients strongly believe in the familial and cultural view that sexual abstinence before marriage is desirable or if they just as strongly hold the familial and cultural idea that sexual liberty before marriage is the custom to follow, REBT would go along with both these views, feelings, and behaviors. It considers them "rational" as long as the individuals who follow them are willing to take the consequences of their choices.

However, if clients believe that under all conditions and at all times they *absolutely must* be sexually abstinent before marriage or else they are *worthless persons,* their REBT counselor would question this view and would show how it well might get them into emotional-behavioral trouble. Their therapist would also question the view and the feeling that clients *absolutely must* be sexually permissive before marriage or else they are *worthless individuals.*

Obviously, then, REBT only questions clients' *rigidly, inflexibly, and unconditionally* following a familial or cultural rule, and it does so when clients are getting results they would like to change. It never questions the *desirability* of the rule itself. It even gives all clients full permission to rigidly follow cultural—and other—rules, as long as they are willing to abide by the consequences of their rigid adherences, which (it holds) often will be feelings of anxiety and depression.

In other words, REBT has always been and still is a *constructivist* or *choice* therapy. It therefore allows clients to personally *select* their goals and values, but informs them about the self-defeating, and society-defeating results of their rigid, absolutistic adherence to their selections. Because this is the case, REBT practitioners are almost intrinsically multicultural. They accept all clients with their many varieties of cultural, religious, political, and other standards; and they only question how *rigidly* clients adhere to their cultural goals and how they sometimes sabotage themselves (and possibly their community) by their absolutism and rigidity.

REBT counselors also, following REBT theory, actually welcome cultural (and other) diversity. They encourage their clients to stick to *whatever* customs and mores with which they were raised and to enjoy the unique advantages of these traditions. But they also, of course, encourage their clients to select the virtues of *other* cultures than those in which they were raised; or to select a mixed bag, consisting of parts of *several* cultures; or to modify those selections or invent their own standards. Chacun à son gout! Each one to his/her taste! If any form of therapy accepts clients with their own preferences and values, it is certainly REBT.

REBT also accepts the practices of some of the leading therapies that favor multicultural diversity. Thus, as I have shown (Ellis, 2001b), it largely accepts the position of Rigazio-DiGilio, Ivey, and Locke (1997) that particularly stresses the inclusion of multicultural values in therapy.

REBT also goes along with therapists of various schools who strongly favor multicultural positions. It largely, though not completely, agrees with viewpoints favoring multi diversity counseling and therapy (D'Andrea, Daniels, & Heck, 1991; Cuellar & Paniagua, 2000; Hall, 1997; Ivey, Ivey, & Simek-Morgan, 1997). It also questions some of the passionate exaggerations of multicultural counseling, as discussed by Weinrach & Thomas (1996).

What are the main practices of REBT multicultural therapy? Let me describe some of them.

Cultural (and family) rules have their distinct advantages. They supply a good degree of order, provide people with attainable goals, award them approval for following the rules, and have various other benefits. But they also usually have disadvantages: They restrict individual choice, provide many life difficulties, encourage social disapproval, present numerous dilemmas, and lead to other disadvantages. Our human purpose may well be to preserve most existing cultures but to hope that they develop and change over the years. Culture seems to have a biological as well as a social learning basis. But many of us have mental-emotional problems when we live in one predominant culture, perhaps also follow the rules of one of its minority cultures, and try to do so in a balanced and unrigid manner. We often do not live peacefully with the fact that large numbers of our citizens choose to abide by the teachings of a different culture; and that they and we have distinct prejudices about maintaining a culturally diverse existence.

How can we solve this problem? Not easily! And how can therapists cope with multicultural issues—particularly if they are working in an increasingly diversified country like the United States? How can they unravel the question of what cultural teachings are "rational" (self-helping and society-helping) and what are "irrational" (self-defeating and society-defeating)? Again not easily!

Here are a few points that may be helpful. First, perhaps therapists had better forego rigidly defining the "rationality" or "workability" of any given culture. For one thing, they are most probably prejudiced by the teachings of their original culture, and therefore will not give the views of other cultures a fair evaluation. Second, even though most people raised in a minority culture follow it well enough, a therapist raised in one culture may personally think that clients who follow a different one are "crazy" and "self-sabotaging." Therefore, to be "rational," therapists had now better accept foreign cultures as they exist—although, of course, these counselors can work, if they will, to change their own culture, and perhaps some of the aspects of other cultures.

Still, therapists have to deal with clients who follow the rules of their original culture *too strictly* and are upset about its restrictions. Therapists may also have clients who follow their original cultural rules *too loosely* and are very ashamed and guilty about doing so.

Let us consider the second case, since I find it much more frequent in my practice with clients who strongly follow a non-"American" culture, though they may be United States citizens. Thus, clients are not devoted to their parents, as their original cultural upbringing tells them is proper; or they masturbate as their original culture tells them they are not supposed to do; or they marry a person from a group that their culture defines as a "wrong" group. So they shame or depress themselves about not following an important rule of their original culture. They want therapy to help them alleviate this shame and depression. But they resist the REBT notion that no teaching is absolute or sacred and they endorse their original culture's view that shame and depression are normal feelings when they break one of its strict rules. So they think that they *should* feel self-downing—and yet they come to therapy because they want to reduce this feeling.

The first thing I would do is agree with such clients that his culture's rules are okay, although they may not make sense to someone raised in the American culture. These cultural rules have a long history, are followed by most of the other people in their original culture, and these others seem to deal well with life when adhering to those rules. If clients choose to rebel against these rules, and still want to be a respectable member of their culture, they are behaving "wrongly" or "immorally." Of course, they can choose to renounce and resign from their original culture—and then have less of a problem in rebelling against its rules. Mostly, however, they do not want to choose this drastic "solution" to their dilemma.

If they use REBT, clients with this kind of conflict can choose to feel "healthy" negative emotions—such as sorrow, regret, disappointment, or remorse. Or, instead, they can choose to feel "unhealthy" negative emotions—such as shame and depression. Both "healthy" and "unhealthy" emotions, however, may result in different results in different cultures and therefore have no *absolute* meaning. In our own culture, and *perhaps* for many other cultures, "healthy" negative feelings usually lead to "good" results and "unhealthy" negative feelings lead to "poor" results.

To produce a healthy negative feeling, clients could convince themselves, "I did the wrong thing because, according to my original cultural upbringing, what I did is bad. But I am not a *bad person* for doing that act—only a person who behaved badly *this time;* and I am still capable of behaving better in the future. If I were a bad person, I would *always* act badly under all circumstances. I would not only disregard my original culture's rules, but I would also have to act against *all* social rules. So I cannot deny that, according to my original culture whose rules I generally uphold and follow, I am wrong in this instance. But since I am *not* totally incompetent and worthless for being wrong, I can change and correct my behavior in the future. So I regret going against my original culture in this instance, and I will try my best to follow its rules in most other cases." Then, according to REBT theory, these clients would be *sorry* about some of their acts, but not *self-damning.*

REBT, then, helps people who do not strictly follow the rules of their original culture to feel *healthily* sorry and regretful about flouting these rules instead of feeling—as many of them do when they first come to therapy—*unhealthily* guilty, depressed, and self-downing. It shows them how to recognize their rigid insistences—e.g., "I *absolutely must* never break my original culture's rule, and I am a *rotten person* if I do!" They can change them to flexible preferences—e.g., "I *dislike* my breaking my original culture's rules and may try to correct my rebelling against them. But I am a *person who* perhaps wrongly failed—and *not* a *failure* or a rotten person!"

If people who "wrongly" rebel against the mores of their original cultural upbringing use REBT to create unconditional self-acceptance (USA), they will surrender their self-damning attitudes. They will learn that it is not the strict rules of their original culture that *makes them* disturbed, but as Epictetus said 2,000 years ago, their *view* of these rules. When they surrender their absolutistic shoulds, oughts, and musts about following rules—whether they be cultural or noncultural—they give themselves a *flexible choice* of whether to follow them, to give them up, or to make some kind of compromise with them. Their therapist helps them, with REBT, to be less rigid and more flexible in their thinking, feeling, and behaving. He or she does not push them to make any cultural—or noncultural—choices, but helps them to have the freedom to make their *own* choices and decisions.

REBT is remarkably open-minded about clients' basic values. It doesn't disagree with any cultural rules or define them as absolutely good or bad. It accepts them as "good" for that culture and as "bad" for members of that culture who choose to go against them. But it holds that dissenters are not "good" or "bad" people—just people who do "good" and "bad" acts. It subscribes to Alfred Korzybski's ideas that overgeneralization is a common mode of thinking that often renders people, as he puts it, "unsane." This especially goes for the overgeneralizing, "I am what I *do*"—the *is* of identity.

Whatever your clients' cultural rules are, they define the behavior of the people in a given culture as "good" or "bad." So in that culture, they had better acknowledge the practical advantages of acting "well" and the disadvantages of acting "poorly." That is their social "reality" and they can choose to heed it or not to heed it and take the consequences. They always have a *choice*. But, REBT says again, *they* are never "bad people" when they choose to act "badly."

Can REBT *prove* this hypothesis? No, it can probably never be proven or disproven. It is definitional rather than factual. But REBT—along with Korzybski—holds that your clients, and particularly those with a culture conflict, will get healthier emotional and behavioral results if they give up the "is" of identity—"I *am* bad if I behave "badly"—than if they overgeneralize and subscribe to it.

Try to be multiculturally open-minded. Know as much as you can know about the rules of the minority cultures in your general culture. See that these rules are not *in themselves* right or wrong, good or bad—but are legitimate for the members of the minority culture who subscribe to them. Your clients can be "rational" and "self-helping" if they firmly stick to their cultural code or if they flagrantly flout it—providing that they are willing to take the social consequences of doing so. That can be their undisturbed, though difficult, choice.

When, however, your clients damn their total selves, their whole beings, for being too culturally conforming or too lax, they usually feel the consequences of their self-damning—such as panic and depression. That, of course, is their privilege. But they still have a *choice!*

Is rigidly sticking to cultural norms or rigidly rebelling against them in itself a disturbed trait? Yes, somewhat, since rigidity limits one's choices and may well have more disadvantages than advantages. Devoutness is the opposite of flexibility, and therefore has its hazards. Studies of devout religionists have shown, however, that their devoutness may be compatible with mental health, as long as they strongly believe in a forgiving rather than an unforgiving God, Higher Power, or Universal Force (Nielsen, Johnson, & Ellis, 2001).

Human forgiveness—or what REBT calls unconditional self-acceptance (USA)—seems to add flexibility to life. For you can believe that you acted badly or immorally (against individual, family, or cultural rules) and still forgive and accept *yourself* for doing so. And you can forcefully criticize certain *acts* of others without thoroughly damning them as *persons.* So you may realistically point out the disadvantages that may well result from your clients' rigidities, without putting them down as persons—and thereby helping them fully accept *themselves* in spite of some of their self-defeating *behaviors* (Ellis, 1962, 2001a, 2001b; Enright & Fitzgibbons, 2000; Ellis & Harper, 1997; Hauck, 1991).

Are there some "rational" or "self-helping" thoughts, feelings, and behaviors that you can recommend that your clients follow in almost *any* culture? Not exactly—since all cultures have significant differences and all your clients, even when they are part of the same culture, have distinct individual differences. It may be important to note, however, that radically different cultures and religions often have similar proverbs and rules that they recommend their adherents follow. Thus, the bibles of the Jews, the Christians, and the followers of Islam, all to some extent copy from each other and endorse some very similar behaviors for members of their religion to follow. They all define different human behaviors as "sinful" but also include—at least to some degree—a God who accepts the sinner but not the sin (as in the story of Jesus and the prostitute, Mary Magdalene). They also fairly strongly endorse high frustration tolerance in the face of real Adversities (as in the story of Job).

In spite of the fact, therefore, that many clients may follow the teachings of their minority culture, and that therapists had better fully respect this cultural diversity, they may choose to recommend, with some degree of caution, beliefs, emotions, and actions that would probably be beneficial to most clients who are adherents of almost any culture. Thus, therapists will probably be safely on their clients' side if they encourage them to work at achieving three of the basic attitudes that REBT heartily espouses: (1) unconditional self-acceptance (USA), (2) unconditional other acceptance (UOA), and (3) unconditional life-acceptance (ULA) or high frustration tolerance (HFT). Not all clients certainly will benefit if they achieve these three Beliefs-Feelings-Behaviors. But a hell of a lot most probably will!

Let me present the case of a woman, Sari, who strongly followed her Indonesian cultural rules but angered and depressed herself about doing so because people in the United States did not feel obliged to keep those rules and some of them thought her a "fool" for following them.

Using the ABC's of REBT, I showed Sari that her angering and depressing herself (at point C) partly followed from A, the Adversities she encountered by living in both a majority culture and a differing minority culture. But it also followed from B, her *Beliefs about* A. Theoretically, she had the choice of rationally and self-helpingly convincing herself, "I dislike following the rules of my Indonesian culture but I would also dislike *not* following them, for I think they have some value. So I'll choose to restrict myself, unlike people in the United States, and make myself feel sorry and disappointed that taking on the Indonesian restrictions leads to my being thought foolish by some Americans. I could choose to insist that American values *must not* be unfairly imposed on me, and thereby make myself enraged and depressed. I could also choose to dislike Americans who call me *a fool* for following Indonesian rules when I am already an American citizen. But I choose not to anger myself against my American detractors and to refuse to put myself down for what Americans call my 'foolish behavior'."

Sari, after some REBT sessions with me, ended up with this sensible philosophy. But at the beginning of our sessions, she had two strong contradictory *musts:* (1) She *absolutely should* follow the rules of her original Indonesian culture—and, for example, not be sexually intimate with any man before marriage. (2) She *absolutely must not* be criticized and put down by Americans—and especially American males—for following her original culture's dictates. Sari rigidly held both these *musts* and thereby made herself quite angry and depressed.

Using REBT in my sessions with Sari, I helped her first see that her following very strict Indonesian rules was desirable—but was *not* absolutely necessary. She had a *choice* of doing so. If, therefore, she chose to follow them, and was put down by some Americans for making that choice, she could tackle her second *must:* "All Americans *must* respect my choice and not put me down for making it!" If she changed both her dogmatic *musts* to *preferences,* she would not severely castigate herself when she failed to rigidly follow Indonesian rules; and she would not enrage herself against Americans who called her "a fool" when she followed them.

I helped Sari dispute her *absolutistic demands* on others and on herself to keep her *strong preferences* for following Indonesian rules. She was able to *wish* but not *demand* that Americans would not denigrate her as a person for following them. She gave up her anger against Americans and began to follow Indonesian cultural rules moderately but not rigidly. She thereby made herself much less angry and depressed.

In many cases like that of Sari—but by no means in all cases!—you can use the REBT Theory of Disputing Irrational *Beliefs* to show confused, indecisive, anxietizing, depressing, and self-angering members of a minority culture how to resolve their conflicts with the majority culture. They will often have problems in deciding which of the two cultures they choose to follow, but they need not upset themselves about their decisions. How? By your showing them how to honor and respect their cultural *preferences* but rarely escalate them into rigid *musts, shoulds, and oughts.*

In other words, culture conflicts that lead to emotional and behavioral disturbance do not merely stem from clients being reared in one culture and residing in another culture where they are a minority. They largely seem to arise from *demands* by people in the minority culture *and* in the majority culture that everyone *must* follow or *must not* follow certain minority and/or majority rules. If everyone followed the REBT recommendation that they keep their cultural *preferences* and not escalate them to rigid *demands,* considerable cultural conflict and disturbances about such conflicts would, I predict, decrease.

The three major *Beliefs* that REBT would like to see culturally disturbed people achieve are similar to the ones it applies to many kinds of self-disturbing clients. These are:

1. "I prefer and wish to follow the rules of my original culture *and* my new culture, *but* I never have to *absolutistically insist* that I do so."
2. "I prefer and wish that others treat me and my cultural goals fairly, considerately, and respectfully. *But* they never *have to* do so."
3. "I prefer and wish that conflicts not exist between my minority culture and the majority culture in which I now reside, but if these conflicts do exist I can handle them and decide what minority and/or majority rules I will follow."

REBT hypothesizes is that if clients consistently and persistently stay with these major modes of preferring, and rarely change them into dysfunctional demanding and commanding, they will be much more able to deal with many life problems—including that of living in a majority culture that has many significant differences from the minority culture to which they also have some strong allegiances.

Now this, of course, does not solve the serious political, social, and other problems inherent in multicultural and in multisubcultural living. But it does indicate how clients can more healthily wrestle with some of the individual Belief-Emotional-Behavioral problems with which they often come to therapy.

It also may help you solve some of your problems when you live in a world that is increasingly filled with *multiversity*. For when you are reared in one culture you almost always tend to see clients in its prejudiced light and this gives you a one-sided view of clients who have strong ties to another culture.

We had better not ignore the fact that you often have strong minority cultural ties, and may be prejudiced against understanding and dealing with clients who were reared in a majority culture. Of course, there are many exceptions to these biased tendencies, but they often clearly exist. It has therefore been suggested that all therapists and counselors work at making themselves unbiased and fair.

Multicultural diversity is a notable answer to this common important bias, and REBT enthusiastically endorses it.

Mary Smith Arnold (1997) a professor of counseling at Governors State University has given the complex matter of multiculturalism serious thought. She concludes that ignoring it will lead to various kinds of oppression and has summarized six important points for counselors to consider if they are to do multicultural and anti-oppression work:

1. Acknowledge that various kinds of oppression, especially that fostered by ignoring multiculturalism, is pervasive among humans but that "all of us—oppressors and victims—can alter our behaviors and emotional responses to systems of oppression" (p. 39).
2. "Oppression hurts everyone." (p. 39)
3. "Oppression is not our fault, [but] we do have responsibility to challenge and ultimately to end it" (p. 39).
4. "The inability to see the parallels and intersections of racism and sexism keeps both in place" (p. 34).
5. "It is not our difference but our attitudes about our differences that generates problems" (p. 34).
6. "I really believe that we each have the capacity to unlearn and unravel the oppression of our lives" (p. 39).

REBT agrees with Mary Smith Arnold, that in our culture and probably every culture all of us oppress ourselves and others—and that we have the ability to stop doing so. Again, REBT holds that if therapists teach themselves and their clients to achieve unconditional self acceptance (USA) and unconditional other–acceptance (UOA) multicultural—and other—oppression would greatly diminish. But, as professor Arnold indicates, "the complexity and depth of oppression cannot be delineated in . . . brief treatment" (1997, p. 36). Alas, true!

Redding (2001) makes the often neglected point that psychologists lack sociopolitical diversity, since most of them are liberal and may therefore have prejudices against conservative views and actions. He recommends that we should encourage conservatives to join our ranks and foster a true political dialogue in our research, practice, and teaching. "It is in our self-interest to do so" (p. 213). A good point in promoting multicultural diversity!

Stephen Weinrach and Kenneth Thomas (1996, 2002) more specifically tackle this complex and difficult problem by recommending seven guidelines that therapists can use to achieve a higher degree of diversity-sensitive psychotherapy and counseling. Let me paraphrase their guidelines.

1. Place the goals of clients above all other considerations.
2. Select therapy interventions on the basis of the clients' agendas, as opposed to imposing an external social or political agenda on the counseling relationship.
3. Recognize that within-group differences among clients are usually more variable than between-group differences.
4. Expand the dialogue on diversity to include, at a minimum, age, culture, disability, gender, educational level, ethnicity, language, physique, race, religion, sexual orientation, and socioeconomic status.
5. Provide sufficient opportunities for practitioners to be trained in the skills associated with diversity-sensitive counseling.
6. Support all those who are qualified to conduct research on sensitivity counseling.
7. Create an environment that supports professional tolerance (Weinrach & Thomas, 1996, pp. 475–476).

These are hardly perfect guidelines to aid multiversity and discourage wide-ranging prejudices against many kinds of minority clients. Let's test them out, however, to see how well they work. Therapists, like all humans, easily succumb to narrow-mindedness and intolerance. Psychotherapy in general and REBT in particular promote unconditional self-acceptance (USA) and unconditional other-acceptance (UOA). How could they not do so if they are to significantly help many kinds of clients much of the time?

How to Deal with the Resistance of Your Most Difficult Client—You

13

As indicated in my first chapter, on multiple reasons for resistance, one may be the disturbing behavior of the therapist. On the whole, therapists may be less disturbed than their clients, even though they are members of the human race and prone to various disturbances. They have often had some therapy themselves, they have read considerable material on how to change oneself, and they are interested in helping themselves and other people. Unfortunately, however, they still may be prone to various aspects of self-disturbing, including even addiction. They also may be defensive and may not acknowledge that they easily disturb themselves, especially since they might consider self-distressing shameful for a therapist to do. Nonetheless, there is a possibility that they have disturbances which interfere with their helping their clients. This chapter will consider some of therapists' disturbances, in case you yourself are prone to having any of them, and will also give the REBT and CBT theory and practice of how to deal with them.

Other systems, of course, have dealt with the problem of disturbing and resisting therapists. The psychoanalytic system, for example, stresses the therapist's being prejudiced in various ways, just as the client is, and therefore being a victim of counter-transference. The Rogerian system emphasizes the therapist's not having unconditional acceptance of his own life and his own problems and therefore being unable to give accurate empathy, genuineness, and unconditional positive regard to clients. Behavior therapists tend to ignore this problem somewhat and recommend that effective therapy includes several kinds of teaching and persuasive skills which the therapist for one reason or another may not have.

I agree with Carl Rogers that therapists may not particularly disturb themselves and that even if they do they do not necessarily require a year or more of intensive personal psychotherapy as part of their training process. Such personal therapy would probably be valuable, but it is not necessary.

At the same time, whether or not therapists receive therapy themselves, it would be good if you personally were well aware of your Irrational *Beliefs* to see whether these might interfere with your therapy. Here are some common RBs and IBs that I have found during my supervision sessions over the years that therapists are likely to hold and that may interfere with their giving maximum care, as well as minimum harm, to their clients. Be honest with yourself and carefully check to see whether you hold any of these irrational convictions and then go on to effective cognitive, emotive, and behavioral Disputing of them.

Rational *Belief:* "I am interested in my clients and I want very much to help them alleviate their distress and achieve the kind of self-fulfilling that they personally would like to achieve." Irrational *Belief:* "I absolutely must be successful with practically all my clients almost all the time. If I do not succeed with them, my manner and my techniques are far from desirable and, if that is so, I am an incompetent therapist and possibly an incompetent person."

If you hold this Irrational *Belief* and hold it strongly, there is a good chance that you will make yourself anxious with your clients and especially with the resistant ones. Of course, it is always likely that you and your methods are faulty; but even when you are succeeding and your clients appreciate your therapy, you will still be anxious when you hold this IB—for you may not do well with particular clients, now or in the future. How can you be sure that you will *keep* succeeding? You can't!

Your dire needing to help virtually all your clients all the time tends to lead to several corollaries: (a) "I must continually make brilliant and profound interpretations with which my client agrees." (b) "I must always have good judgment." (c) "I must help my clients more than I am now helping them, even when they are showing progress." (d) "If I fail with any of my clients, it has to be my fault and not merely because they resist my good efforts." (e) "When I fail, as I must not, I am a pretty bad therapist and perhaps, since this is a very important aspect of me, a bad person." (f) "My succeeding with a client doesn't count if I later seriously fail with him or her."

When you place golden ideals like these on your therapeutic back, how can you fail to feel inadequate, interfere with your therapy, and make yourself a prime candidate for early burnout? Not very easily! How can you risk experimenting with different techniques? You're stuck!

Rational *Belief:* "I would greatly prefer to be an outstanding therapist, but this is not absolutely necessary, and I will do the best I can." Irrational *Belief:* "I absolutely must be an outstanding therapist and continually succeed with my clients, including the difficult and resistant ones!" This is another preferential goal that, when escalated to a necessity, tends to make you anxious. Some corollary self-defeating convictions to which it leads include: (a) "I must succeed even with practically impossible clients!" (b) "I must have all good sessions with clients and very rarely a poor one!" (c) "I must use the best possible system of therapy and be outstanding at using it!" (d) "I must be an outstanding and famous therapist!" (e) "Because I am a therapist and am ultimately responsible for helping my clients, I must have no emotional problems myself that will interfere with this, and it is shameful if I do!"

Like the Irrational *Belief* mentioned above, this second one leads to frantic endeavor and to inefficiencies that accompany such making yourself frantic. It also may very well lead to panicking when it appears that you are not achieving this unrealistic goal.

Rational *Belief:* "I want to be greatly respected and even loved by all my clients." Irrational *Belief:* "I absolutely have to be greatly respected and approved by all my clients, and if I am not there is something very wrong with me and I probably should not be a therapist." If and when you have this form of dire needing instead of preferring, you again frequently have several perfectionistic corollaries: (a) "I must not dislike any of my clients and, especially, must not show that I disapprove of them in any way." (b) "I must not push my clients hard, lest they dislike me or hate me and resist for that reason." (c) "I must avoid ticklish issues that might upset and antagonize my clients even if we don't get to their serious problems." (d) "The clients whom I like and who like me must remain in therapy as long as I want them to, because I don't want to lose them." (e) "My clients must see that I am thoroughly devoted to them and that I never make serious mistakes." (f) "It's horrible to be disapproved by any of my clients, because their disapproval makes me a bad therapist and perhaps even a bad person."

Rational *Belief:* "Since I am doing my best and working so hard as a therapist, my clients should preferably work equally hard and be equally responsible, listen to me carefully, and push themselves toward change in the areas where I think it would be better for them to change." Irrational *Belief:* "Since I am doing my best and working so hard as a therapist, my clients *have* to work equally hard and be very responsible, *must* listen to me carefully, and *should* always push themselves in the direction in which I lead them."

This Irrational *Belief* leads to low frustration tolerating (LFT) and to anger. It helps you to blame your clients for being disturbed. It frequently has several unrealistic corollaries, such as: (a) "My clients should not be difficult and resistant!" (b) "They should do exactly what I helpfully tell them to do!" (c) "They should work very hard between sessions and always do the homework that I point out it would be good for them to do it!" (d) "I should only have young, bright, attractive and easy clients!"

Irrational *Belief:* "Because I am a person in my own right, I must be able to enjoy myself during therapy sessions and to use these sessions to solve my personal problems as well as those of my clients." This irrational conviction contradicts the nature of paid psychotherapy, which indeed may be of help to therapists but which ethically puts the interest of the clients first. The philosophy of low frustration tolerating and self-indulgence that underlies this belief often leads to several corollaries that also interfere with effective therapy: (a) "I must mainly use the therapeutic techniques that I enjoy using, whether or not they are helpful to my clients. (b) "I must only use techniques that are easy and that do not wear me out." (c) "I must make considerable money doing therapy and must not have to work too hard to make it." (d) "If I use some of my clients amatively and sexually, that will do both them and me a lot of good." (e) "Because I am so helpful as a therapist, I should be able to get away with coming late to appointments, canceling them at the last minute, sleeping during sessions, and indulging myself in other ways."

I could go on almost endlessly listing some of the important Irrational *Beliefs* of therapists that prevent them from being more helpful to their clients. Let me list one more set. "My clients absolutely should listen to me, never resist my treatment, keep working hard to improve, appreciate my efforts to help them, etc." These are some important points about the REBT theory and practice of treating resistance. Let me now apply some of these practices to resisting therapists. If you have been consciously or unconsciously subscribing to some of the Irrational *Beliefs* listed above, if you have consequently felt disturbed about yourself as a therapist, and if your effectiveness has thereby suffered, here are some of the cognitive, emotive, and behavioral techniques of REBT and CBT you can use to deal with your most difficult client—you.

1. Assume that some strong Irrational *Beliefs* lie behind your own upsetting and that these include one or more absolutistic shoulds, oughts, or musts, such as those listed above.

2. Search diligently for those that specifically apply to you and your therapy. Don't give up until you seem to be finding a few.

3. Consider your own irrational convictions as hypotheses—not facts—that you can dispute and surrender. Use the same methods to

challenge them as you would employ to question any other IB and that you also presumably are using with your own clients. For example, "Where is the evidence that I have to be successful with all my clients practically all the time?" "Who says that I must be better than other therapists?" "Where is it written that it is necessary for me to be respected and loved by all my clients?"

4. Carefully think about your Irrational *Beliefs* until you come up with disconfirming evidence and are really willing to give them up.

5. Create alternate rational, preferential statements to substitute for your unrealistic, unconfirmable *Beliefs*. For example, "I clearly don't have to be successful with all my clients, though that would be great! Because I would like to help most of them, let me do the best I can to work at that goal!"

6. If you seem to only hold your rational coping statements lightly, then Dispute them, too. For example, "Why don't I have to be successful with all my clients?" Answer: "Because practically no therapist is that successful, including me. Because even if I do great therapy, many clients may stubbornly resist using it. Because there is no law of the universe that says that because I *preferably* would like to do something I *have to* succeed at doing it. Because I am a fallible human, and consequently a fallible therapist, I may, even with the greatest caution, make some serious errors."

7. Work on achieving unconditional self-acceptance (USA) for yourself just as you would work to help your clients achieve it. Strongly convince yourself that you can unconditionally accept yourself as a person *whether or not* you are succeeding as a therapist and *whether or not* your clients and other significant people approve of you. Acknowledge that some of your acts may lead to ineffective therapy and are therefore ineffective and deplorable, but stubbornly refuse to lambaste your *self* or your *being* for having these failings.

8. Work on refusing to awfulize about anything. See that it is most inconvenient and annoying when your clients refuse to do their agreed-upon homework, but it's not awful, horrible, or terrible. Just annoying!

9. Instead of mainly looking at the ease of staying the way you are, and the discomfort of changing, do a cost-benefit ratio of the advantages and disadvantages of continuing on your present pathway. Make a comprehensive list of the pains of maintaining your disturbance and the advantages of giving them up. Review and think about this list every day, until you are more motivated to change your ineffective therapy behaviors.

10. Give yourself the strong challenge and excitement of doing one of the most difficult and most rewarding things you can do in your life—pig-headedly refusing to make yourself miserable about anything.

Then you are more likely to be able to work effectively at helping your clients accomplish this same thing.

11. Reduce some of your self-defeating *Beliefs* to absurdity and see the humor in some of the profound stupidities that you keep rigidly holding. Tell yourself, for example, "I really should do only what I enjoy doing during my therapy sessions. What do you think those blasted clients are paying me for anyway, to get better?"

12. You can use virtually all the emotive-evocative-experiential techniques that you employ with your clients to cope with your own problems. Thus, you can use rational emotive imagery and vividly imagine yourself failing miserably as a therapist. Then let yourself feel any anxietizing, depressing, or self-downing that you would often feel under those conditions. Really get in touch with your negative feelings and then, while still imagining this abysmal scenario, make yourself feel only disappointed and regretful about your failing but not self-downing about *you*. Practice this rational emotive imagery every day for at least thirty days until you automatically begin to feel regret and disappointment instead of depression and self-depreciating whenever you think about failing badly at therapy.

13. Whenever you can do so, unequivocally, strongly, and persistently act against your Irrational *Beliefs*. If, for example, you hate difficult clients and think that you can't stand them, deliberately take some on and show yourself that you can tolerate what you don't like and that you can accept these clients and learn from them how to deal with their obnoxious behaving, including their hateful attitudes toward you. By the same token, if you find yourself using only techniques that you find easy and enjoyable, sometimes force yourself to try some difficult methods and keep trying them until they become familiar—and probably rewarding.

As you can see from the foregoing suggestions, dealing with your own personal problems and problems as a therapist involves some of the same techniques that you would presumably enjoy with your own resisting clients. However, it may be more difficult to do this in your own case, because you can easily monitor your clients' progress in following your techniques, while you only have yourself to do the monitoring when you apply them to yourself. This is tough, but not impossible. You can, if you deem it desirable, go back into therapy yourself and thereby acquire a monitor. But unless you are an unusually difficult customer, it might be better if you go it alone. Why? Frankly, to make things a bit more troublesome for yourself. For if you try to change yourself, at first, without guidance and support from another therapist, you might be able to better appreciate the struggles of your own clients when they strive for self-change. You may thereby come to accept them with their struggles and their setbacks. In any event, if you do find that you do not satisfactorily change on your own, you can always work with another therapist—and had better do so!

If you persist in looking for your own problems and failings as a therapist, if you honestly confront them, and if you use REBT and CBT methods of thinking, feeling, and acting against them, you may still never become the most accomplished and sanest therapist in the world. But I can safely guess that you will tend to be happier and more effective than before.

IMPROVING THE PERSONAL CHARACTERISTICS OF EFFECTIVE COUNSELORS

Pope and Kline review the literature on the personal characteristics of effective counselors and therapists and find that there is considerable agreement that some counselors have "good" personal traits that enhance therapeutic effectiveness. They did a special study of ten experts in the field of counseling and counselor education who were asked to rate how important personal characteristics of counselors were and how responsive to training these important characteristics were. They found that ten traits ranked highest in importance but that often these traits were least responsive to counselor training.

Let us assume that this ranking of counselor importance is fairly accurate, though it well may not be from the standpoint of REBT and CBT. For the traits listed by these expert counselors and supervisors as most important for therapy may help clients *feel* better, which is fine, but may not help them *get better*—which, according to REBT is fine. However, this study of therapist's personal characteristics is still valuable, since several of the personal traits that make for close, trusting alliances between therapists and their clients would most probably work best with difficult and resisting clients.

Assuming that this is at least partially correct, how can you improve your personal characteristics, even though Pope and Kline found these unresponsive to change in counselor training? In many ways, I am sure. But let me show you how to use REBT if you would like to improve some of your important personal characteristics.

Acceptance. REBT especially concentrates on people's achieving unconditional self-acceptance (USA) and unconditional other-acceptance (UOA). But, unlike Carl Rogers, who modeled USA and UOA for his clients, you will *also actively teach* it to your clients (as I

show in chapter 6). Following REBT, you can *teach* yourself to unconditionally accept your clients *just* because they are alive, human, and
unique; and, of course, you can use the same method to unconditionally accept yourself—yes, with all your failings and errors. Unlike even
existential therapy, which tries to get you to see the value of USA and
UOA for *yourself* (with some help from your therapist), REBT much
more definitely *shows* you their importance—and how to acquire these
personal characteristics.

Emotional Stability.   REBT does not insist that therapists be thera-
pized themselves and thereby increase their emotional stability, though
it recommends that they *preferably* have some individual and group
therapy sessions of Rational Emotive Behavior Therapy. Whether or
not you have such therapy, you can improve your emotional stability
by looking for your musts and shoulds when you feel upset, Disputing
them vigorously, and using REBT methods to help you feel and act
against them. Moreover, as you employ REBT to strongly help rid your
clients of their IB's, you will most probably consciously and unconsciously reduce your own dysfunctional *Beliefs* and behaviors. Not necessarily! But sometimes quite effectively.

Open-Mindedness.   REBT especially crusades against closed-mind-
edness, absolutism, and bigotry, as it identifies all these characteristics
with emotional-behavioral disturbance. If you use REBT on yourself
and, as noted in the preceding paragraph, keep using it to help talk
others out of their closed-minded thinking, you will most probably
become more open-minded.

Empathy.   As I have shown in chapter 6, REBT fosters at least two
kinds of empathy: (1) listening caringly to client's disturbed thoughts
and feelings and showing them that you really *want* to help them feel
better and get better, and (2) listening for their Irrational *Beliefs*—their
absolutistic shoulds and musts, that they are usually aware of, and
pointing these out and collaborating with them on Disputing them. You
can use this mode of *double* empathy to listen to your own problems
with unconditional other-acceptance (UOA), an important ingredient
of empathy, and listening for and Disputing your own behind-the-
scenes Irrational *Beliefs*. You thereby give REBT's double empathy to
yourself as well as to your clients.

Genuineness.   To help your clients, you had best genuinely want to
aid them for their own sake (and not mainly to rate as a noble savior);
honestly use methods with them that you think will work and ignore

methods that you think will not work; show them that you strongly believe in your therapy but that it may well have limitations and contraindications; and often risk their disapproval of how you are behaving with them. If you use REBT on yourself, you will likely aid these forms of genuineness by showing yourself how not to care *too much* about your client's approving of you and how not to absolutely *need* to be effective with your therapy in general (or with your particular client).

Flexibility.   REBT and CBT specialize in helping people think and act flexibly, unrigidly, and, in the light of possible alternatives to their believing, feeling, and acting. As you use them and keep seeing the value to your clients of making themselves more flexible, you can similarly employ them to aid your own cognitive-emotional-behavioral flexibility. You can consciously see that even REBT, if rigidly used with all clients, simply will not work with some of them. You can therefore distinctly modify it in some instances or even abandon it for "irrational" methods that seem to work better than the "rational" ones you are using. In one sense, human disturbance is "irrational" because it doesn't work for the good of the individual or her social group. Therefore, any technique of therapy can be said to be "rational" if it really works for the individual client and his/her social group. Unrealistic and illogical therapy techniques can therefore *sometimes* be "rational." Sometimes!

Interest in People.   This characteristic seems to be almost synonymous with your doing good therapy, though an occasional client may work harder at helping herself because she thinks that you are *not* sufficiently interested in her and works hard at herself to *get you* interested—or even to spite you! Since you are a therapist, you obviously started out with *some* real interest in helping your clients. But you could considerably interfere with that interest by having low frustration tolerance and by making yourself impatient with and bored with clients. Or you could think you are doing poorly with clients and withdraw from your interest in helping them. If so, you obviously can use REBT and CBT on yourself to stop your irrational awfulizing about therapy being *too* hard and *too* boring to continue. And you can Dispute your Irrational *Beliefs,* "I must always succeed remarkably well with my clients and if I don't what's the use of continuing to practice it and making myself an incompetent person." Of course, you could genuinely and rationally lose interest in doing therapy and involve yourself in another vocation. Fine!—but first see if your LFT or self-downing is making you "genuinely" retreat.

Confidence. Therapists who have no confidence in their practice or, worse yet, in themselves will hardly be able to offer effective treatment. The more difficult they find their clients, the more they will lose confidence. Lack of confidence in what you do, I called lack of achievement confidence in *Reason and Emotion in Psychotherapy* in 1962. In the 1970s, Albert Bandura (1997) called it lack of self-efficacy.

If you suffer from self-inefficacy, Bandura has shown several ways of making yourself feel more efficacious—and, as a result, usually acting more efficiently. REBT and CBT also recommend several ways to increase your confidence in your therapy, including these: (1) Give up your perfectionistic standards of what a "good" therapist *should* be teaching. (2) Check with your clients to see if they are being helped from their *own* frame of reference. (3) Practice steadily and vigorously imagining that you *are* to some degree succeeding with difficult clients and that you are able to keep succeeding with them. (4) Take some workshops or extra supervision that will help you succeed better. (5) Talk to other therapists to see that they often do no better than you. (6) Refuse to see clients with whom you seem to do poorly.

If you suffer from lack of *self-*confidence or *self-acceptance* and keep putting yourself down for your supposed or actual inefficacy with your clients, use REBT's principles and techniques of giving yourself unconditional self-acceptance (USA), as I keep showing throughout this book.

Sensitivity. Sensitivity means honing in on the main nuances of your client's thinking, feeling, and behaving and especially on how disruptive it is and what can be done about it. A good deal of sensitiveness may be partly innate—as, probably, is sensitivity to art and music. But just as these kinds of sensitivity can be increased and developed—as, for example, with music appreciation—so can your sensitiveness to people in general and clients in particular be assessed and increased. Individually, with a tutor, book, or materials, you can arrange for sensitivity training. Or there are many courses, workshops, and other presentations in which you can have group experiences that aid your people-sensitivity.

Often, however, you may be innately quite sensitive to people but block your cultivating your own use of its potentials by irrationally addicting yourself to one, two, or three of the main dogmatic musts that impede so much of your human functioning:

1. *Self-downing:* "I really don't understand and be as sensitive to people as I must be! I'll never be good at this, so I might as well give up and stop trying to be a therapist!"

2. *Anger:* "People in general, and my clients in particular, are a pain in the ass and make it almost impossible to let me understand and empathize with them! They *absolutely shouldn't* be so difficult for me to work, so I'll stop trying to do so!"
3. *Low frustration tolerance.* "Conditions and situations of being sensitive to people and of helping my clients *must not be* as difficult as they are! It's *too hard* to try to keep my sensitivity and empathy alive! If I'm really sensitive to myself, I'll stop trying to be so goddamned sensitive to others!"

If you zero in to any of these three—or all three—Irrational *Beliefs* that block your sensitivity potential, and if you think, feel, and act against them, you can creatively unblock your *in*sensitivity and achieve good measure of sensitivity.

Fairness.   Fairness to your clients means putting them at least equal to and in some ways ahead of yourself. Usually, they are paying you or your agency for help; therefore, in many ways they come first—over your own leanings and comfort. Thus, you are ethically required to come early to sessions; give them their full therapy time; not to go to sleep on them; to attentively listen; and to not have personal relations, especially sex or love relations, with them. Your professional therapy organization and your licensing board has a good many rules of ethics for you to follow. Do so!—even if some of these ethical rules restrict or deprive you. Else seek another profession!

As usual, your emotional problems and the Irrational *Beliefs* (IB's) that accompany them may encourage you at times to act unethically with your clients. Thus, if you think you absolutely *must* get paid well by your clients, *must* have them utterly devoted to you, *must* have them follow the therapy procedures you are prescribing for them, *must not* have them argue with you or resist you, *must* have them persuade their friends and relatives to see you for therapy, or you have several similar demands and commands that they *must* meet, you will likely treat them unfairly in various ways.

Some Remarks on "The Best" Techniques for Coping with Resisting Clients

14

Practically all clients resist changing to some considerable degree, and the kind that we are discussing in this book, resistant clients, present more difficulty. What are the best styles and stances with which you may experiment in dealing with them?

There probably is no best in this respect. All clients are different individuals in their own right, and resistant ones, though they have some similarities in common, are still unique individuals. Therefore, your style and stance that works beautifully with one of them, or even with most of them, may work miserably with another. Are there, therefore, no guidelines that you can use to select the best style you can think of for any particular client? There probably are several, but at the same time they all have their limitations and restrictions. Let me list a few styles that I have found particularly helpful with resistant individuals.

THE USE OF PERSONAL DISCLOSURE

When selectively used, I have found personal disclosure to be quite helpful with many clients. In some respects, my clients presumably want a perfect therapist, who knows everything there is to know about therapy, has used this knowledge on himself or herself, and definitely does not act self-defeatingly in important ways. Such a perfect therapist, of course, does not exist, and if he or she did exist, some clients would take it amiss. In comparing themselves to this therapist, they might feel that they could not do as well and might look for a much less perfect member of the species.

Nonetheless, the classic psychoanalytic model of the therapist who never reveals himself or herself but keeps strictly to the client's problems does not work for me in many instances. I find it much more useful to mainly be myself during the therapeutic session and reveal several things about myself, particularly when the client asks about them and seems to desire an answer. Putting the client off and saying practically nothing about myself doesn't seem to work very well.

So I frequently reveal a good many of my personal problems and personal tastes but try to structure them to help the client. Thus, I have no hesitation about showing that I have sometimes anxietized and phobicized. However, I also show them that I use the same kind of techniques that I am using with them to overcome my own difficultizing. In this way, they can see that I am human and fallible, that I am not ashamed to admit my own failings, that I definitely work on them to alleviate them, and that I succeed to some degree in doing so.

That is all very well and seems to do considerable good and very little harm, but I still have to watch it. I have to watch closely to see how the clients react to my self-disclosure and whether they use it to serve as a good model for themselves or whether they have other negative ideas and feelings about it.

Second, it almost goes without saying, that I do this self-revelation very briefly and intermittently, so that the outstanding focus of each session is on the client and hardly on me! I also experiment by telling some clients certain things about myself that I do not tell to other clients. Harm avoidance is ever-present in my thinking and therapy. Therefore self-disclosures that seem to work well with some clients are avoided with what I think are more vulnerable clients who would be harmed with it. Good perception and good judgment in this respect is required—and there is no perfect way to achieve these important aspects of therapy.

ENCOURAGING CLIENTS TO EXPERIMENT

Clients frequently, especially some resisting clients, are skeptical. Before they can induce themselves to try certain therapy techniques, they rightly ask significant questions about these methods and they hardly jump into them enthusiastically.

This is all to the good, since we therapists are trying to help people think for themselves and not cavalierly take over the suggestions of others. So it is often wise to frankly admit that the methods that you are now encouraging particular clients to use have worked with many other clients, but that they may not work for them and therefore are to be used experimentally. They can only find out what truly is effective for them by taking some experimental chances and risks.

At the same time, I frequently point out to resisting clients that because they are going to have difficulty in working with a special method and because there is no guarantee that it actually will be effective for them, they still had better try it. That is because they are unusually stuck in their present position, are getting nowhere, and may well be in considerable pain. Therefore, I point out that the technique that I am now advising may well not work but that it is worthwhile finding out whether or not it will.

Now this attitude again has its disadvantages, because if I am very authoritative about the effectiveness of the technique I am suggesting and hold that it definitely works most of the time with practically all clients, some of the more suggestible ones will accept my authoritativeness, use the method, and use it successfully mainly because they think I think that it will bring them great results. This will work temporarily or palliatively, and may be used in exceptional cases; but it still probably would be highly desirable if clients more open-mindedly experimented with various techniques and found out whether recommended ones work for them.

The more consistently and vigorously you insist that one of your interpretations is correct or that one of the methods you are suggesting will be effective, the more your very suggestible clients may take to it and even benefit from it, even though it is ineffective with most people most of the time. So you'd better watch how much you authoritatively point out that a technique is very effective when it may work *because* your clients are suggestible. There is no perfect way out of this difficult situation, and you'd better listen to your clients and judge the results you get in each instance, and often take a new tack. The new tack may be less effective in the short run but more effective in the long run and help people, as you hope, get better rather than merely feel better.

WHEN CLIENTS AVOID "DANGEROUS" TOPICS

When you see that clients are trying to avoid discussing "dangerous" subjects, you can of course let these go for a while and hope that they will get around to dealing with them later. But too much queasiness on your part, for fear of making your clients uncomfortable, or out of your "horror" that you will offend and lose them, can result from your own dire need for approval. But even if you have no such problems, you may be undecided as to whether to barge in and encourage clients to talk about ticklish subjects or whether this would help them resist more. As usual, there is no perfect way to answer this. First, you can work on your own queasiness and diminish your anxiety about bringing up a difficult subject. Once you have that under control, you still have to decide whether you think confronting your client will do more harm than good. You can take the tack of going ahead and seeing what happens, and retreating if it turns out fairly badly, or, once again, you can simply wait for a more suitable time to bring up this difficult subject.

You can sometimes say something like this to the client: "I know that what I am about to discuss may be a difficult area for you, and frankly I am having some problems of my own in bringing it up. Nonetheless, I would like you to consider this area and think about the advantages of discussing it even though you may be uncomfortable doing so." If you then get the client's permission to go ahead, there will probably be less difficulty. But there is no perfect rule to follow in this regard.

THE DANGERS OF FORCEFUL TEACHING

You may decide that the best way to help clients change would be to forcefully bring to their attention the grim consequences of their behaving. However, you risk your client thinking that you are too preaching, or too condemning. You therefore can do your so-called preaching in a fairly tactful way. You can say for example, "Yes, I see that you often got away with borrowing money from your friends and not paying it back, and perhaps you will continue to get away with it. But in the long run, some of your friends will probably tend to resent this and you will therefore lose them as friends. Not that's all right if you're willing to take that consequence. But you will probably lose out to some extent; and even if you don't, you may train yourself to keep avoiding facing responsibilities and thus enhance your low frustration tolerance. That won't make you a worm or a totally weak individual, but it usually has distinct disadvantages. So give the matter some thought and see if your behavior is really worth it in the long run."

Of course, your tone and manner are crucial in doing this sort of thing. Some clients will take it amiss no matter what tone you use. Especially when you think and feel that there are not many other good approaches to take with this kind of situation, you can risk being critical in a very tactful manner. You can even show clients that your showing them some of the bad consequences of their behavior is not really criticizing them. You're merely trying to get them to assess the behavior in terms of their own good and see whether it is best for them to perform.

Some therapists advocate avoiding all confrontations because they lead to resistance. To some extent, they have a good point. But following this view, you may have to avoid discussing some crucial aspects of the client's self-defeating behavior. No general or universal procedure is likely to be suitable with most clients. Some resistors will benefit from a "hard line" and some from a softer approach (Leahy, 2001). Your discretion would seem to be the better part of valor!

To get around the difficulty of making confrontations, it has been suggested that you use what is called action language and simply describe the things that the clients do instead of adding interpretations to them. Thus, instead of saying to a client, "You actively expressed your aggression," you say, "You ignored the points that he was making." Instead of interpreting, "You sabotaged your plan to confront your boss," you say, "You failed to ask your boss to discuss things with you." If you show people what they actually did instead of making an interpretation, and sometimes a dubious interpretation, they may not resist your confronting them.

DISCUSSING CLIENTS' RESISTANCE

John Vriend and Wayne Dyer (1977) point out that you had better have some idea about why your clients are resisting and ask yourself whether their non-compliance is typical of their general reactions or is specifically related to their interactions with you and their conceptions about the kind of therapy you do. Assuming that you believe that their resisting is specific to you, you can then discuss their resisting somewhat along the following lines:

1. Show them that you acknowledge and understand their resisting feelings.
2. Inquire whether these feelings are an important part of their personality or more specifically limited to the therapy with you.
3. You and the clients had better explore any Irrational *Beliefs* (IB's) involved in their kind of resistance.
4. Show the clients that you are strong and competent enough yourself to handle their resisting without being personally threatened.
5. As I keep stressing in this book, show your clients that you can unconditionally accept them, even when their resisting blocks you and their therapeutic efforts.

By dealing honestly and openly with your clients' resistance, you can indicate that therapy is not a process in which they merely express their feelings and passively listen to you. It is a two-sided effort in which both of you had better face difficult problems and work hard to help each other aid the therapy process.

EXPLORING DIFFERENCES IN THE THERAPIST'S AND THE CLIENTS' GOALS

You may have different goals and values from your clients and these may contribute to their resisting therapy with you. By all means investigate whether these differences exist.

Particularly investigate how your therapeutic goals and those of your clients may clash. Is your client, for example, aiming for mere symptom removal—such as overcoming social anxiety—while you are aiming for a more profound personality change—such as unconditional self-acceptance? Which goals can the two of you agree upon and mutually work for?

If your therapeutic goals are more pervasive and far-reaching than are your client's, and you are willing to allow this discrepancy, at least be aware of it and consider the advisability of making the client aware of it too. You can then expect the client's resistance and either work harder to overcome it, choose to live with it, or help the client look for another therapist (Reis & Brown, 1999).

Your goals, especially if you use REBT or CBT, may be to first get at your clients' Irrational *Beliefs* and thereby get to their dysfunctional feelings and behaviors. That is all very well, but the client's main goal may be to improve their Adversities and thereby change their dysfunctional behaviors. They may be waiting for a significant change in events before they want to change their IB's. For example, I saw a 30-year-old male salesman who ceaselessly complained about his wife, his children, his boss, and his conditions of work. Although he admitted he was childishly temper-ridden, he kept refusing to accept and gracefully lump the "grim" conditions of his life. For a while, I tried to show him that he had better accept these conditions, not whine and wail about them, and therefore increase his blood pressure. Because he stuck to his goals and I foolishly stuck to mine, we were making no inroads into stemming his frequent angry outbursts.

After I gave some careful thought, I decided to take a different tack and focus mainly on how this client could get a better job and how he could deal with his new boss and customers and act less angrily toward them. He cooperated much more readily with these goals than he had ever worked at changing the Irrational Beliefs that led to his angry feelings. Four months later, he had a new job, was making almost twice as much in commissions as he had previously made, and was getting along almost famously with his boss and his customers.

At first, this client still displayed many temper tantrums with his wife and children. But after he had been on the new job for seven months, his outbursts at family members decreased significantly and he was much more tolerant of their "stupid" behaviors. His own view of his improved family relations was that, "I get along better with them because things are going so much better in my business life."

Through working with this client on his relations with people at his business I was able to help him change some of his Irrational *Beliefs* and emotional consequences. I think that without helping him to change the Adversities (A's) of his life, his rantings and ravings about his family "injustices" might well not have lessened. Though at first I thought this was the wrong thing to do, I reorganized my own thinking and worked on his A's more than his *Beliefs* and thereby reduced his resistance.

In another instance, a 47-year-old woman with a lifelong history of lack of deciding, depressing, and failing to achieve intimacy with any man, kept clinging during the first nine months of my sessions with her to her narcissistic need to be everyone's center of attention and felt abysmal self-downing whenever she was rejected by people. In spite of her having graduated from college magna cum laude, she worked as a claims adjuster, made little money, overspent on clothing, and complained bitterly about her poverty.

After my getting almost nowhere with this borderline client for a year, I focused on helping her change the Adversities of her life by marrying a "nice" man whom she had dated for six years but found physically unattractive and below her intellectual level. Once she decided that he had several desirable traits and worked on satisfying him sexually—sometimes giving him seven orgasms a week although she only occasionally had one herself—she encouraged him to fall enthusiastically in love with her and devote himself to pleasing her, as he had only mildly done before.

Married to this husband, her life changed radically. She worked only part-time, got involved with fixing up their new home, was busily drawn into her husband's social and business life, and had little time for her previous moaning and wailing. She accepted herself—wrongly, in REBT terms—because of her better material and financial status; and although her irrational philosophies had not changed that much, she lived happily with her husband. They frequently come to my Friday Night Workshops at the Albert Ellis Institute in New York, where I demonstrate REBT in public with volunteers from the audience. From talking with them from time to time, as well as talking with several of her friends whom she had referred to me for therapy, I would say that for the past several years she has been functioning only in a moderately disturbed manner. Mainly, I hypothesize, because by changing some of the Adversities in her life, she has thereby helped herself change some of her emotional and behavioral consequences—as well as a few of her Irrational Beliefs.

Still another instance may be instructive. An 18-year-old college student came to see me several years ago, and although I tried very hard to help her overcome her procrastinating in her school work and her anxiety about talking to personable males, I got nowhere for 17 months. She almost was thrown out of college several times because of her incompletes; and although she was unusually attractive, she rarely dated and was horrified because two of her best woman friends were already engaged to be married.

Seeing that I was getting nowhere with regular REBT and that I was not helping her give up her Irrational *Beliefs* that she shouldn't have to do onerous work and was worthless if a personable male rejected her, I experimented with a different tack. I encouraged this resisting client to dress beautifully, to indicate to her schoolmates that she was sexually liberal, and to say only flattering things to the males she encountered. Doing this, she was soon besieged with dates, even though she did little to overcome her anxiety about meeting suitable men.

After a few months of social success, this woman's confidence in her ability to win males enormously increased. She had fun dating, and she gave up her goal of marrying soon because she wanted to keep enjoying playing the field. She did not unconditionally accept herself with her failures, as I would have preferred her to do, but conditionally accepted herself because of her successes. However, she gained such a degree of achievement-confidence and self-efficacy about her social life, though not the self-confidence of unconditional self-acceptance, that she realized that she could, with effort, get more of the things she wanted and that this could apply to her studies as well. She began to work harder at school, diminished her procrastinating, and for the first time since she entered college, began to get good marks. Her increased confidence in her social ability apparently helped her to see that she could do better at her school work and that it was not too hard for her to do so. By showing her how to change some of the Adversities in her life, I presumably helped her to change some of her major Beliefs and Consequences as well.

I won't say that all resisting clients are like the three I just mentioned and that therefore they find it impossible to change themselves unless they can also be shown how to change the adverse conditions under which they live. So be it. Using REBT and CBT, you can often show them how to change A—and therefore make themselves more likely to change B and C. This, of course, has its disadvantages and dangers, for many resisting clients will only work at modifying their life conditions rather than change their disturbance-creating Beliefs. They are distinctly more interested in feeling better rather than getting better.

I have seen hundreds of people who temporarily overcame their feelings of anxiety as soon as they formed a presumably lasting relationship, usually with a member of the other sex or, if they were gay, of the same sex. When they considered quitting therapy, I advised many of them to continue, but they quit anyway. Some of them later returned, to confess that their leaving had been premature. Many others, however, from what I heard from their friends and relatives, were ashamed to return and thereby admit that they had mistakenly thought that changing some of their important A's automatically and permanently changed their B's and C's.

Nonetheless, part of efficient therapy is helping people to change the Activating events or Adversities of their lives as well as their Irrational *Beliefs*. Therefore, I use Rational Emotive Behavior Therapy to deal with them in their life situations. Although I would prefer them to make themselves disappointed and sorry rather than severely anxiety-ridden and depressed about almost any situation they find undesirable, I often settle for getting them to feel better by modifying the situation itself. Inelegant, but sometimes what else can you effectively do?

Some of the ways in which you can use REBT to help resistant clients change the Adversities of their lives include the following:

1. Instead of giving up their whining and wailing about a partner they seem to be losing, they can increase their efforts to be nice to and possibly win back the partner, or at least use their newer nice techniques to win another partner.

2. Similarly, if they refuse to give up their self-depreciating about their job performances or angering about their conditions at work, they can put their energies into finding an easier or more enjoyable job. You can help them do better at their jobs as well as accept themselves when they don't do well.

3. When clients retain their philosophy of addicting themselves to harmful behaviors—for example, still believe that they need to smoke, overeat, or procrastinate and that they can't stand immediate pain to arrive at making themselves nonaddicting—you can help them switch to a less pernicious form of addicting. For example, caffeine rather than cigarettes.

4. When resisting clients won't do their in vivo desensitizing homework—such as taking elevator rides that they terribly fear—you can let them take toned-down assignments, such as riding on escalators or going in one elevator every month. Or you can assign them concomitant security measures, such as only riding in elevators when accompanied by a "safe" person with whom they are friendly.

5. When clients won't do a difficult task—such as writing a book they want to write—you can show them how to get a competent collaborator, such as a co-author.

6. You can give resisting clients a choice of working on an elegant or philosophic solution to their main emotional-behavioral problems or figuring out practical solutions to partially resolve it. But you can show them that if they pick the less elegant pathway, they have a right to this choice and never need put themselves down for taking it.

7. When resisting clients refuse to give up their philosophy and feelings of angering, you can help them to stay away from people at whom they are angry and to make greater efforts to be with those they can more easily accept and take a liking to.

In many ways, you can help clients, even when they do not elegantly solve their emotional behavioral problems, to act to change the Adversities (A's) of their lives. This will not be easy, because a great many resisting clients have low frustration tolerating. But they will much more likely work at changing practical situations that they don't like than they will sometimes work at changing their basic *Beliefs* that make and keep them emotionally disturbed.

QUESTIONABLE TECHNIQUES
OF OVERCOMING RESISTANCE

Some techniques for helping clients overcome their resisting actually work, and sometimes quickly, but have their own limitations and disadvantages. Some are also inherently dangerous and antitherapeutic as has been shown for many years by several therapists and by the harm avoidance-movement in addiction and other forms of therapy that are becoming popular today. Even reputable and good techniques of psychotherapy, as I pointed out in a paper on the limitations and disadvantages of behavior therapy in 1983, can distinctly distract people from using still better techniques and therefore can be relatively harmful.

On the other hand, as Kirsch (1999) has shown with a series of experiments, profound belief in almost any kind of therapy, physical or mental, may have a pronounced placebo effect and may definitely work for some people even though it is ineffective or harmful for many others. Jerome Frank (Frank & Frank, 1993), as early as 1969, pointed to this same state of affairs—namely, that a large number of clients improve mainly because they like their therapist, believe that he or she is competent, strongly favor the theory of their therapist, and feel much better mainly because of their optimistic beliefs.

In view of these facts, it is most difficult to say that any kind of therapy or manipulation by the therapist will not work or is inherently harmful. Statistically, it can be shown that certain therapies and techniques within these therapies harm a number of people. But it cannot be shown that they are useless or harmful for practically everyone.

This is particularly true of resisting clients. They are often so stuck in their ways and so unwilling to work at changing that you can sometimes try peculiar or bizarre methods that you normally would not use with regular clients. It may be argued, however, that since some resisting clients are harming themselves enormously, even risky techniques had better be used with them when you are practically certain that your regular methods will be ineffective. So give this matter some serious thought and resist using techniques that you believe are risky. But perhaps you'd better have a few exceptions!

Types of therapy that are not likely to work with clients and that may harm them include the following:

1. Inducing clients to follow dogmas and bigotries and become even more absolutistic and rigid than they usually are.
2. Using magical rituals, such as shamanism, witchcraft, and voodooism, that may help clients temporarily but that they are likely to be disillusioned and disappointed with later.
3. Convincing your clients that they are immortal and god-like, that they can have practically anything that they wish for, and that they can ward off all evil.
4. Showing clients that they are members of some superior race, ethnic group, religion, or therapy group that by virtue of their following will favor and protect them.
5. Convincing clients that if they truly understand the causes of their disturbing they will easily and automatically change themselves by having this insight.
6. Making your clients completely dependent on you and devoted to your therapeutic dictates.
7. Showing clients that you distinctly despise them because they are resisting your noble efforts to change and are stubbornly refusing to do what you are trying to help them do.

Once again, all the above techniques of trying to overcome resistance may work at certain times and under special circumstances with certain clients. You may therefore, in a pinch and when you think that all other methods will fail, consider using risky methods—but with due consideration and caution. These techniques may work at certain times and under certain conditions but are not generally reliable. If at all, use them rarely!

ADDITIONAL WAYS OF HELPING CLIENTS
MAINTAIN THEIR THERAPEUTIC GAINS

It is important that clients maintain their therapeutic gains. It is not exactly true that if clients make the profound kind of philosophical changes that we favor in REBT they will not only reduce their presenting symptoms but also maintain their gains and make greater ones. This is true of some clients, but hardly all!

You had better, therefore, give considerable thought to helping your clients maintain their symptom-changes and their basic personality changes. Some of the things you can do in this respect are the following:

1. Recognize the complex nature of the skills that you are teaching the clients and the interactional factors in their accepting and using these skills. Emotive as well as cognitive and behavioral methods are important in facilitating generalizing and maintaining aspects of change.

2. Where feasible, include clients' relatives and encourage family members to help clients achieve and maintain changes.

3. Help clients to change their environments, as well as themselves. You don't have to, but can consider therapy intrinsic to social and community change (Ellis, 2001b; Rigazio-DiGilio, Ivey, & Locke, 1997).

4. Assume that your treatment of clients will not necessarily lead to their generalizing and maintaining their changes, and try to give them specific encouragement and instruction in how to do this.

5. Encourage clients to make recordings of their sessions and to listen to them during therapy and also to listen to some of them after therapy has ended. They will then be reminded to forcefully talk themselves out of their Irrational *Beliefs* and to keep working at resolving their practical and emotional problems.

6. Clients can be encouraged to return for booster sessions after their regular sessions have ended. You can arrange for them to have a follow-up session every year or at some other regular interval.

7. I. W. Miller (1984) and his associates have found that if clients are instructed to practice their newly acquired coping skills and skill training beyond a competence level, they are more likely to maintain their therapeutic gains. Therefore, it is often advisable to have clients review their coping skills and their skill training methods toward the end of therapy.

8. Although you can be quite directive and didactic during the first sessions of therapy, it is wise to encourage clients to take over themselves and assume greater activity and responsibility for their changing as therapy proceeds.

9. Rational-Emotive Behavior Therapy and Cognitive Behavior Therapy usually focus on clients' between-sessions activity, especially as therapy is coming to a close. This between-session activity helps clients maintain their therapeutic gains.

10. Don't forget to keep informing the clients during the sessions that they had better keep working at therapy during and after their sessions. It is their steady work and practice that helps them get better. If, moreover, they acquire a philosophy of commitment, they are likely to keep maintaining their gains.

CAVEATS AND CAUTIONS

1. Clients resist making therapeutic changes for various reasons at various times. Therefore, don't dogmatically assume that you clearly know why a given client resists and are sure what to do about his or her resistance.

2. Both you and your clients may be prime contributors to resisting. Remain open to this possibility.

3. Whatever your main theory of psychotherapy, don't assume that it fully explains and will help you deal effectively with every client's resistance. Explore possibilities as well that are not especially covered by your regular theory and practice.

4. If one cognitive, emotive, or behavioral technique doesn't help with a particular client, and he or she still seriously resists, try another technique. Experiment and use several methods, if necessary, with a single resisting client.

5. Persist! Just because your chosen methods of helping clients overcome resistance do not work for awhile, don't assume that they are totally ineffective and will never work. Keep persisting before you give up certain techniques.

6. If you think a client is resisting so much that it is almost impossible to resist this resisting and you are ready to abandon therapy with this individual, consider consulting with other therapists to check out your hypothesis and to consider their suggestions about how you might successfully continue. If this still does not work, then you may refer the client to another therapist.

7. If you have anxious, depressed, or self-downing feelings about your ability to reach resisting clients, check your Irrational *Beliefs* about yourself and your demands that you *must* be helpful to resistors. Work hard to surrender these beliefs, and if you don't succeed, consider going to therapy yourself for help.

8. Try to be honest with yourself about your therapeutic failures and about the limitations of psychotherapy in general. As I point out in the final chapters of the original and revised edition of *Reason and Emotion in Psychotherapy,* therapy has distinct limitations and shortcomings. Yes, all psychotherapy, including REBT and CBT! Don't be grandiose, but acknowledge the possible limitations of therapy and do not depreciate yourself because of your or psychotherapy's distinct limitations.

How to Choose Special Styles of Therapy for Different Clients

15

s noted previously in this book on *Overcoming Resistance,* REBT and CBT, especially when they are integrated with some of the other major forms of psychotherapy, have many techniques that you can use with your regular and resistant clients. But, as I also keep pointing out, each of your clients is a unique individual who may well require different methods, and also different styles and emphases when you use the same method.

Take the technique of Disputing one of your client's main Irrational *Beliefs,* for example. For individual clients, you may do this in a number of different ways. You may start Disputing in the first few sessions— or after you have built up rapport with the client for several sessions. You may do it strongly or weakly; indirectly or directly; by means of Socratic dialogue or by creative metaphors; calmly or emotionally; tactfully or head on; etc.

You may continue one style of Disputing with a given client, or you may keep changing it to fit the same client's varying moods; the stages of therapy he or she is in; how well the client is progressing; what Adversities keep occurring in his or her life; how much homework the client is doing; and in relation to several other variables that are occurring with the client.

You and the client have a wide choice of the particular techniques you can use, in what manner and style you use them, and whether they seem to be working or not working. Quite a choice! What is more, you and your client can change your choices; preferably should change them as therapy progresses—or doesn't progress! Your using flexibility in this regard is quite important.

What can you do to make these many possible choices? Several things:

- Start with the techniques and styles of presenting them that you have found effective with many of your clients much of the time.
- Watch your client closely to see how she responds to your starting techniques and styles. If you are reasonably active-directive with REBT and CBT methods, the ways in which clients respond to them—as I have noted for many years—will often provide you with a better diagnosis and prognosis than other assessment methods.
- However, your usual assessment methods will give you some indications how to start and to proceed with difficult clients, particularly those who have psychotic or severe personality disorders. So, use them, too, to check on what you think would be the best procedures to use with particular clients.
- Keep flexibly experimenting! None of your usual techniques and styles will work best for all your clients—especially the resistant ones. Some of your "best" methods will hardly work at all for some clients; and some of your "worst" procedures may be the only ones you can use effectively with certain difficult customers (DC's). Too bad! Now what are you going to flexibly try?
- Don't assume that because a favorite method does not work with a few of your clients, you should abandon it completely. It still may be effective for many or most other clients.
- Don't assume that because one of your unfavored procedures works with a difficult client, it will work with many other clients, too. Maybe it won't!

SOME CONTRADICTORY THERAPY PROCEDURES AND HOW THEY WORK WITH RESISTANT CLIENTS

As I noted in the previous section of this chapter, you may use some techniques and styles that seem rather contradictory. So, what should you try with what kind of clients? None are guaranteed to produce great results. But let me consider some of them and see how they can be used with integrated REBT and CBT procedures. I shall try to fairly present both sides in regard to opposing techniques but shall also present my prejudiced view of what I usually—and not always!—do with my own resistant clients.

Active-Directive and Less-Active-Directive Procedures

At the start of therapy, I am usually quite active-directive even with my difficult clients. I assume that 20% or 30% of them can quickly agree with the basic premises of REBT: that they have partly upset themselves, have importantly done so with their strong and persistent Irrational Beliefs, and that they can constructively reduce their disturbances by using their thinking, feeling, and acting processes. Because these clients are in trouble and because I think that they *may* be able to quickly diminish it, I start out quickly to show them REBT's ABC's of emotional-behavioral disturbance, and show them how to thoughtfully, emotively, and actively minimize their IB's.

With my slower-moving clients, and with those who first make fast progress and then return to their dysfunctional ways, I curb my own active-directive pace and become more passive. I listen more, push them encouragingly, perhaps reduce their homework, keep reassuring them that they can (with some hard work) keep changing, show them that change is indeed difficult for most people, fully accept their slow moving, and settle in for a longer haul. I may also coach them more and give them additional skill training and I particularly show them how to cope with and change bad environmental Adversities. With my more resistant clients, then, I am often less active-directive, more supportive, quite patient, and more giving of unconditional other-acceptance (UOA) than with my harder-working, more energetic clients (Ellis, 2001b; Leehy, 2001). I often persistently and patiently keep plugging away at their self-downing and low frustration tolerance until they start to feel USA and HFT. Even with my faster-moving clients, if they stay in therapy for ten sessions or more, my active-directive pace tends to slow down, and we keep persistently working for the consolidation and deepening of their initial changes. So, I modify various of my fast-moving active-directive methods with certain clients.

Didactic Teaching and Socratic Dialogue. There is a difference in REBT and CBT practitioners, as well as in therapists of some other modalities, as to whether it is best to use didactic teaching or Socratic dialogue with resistant (and other) clients. Most therapists, such as James Overholzer and Aaron Beck favor using Socratic dialogue, because it is presumably less directive and more collaborative then didactic teaching. However, I don't always go along with their recommendations, for several reasons:

- A Socratic interchange confuses some clients, especially those who are very anxious, have severe personality disorders, or are not too educated. They give vague answers to such questions as, "Why is a *must* or a *demand* more likely to make you disturbed than a preference?" "When you tell yourself that you can't stand your Mother-in-law's chatter, why is that statement false?"

- If Socratic dialogue is used too soon in therapy, many clients do not yet have sufficient knowledge of REBT and CBT to be able to come up with the correct answers to the therapist's questions. They would not be able to answer the question, "Why are you not a bad person if you kill somebody?" unless the therapist had previously shown them, quite didactically, that a "bad person" would only and always do bad things, now and in the future, therefore the term "bad person" is an inaccurate over-generalization.
- Some clients can only answer Socratic questioning correctly after they have been didactically taught a number of times what the answer is likely to be. Thus, if they are shown several times that drinking and smoking are pleasurable in the short-run but not in the long one, they may *then* be able sensibly to answer the Socratic question, "If drinking and smoking give you great pleasure, why should you preferably not indulge in them?"
- When your clients fail to give you accurate answers to your Socratic questions, they may easily think that they are "stupid," may feel ashamed of their "stupidity," and may avoid continuing to answer them.

Because of these limitations of Socratic questioning, I often use it sparingly, especially with clients who do not respond favorably. In my initial sessions, I give several fairly long lectures on the causes and cures of the clients' dysfunctional thinking, feeling, and behaving. I also recommend that my clients soon read the dozen pamphlets on REBT that we give them in their intake packet. I further recommend that they read some of our simpler books on REBT, such as *A Guide to Rational Living* (1997), and that they listen to some of our audio taped lectures on it.

When I think that my clients have fairly well comprehended the didactic presentations on how to use REBT, I then use a good deal of Socratic questioning to see whether they really understand what they are doing to make themselves disturbed and what they can think, feel, and act to significantly reduce their dysfunctioning. I also authoritatively answer their questions and throw in, from time to time, several brief therapeutic lectures. On the basis of much experience, I observe that this kind of combination of didactic teaching and Socratic questioning often works very well. As is usual with REBT, I use both/and instead or either/or.

Stressing the Dire Costs of Disturbed Behavior and the Great Benefits of Working to Overcome It. Some therapists try to help resistant clients by stressing the dire costs of their dysfunctional behavior (especially, drinking, drugging and smoking); and, almost contradictorily, other therapists try to motivate clients by stressing the great pleasures and joys they can achieve by resorting to constructive, self-fulfilling thoughts, feelings, and activities. Which of these procedures helped you better with resistant clients? Again, I would strongly say, "Both/and instead of either/or."

Frankly, right at the start of therapy, I often emphasize the decided penalties of my clients' continuing their destructive ways. Thus, I firmly (but not accusingly) said to one of my clients at the end of the first session, "You see. I've been trying to show you that it's not your taking an important and difficult test that makes you panicked, but your insistence, your demand that you *absolutely must* pass it well—in fact, *perfectly* well, one hundred percent well! Fat chance! I think I've briefly shown you that your *musts* are quite deadly—and that your profound belief that you *absolutely must not* be panicked is even deadlier. Those arrogant musts will screw you. In fact, I would be irresponsible if I did not tell you that if you stubbornly keep repeating those foolish musts to yourself—as you have been doing for the past twenty years—you will almost certainly suffer from panic for the next fifty or more that you live. Yes, 50 more years of misery—think of it! So it's your choice—to suffer from panic, wrought by your perfectionism, for the next many decades, or give up that foolish perfectionism, which you damned well can, and only rarely panic. Well, which choice are you going to make? Be my guest!"

Fortunately, my highlighting to this client the likely future results of his perfectionism and his panic about his panic worked. He determined to work at REBT and decrease his states of panic and he did so. I had no such luck however, with a number of other clients with whom I used this technique. So with some of them I tried a more optimistic approach.

For example, with Sally, a 37-year-old teacher, who in spite of her high intelligence and remarkably good looks, got nowhere in her quest for a suitable man because she fearfully picked "weaklings" who were not up to her level and then cravenly catered to them to prevent her being "eternally alone." She was, as I termed it years ago, a "love slob," who *absolutely needed* a man, or else she was "utterly worthless." After staying a year or two with unfulfilling men, she finally got up the guts to leave them—and to look for another basket case.

When I warned Sally that years of misery were ahead of her if she continued to be so desperately needy, my painting a grim picture of the future only partly worked. She half-decided to become less needy, but still resisted changing. Whereupon I took a more positive track and emphasized the fulfillment she could probably have if she more risk-takingly tried for the kind of men she really wanted.

"Look, Sally," I said. "You've picked several shnooky men for hus-
bands, and catered to them to no avail. Let's suppose that you now find
a stronger and more suitable man and risk his finding you undesirable.
But also let's suppose you hold your ground, refuse to cater to him too
much, and show him your strengths instead of your weaknesses. You
risk it indeed, but you place yourself in the path of finding a lasting
mate for the next 50 years or so. Nothing ventured, nothing gained—as
you have proven several times up to now. Instead of staying with a suc-
cession of inadequate men for a short period of time, you may well end
up with a long-term mate who is sensibly avoiding love slobs like you.
Make yourself non-needy and see!"

I kept showing Sally the potential joys of her future mated life, as
well as the strengths and pleasures she herself would experience, if she
scuttled her neediness and took the hard but rewarding road to being
her own person. My highlighting the future gains of changing herself,
rather than the future pains of remaining dependant, finally convinced
Sally to take the risks of non-neediness and to determinedly seek for
the special man she really wanted rather than a series of easily found
partners who were clearly not for her.

Moral: stressing the dire costs of your clients' inactivity will sometimes
prod them into healthy action. But so will stressing the real benefits of
their overcoming their inaction. Tactics that work with one resistant
client may hardly work with another; and sometimes your integrating
threatening with potentially beneficial scenarios may bring better
results than using either one of these tactics.

A Hardheaded and Gentle Approach to Religiosity and Spirituality.
Your taking a hardheaded approach to your clients religiosity and spirituality can consist of showing them there is no empirical evidence for
supernatural gods and spirits and that therefore their devout beliefs in
divine powers to help them with their emotional-behavior problems is
chimerical and detracts from their constructivist ability to help themselves. I took this hardheaded position some years ago and held that
devout religiosity and spirituality often did clients more harm than good.

In the last few years, I have largely abandoned this position. I now
see that devout faith in supernatural entities—in faith unfounded in
fact—is hardly always irrational or self-defeating, though it has some
hazards. Research has shown that when people believe in a kind and
loving God, rather than in a damning and punishing one they tend to be
mentally healthy.

Actually, faith in almost anything, however absurd it logically seems
to be, may sometimes lead to good results. Suppose, for example, a
person has severe recurrent depression and does not respond to any of

the regular types of therapy, including REBT, CBT, and medication. She, Mary, let us again suppose, meets a man, Dan, who convinces her, that he is buddy-buddy with the Devil and that he can arrange for her to be favored by the Devil, too. So Mary gullibly goes along with Dan and he introduces her to the Devil—or at least has the Devil talk with her by a special telephone connection. Mary has several conversations with the Devil—or with his phone voice—and he promises to help rid her of her depression and to provide her with an almost perfect husband and children.

Let us still suppose that Mary completely believes the Devil—or his voice she hears on the special phone—and looks forward to his fulfilling her great desire for a near-perfect husband and children. Although she has no direct contact with the Devil, and cannot be sure that Dan has such contact either, she devoutly believes that the Devil exists, that he is talking to her, and that he has the power to help her achieve her outstanding heart's desire.

I now ask: If Mary has this kind of devout faith, do you think that she would be considerably helped by it to alleviate her state of depression? Personally, I think that, at least for a while, she would become considerably less depressed. Why? Not because the Devil actually exists—for he most probably doesn't. Not because he has promised to help her. Not because he has the power that Dan says he has. No, not for any of these reasons—but because Mary has devout *faith* in the Devil, his power, and his agreement to help her achieve her greatest desire.

Faith, as Jerome Frank (Frank & Frank, 1991) has said for many years, is remarkable, and REBT sees its remarkable power and considerably uses it. For REBT hypothesizes—together with Epictetus and other constructivists—that unfortunately events (Adversities) do not by themselves upset people. Instead, it is these events plus their *view* of them. People's *beliefs,* says REBT and the other cognitive behavioral therapies contribute greatly to their disturbances—and, also, to their restructuring themselves to ameliorate their self-defeating thoughts, feelings, and behaviors.

But a belief, of course, is a form of faith. You believe something is true or false because you have faith or lack of faith in it. Faith may be founded on fact—as when you believe that the bridge you walk over is built according to the laws of physics and the competency of its architect. Or faith may be anti-factual as when you believe that you are a *total fool* who will *always* behave foolishly when you have merely committed a foolish act. REBT, like most psychotherapies, favors science and therefore promotes faith founded on fact, such as Mary's faith (or belief) that psychotherapy and medication may possibly help relieve her depression. It does not favor faith that is little bolstered by fact, such as Mary's faith (or belief) that there is a powerful Devil who agrees to help her and will definitely do so.

REBT and CBT, however, had better not ignore the fact that Mary's faith in the Devil's power and his willingness to use it to help her—which is most probably based on illusions—*can* help her to become less depressed. Whether or not there *is* a Devil who will help Mary is somewhat irrelevant to the point that if she solidly *believes,* has *faith* in, this empirically unvalidated "fact," she may well benefit from her faith.

Although I have personally been an atheist since the age of 12 and do not believe (have faith in) any supernatural phenomena, and although I also believe that devout faith in supernatural gods, devils, spirits, and other entities has led to considerable human harm for many centuries, I cannot deny that faith in supernatural and transcendental entities has brought many people emotional-behavioral benefits. As a scientist, I had better face the fact that what I personally think is faith in some highly questionable phenomena, has often helped disturbed people to think, feel, and believe in a healthier manner. I often wish that this anomaly did not exist. But quite apparently, it does.

My recent thinking gives a distinct place to faith founded in fact—*and* on some forms of faith unfounded in fact. As I have noted, the Judeo-Christian tradition, in which I was raised but no longer follow, has many philosophies that are similar to the main philosophies of REBT. I don't like the devoutness and rigidity with which many Jews and Christians subscribe to these tenets and would prefer less dogmatic versions of them. But even when religious dogma is firmly and devoutly held by Jews, Christians, and members of various other religions, it still can considerably aid mental health. In fact, as shown in the book, *Counseling and Psychotherapy with Religious Persons,* which I have co-authored with Stevan Nielsen and W. Brad Johnson (Nielsen, Johnson & Ellis, 2001), we show how certain specific Jewish, Christian, Muslim, other religious dogmas can be used by REBT and CBT practitioners with excellent therapeutic results.

As a therapist, you can still hold my former hardheaded attitude toward your clients' religious beliefs and try to help them become emotionally healthier on their own, without their relying upon any Higher Powers. But in many instances you can also use their mild and devout religious tenets to promote greater mental and emotional health.

For example, I had an orthodox Jewish client who had an enormous fear that deadly germs were everywhere and were going to destroy him and his family unless he engaged in "protective" obsessive-compulsive rituals (such as constant bathing and hand washing) that preoccupied much of his life. I convinced him that although God allowed some deadly germs to exist, He kept them in balance so that my client and his family could take reasonable precautions to cope with them. I used his faith in God as a protector rather than a destroyer of people to cut his OCD washing rituals down to moderate proportions.

Using a Forceful or a Calm Style of Therapy. As indicated throughout this book, REBT practitioners often use a forceful, dramatic, vigorous style of therapy—and I have personally favored this kind of style in my own individual and group sessions. Why? Because as I pointed out in chapter 6, clients, and particularly resistant ones, forcefully and emotionally hold on to their dysfunctional beliefs, feelings, and behaviors and if their therapists are meek, and mild—are "too rational"—they may fail to reach some clients. As I noted in 1956, IB's have strong emotional and behavioral components—hence REBT is cognitive, emotive, *and* behavioral.

Moreover, resistant clients frequently have to be *motivated* to change—which may involve their being practically *pushed, shoved, and persuaded* to do so. Hence the use of many REBT experiential and behavioral methods. But for a variety of reasons, force of this kind may not work with resistors. Thus:

- Some clients have *reactance* and feel that their freedom to be themselves is usurped by therapist pushing.
- Some clients feel "dominated" by a forceful therapist and "righteously" resist such "domination."
- Some clients like to win arguments with their therapists—yes, even at their own expense.
- Some clients are uncomfortable about responding adequately to their therapist's forceful interventions and therefore fail to respond or quit therapy.
- Some client's ostensibly agree to follow the therapist's forceful interventions but only passively and half-heartedly follow them.

For reasons such as these, I still start off by forcefully using some of the most useful REBT techniques—such as recommending rational emotive imagery for homework assignments. But if this fails with certain clients, I switch to slower-motion methods—such as calmly and repetitively teaching clients to do cost-benefit analyses of their hanging on to their dysfunctional behaviors. Frequently, however, I include both forceful and easy-going styles of REBT with the same clients at different times in their therapy sessions.

Stressing Individualistic and Socially Oriented Aspects of Therapy. To a large degree, psychotherapy has to be helpful to individualistic goals because most clients come to therapy because they *personally* suffer from unwanted thinking and feeling, and behaving and want to know how to relieve their individual suffering. Even those who have social problems—such as being rejected by other people—primarily want to know how they, as unique individuals, can get along better with other individuals groups. Few people come to therapy just because they see the suffering of others and want to discover how to help these others suffer less and enjoy living more!

Your clients—including your resistant ones—want you to help them to achieve less debilitating anxiety, depression, and other unhealthy feelings and to gain more of what they prefer. Fair enough—so you discover their special individual goals and try to help them achieve them.

Practically all therapies, however, also stress what Alfred Adler called social interest. For few clients enjoy isolations—and those that do rarely seek therapy. All of us, as Martin Buber especially pointed out, live with other humans (and often other animals); for fulfilling our lives greatly involves interpersonal and group-oriented relating. Most species and distinctly *social* animals, and certainly humans importantly are. Moreover, modern society makes it more important than ever for us. We cooperate economically and politically with other community members; and modern weapons, which are much more lethal than in the past yes, make it imperative that we not fight too much with the other.

As I indicated in the 1960s, and as many therapists are increasingly noting, if your clients fail to accept other people with their differences and uniqueness, they not only will easily upset themselves but will also damn others, make themselves hostile and uncooperative, and endanger their community (or the entire world). Therefore social interest and involvement is required for both personal functioning and for good community living. Some therapists even insist that there is really no other good alternative—good relationships with other humans are a real necessity for personal health and for continuation of the human species.

Assuming that you, as a therapist, favor your clients achieving a fair degree of social interest, how can you aid their doing so without seriously interfering with the main goal with which most of them come to therapy—their self-interest and their "selfish" individuality? Answer: you probably cannot bridge this gap perfectly but you can deal with it quite well if you recognize—as do REBT and several other systems of psychotherapy—that you can simultaneously encourage your clients to practice unconditional self-interest (USA) *together with* unconditional other-interest (UOA). These two practices, if you properly present them, are mutually reinforcing.

Carl Rogers said that if therapists firmly showed unconditional other acceptance to everyone, their clients would see its great value and therefore themselves adopt unconditional self-acceptance. Well, maybe! As I keep pointing out, *conditional* self-acceptance (CSA) is normally both innate and socially learned, and is usually so strong that when a therapist gives UOA to clients, they often conclude that he or she really favors them, and perhaps likes them, and that *therefore* they are okay persons who can accept themselves. But this is *conditional* and not *un*conditional self-acceptance! (Ellis, 2000, 2000a, 2000b, Ellis & Blau, 1998, Ellis & MacLaren, 1998).

The REBT solution to this important problem, which you are free to adopt or not adopt, is to have therapists teach their clients *both* USA (thus preserving their individualism) *and* to achieve UOA (thus encouraging their social interest). Again, if there is to be a case of both/and rather than either/or, this REBT approach seems to be it.

In actuality, USA and UOA seem to intrinsically *include* each other: Because when they are adults, people personally *choose* to live in a group or community—and rarely choose to be hermits. And in the course of their lives, some of their greatest satisfactions usually include caring for and being cared for by others. Practically all individuals are distinctly *social* creatures.

At the same time, social groups survive and thrive because they largely fulfill individuals' desires and goals. Where individuals are little satisfied and are too restricted in their goals and purposes, even strict dictatorships eventually go out of business and are replaced with rules that better satisfy wants of the populace.

Leeway to be oneself and to fulfill one's personal desires therefore interacts with and partially matches social interest. Although the two sometimes conflict with each other, if individuals and their communities do not considerably bolster each other considerable problems will occur. As human history has shown!

REBT hypothesizes that USA and UOA basically include an outlook or philosophy—namely, that all humans are fallible but are deserving of life and happiness in spite of their frequent mistaken and "wrong" acts. Their thoughts, feelings, and behaviors can be judged as "bad" when they sabotage their personally chosen goals and purposes; and may also be judged as "immoral" when they sabotage the social rules of the community in which they reside. But none of their behavior is absolutely "good" or "bad" in itself, under all circumstances at all times. Their value or worth as a whole *person* cannot be accurately judged by their specific behaviors because, first (as already noted) they are very fallible and therefore have to commit *some* "bad" acts; and second, they are complex and variable people who inevitably enact many "good" and many "bad" behaviors. Therefore, as Alfred Korzybski sagely observed, they cannot *be* either "good" or "bad" *persons*. They can easily think that they *are* "wonderful" or "damnable," but sadly mistaken. If they *were* wonderful, they would always live perfect or heavenly lives; and if they *were* damnable, they would always lead totally hellish existences. If they say "I *am* what I do" they are overgeneralizing.

REBT therefore views no humans as super humans or as subhumans. It not only gives all clients unconditional other-acceptance—or what Carl Rogers called unconditional positive regard; but it actively and persistently encourages them to give it to themselves. Doing so, they may still rate their thoughts, feelings, and behaviors as "good" and "bad" and may strive to improve them—thus aiding their getting more of what they want and less of what they do not want. But they work at never devaluing or damning their *selves,* their *personhood* when they behave "badly." For if they consider their *totality* "worthless" how are they going to be able to help this "worthless" and "inadequate" self to change its ineffectual ways? Not easily!

Even if clients commit "bad" or "immoral" acts against other people, they see these behaviors as "wrong" and they may be shunned by other people and penalized for their antisocial deeds. But REBT holds that they are not to be devalued or damned as *persons* for their unethical acts. For if they were really totally damnable, how could they possibly change and behave more normally in the present and future. That would be a neat trick!

As can be seen by what I have just said, the philosophical positions of USA and UOA are closely related. If both these important attitudes are held and followed by your clients, they may well strive for their individual and somewhat unique preferences and avoid their personal dislikes; and they will then be unique individuals in their own right—each one different from other individuals. So they will tend to achieve what Carl Jung called indivination and self-actualization.

At the same time, clients who are influenced by REBT attitudes will "rationally" and responsibly live and let live and not seriously sabotage the desires of other members of their community. In fact, they will probably often help others get more of what they want and less of what they dislike. Again: live and let live!

How about your clients loving other people? Will having unconditional other-acceptance necessarily help them be more loving to other people? No, not necessarily. Acceptance doesn't mean caring. UOA means harm-avoidance, but not necessarily specific affection for others. Actually, we tend to *like and love* people that have what we (prejudicedly) consider "good" traits. But we can unconditionally *accept* all people, even when they have what we personally consider "bad" traits. We don't hate or despise *them* but we may easily dislike many of their *behaviors*. Quite a difference!

As a therapist, you can give UOA, so that your clients—especially your self-hating ones-will appreciate it and perhaps model after you and give it to themselves; and you also can actively teach them to respect others, even when they abhor some of their actions. Similarly, you can assume that the great majority of your clients are prone to accept themselves conditionally—that is, when they behave well and win the approval of others—and that they have been born and reared to be almost allergic to achieving *un*conditional self-acceptance. Therefore, you model it *and* actively and persistently teach its virtues to your clients. Yes, you *stress* its importance for mental, emotional, and behavioral health. Moreover, you assume that many—indeed probably most—of your clients, even when they acknowledge how important USA is still haven't the foggiest idea how to achieve it. So, you active-directively can show them REBT's two favorite ways to get USA, or any of the other ways that other systems of therapy may employ. You keep assessing, by checking your clients feelings and actions as well as their thoughts, how accurately and strongly they "get" UOA; and when you find they hold it only partly and lightly, you firmly—not blamefully!—return to teaching it to them, sometimes again and again!

To sum up what I have said in this chapter, you have many possible styles of trying to help your resistant clients stop blocking their going through the often difficult task of changing themselves. By all means use the styles that you feel comfortable using, enjoy using, and have practiced using. But use your style unrigidly. Check your results, of course, and consider modifying some of your habitual styles. But even when you like your favorite ways and are convinced that they *generally* work, when you come up against stubborn resisters, watch it. Yes, they often have their own agenda and their own rebellion against changing. But don't you possibly have your own stick-in-the-mudness, too? Honestly, investigate whether you do.

Think about it! Maybe the style you are choosing is good—even excellent—for most of your clients most of the time. But for *all* of them? Consistently?

Maybe you'd better loosen up—especially with some of your *real* difficult customers (DC's). Try, at least tentatively, a different style or two. Experiment. Risk some discomfort. Surprisingly, your rarely used therapeutic styles may actually work with client Z even when they were usually ineffective when you used then, with clients A to Y. So now try something different with Z, while you keep generally using your tried and true styles with A to Y. Client Z, of course, may still be resistant—in fact, nothing that you do may help him or her change. But what have you got to lose by trying? Only your self-shackling chains!

How to Integrate REBT and CBT Theory and Practice with the Useful Aspects of Other Leading Schools of Therapy

16

L ong before psychotherapy integration became popular in the 1980s, REBT promoted integration and, to some degree, selective eclecticism. It was the first major therapy to be both heavily cognitive and behavioral, since the other popular cognitive behavioral therapies (CBT's) were devised ten or more years after I started REBT in 1955. Aaron Beck (1976), William Glasser (1999), Donald Meichenbaum (1977), Albert Bandura (1997), Michael Mahoney (1974) and other proponents of CBT published their own versions of it sometime after I had already published a number of widely read articles and books on REBT (Ellis, 1957a, 1957b, 1957c, 1958, 1962).

Moreover, REBT espoused several forceful and vigorous methods of Disputing clients' Irrational Beliefs during its first years and kept adding emotional and experiential exercises in the late 1950s and early 1960s. Arnold Lazarus, after he added cognitions to behavior therapy in the 1960s, also went on to create multimodal therapy (MMT) (Lazarus, 1997). So REBT and MMT seem to be the pioneering cognitive-emotive-behavioral therapies, though a few unusual therapists like those Alexander Herzberg (1945) and Andrew Salter were ahead of them in some respects in the 1940s.

REBT's goal of integrating many different kinds of therapeutic procedures in its theory and practice stemmed from my being trained in graduate school in Rogerian methods; and then, after I received my Ph.D. in 1947, I was trained in psychoanalysis and practiced it for six years. I also trained myself in active-directive, eclectic therapy, for several years. I adopted many techniques from articles and books on psychotherapy in the course of writing two monographs, *New Approaches* to *Psychotherapy Techniques* (1955a) and *Psychotherapy Techniques for Use with Psychotics* (Ellis, 1955b). So in formulating REBT, I incorporated what I thought were the most effective therapy methods used by many systems of therapy.

Psychotherapy that is purely eclectic, as Arnold Lazarus has pointed out for many year, includes contradictory principles and practices. REBT often eclectically chooses certain techniques that seem to work well with different clients—especially, with resisting clients. But it includes some solid theories about the origins of human disturbances and the more effective ways of treating them. As noted in this book, REBT is constructivist, it sees absolutistic *should* and *must* Beliefs as harmful, and it encourages therapists to help clients achieve USA, UOA, and ULA (unconditional life-acceptance or high frustration tolerance). It especially investigates clients' inflexible, rigid, absolutistic thoughts, feelings and actions, clearly reveals them, tries to show clients exactly how they *choose* to disturb themselves, how they can choose healthier pathways, and how to internalize and habituate themselves to more effective techniques and principles for the rest of their lives. REBT theorizes that they then become constructively *self-therapizing* and can largely dispense with their therapist.

While I was training myself and being trained in several therapeutic methods. I also saw that most of them, if rigidly and exclusively practiced, lead to some good and also some dubious results. Thus, I saw that Rogerian therapy had some excellent principles—especially that of giving clients unconditional other acceptance; but I also saw that it was too passive, unrealistically optimistic, and lacking behavioral homework. I saw that classical psychoanalysis was also too passive; that it was unbehavioral; that it was too past-oriented; and that it placed much too much faith in client's insights easily leading to remarkable change. I saw that Gestalt therapy had many useful experiential methods but that cathartic release and "real" awareness were often useful to disturbed people but were far from sufficient in helping them to modify their irrational philosophies and dysfunctional behaviors. Consequently, I have opposed these kinds of therapies when they are practiced in orthodox or pure forms with practically all clients. I have considered them, to say the least, highly inefficient and often harmful to many clients.

I especially point out in my book *Feeling Better, Getting Better, and Staying Better,* that classical person-centered, psychoanalytic, and Gestalt therapy, not only lack elements that might appreciably help many people if they were included; but I also show that they often palliatively help clients feel better *instead* of get better. Thus, all three of these therapies, along with several other forms of psychological treatment, provide clients with a good friend who obviously is interested in them and cares for them. But they concentrate so heavily on the relationship between the therapist and client and thereby provide good vibes for the latter, that they frequently sidetrack her or him from working very hard—and persistently—at devising and practicing new helpful philosophies and actions. In other words, some forms of therapy make individual and group sessions themselves, so enjoyable, supportive, and full of feeling that they distract clients from their basic purpose in getting therapy—namely, minimizing their mental-emotional (and perhaps physical) pain in their present and future lives.

Be that as it may, practically all major systems of therapy have some useful principles and methods. So REBT tries to integrate some of these into its own unique helpful teachings and relationships. Here is how you may practice REBT and CBT and integrate them with other leading schools of treatment.

INTEGRATING REBT AND CBT WITH PSYCHOANALYTIC METHODS

REBT often favors the psychoanalytic rule of uncritically listening to clients. It doesn't let this listening go on interminably but encourages clients to relatively *briefly* tell their woes, particularly their present troubles. You, as the therapist, if you practice REBT or CBT, do not doubt your clients' narration but assume that much of it is accurate and show that your clients really have had and are still having a rough time with relatives, friends, bosses, and colleagues. You thereby, partly show your clients that even if you fully acknowledge that unfortunate things *have* happened to them, they had a *choice* in the past, and particularly in the present and future, to unhealthily upset themselves *about* these real Adversities—or to take them, much more healthfully, in stride.

So you can encourage gruesome narrations, as in psychoanalysis or narrative therapy, while you show clients how they could have reacted differently to them in the past—and particularly how to stop awfulizing about Adversities now and tomorrow. At the same time, you fully allow and encourage catharsis of old and new intense feelings, not just to let them be abreactively dissipated, as in psychoanalysis and other therapies that stress abreaction; but to show your clients how to think about and cope with disruptive emotions in a more constructive manner. Combing REBT in this manner with psychoanalysis has been done by Paul Meehl (1962) since he first read my writings on REBT in 1960.

As in psychoanalysis, you may use REBT and CBT to encourage your clients to bring our their "natural" and "perverted" sex thoughts and feelings to show them that even their "perverted" indulgences are amazingly widespread and "normal." You can be much more liberal than classical psychoanalysts, however, in that you do not arbitrarily call certain sex acts, like satisfying a woman clitoraly instead of through "normal" penile-vaginal intercourse, "perverted" or "abnormal." Unlike psychoanalysts, you also do not hold that sex leads to neurosis, but instead show clients that dysfunctional Beliefs lead to neurosis, including various kinds of sexual dysfunctioning.

REBT agrees with psychoanalyses, that some clients repress their gruesome, painful and "shameful" thoughts and experiences and refuse to remember and face them because they would denigrate themselves if they did so and because they think it is *too* painful to remember them. But instead of using free association or dream analysis to get at repressed feelings, both of which tend to be inefficient, you can use the REBT method of helping your clients to achieve unconditional self-acceptance, which directly attacks their repressed (and nonrepressed) feelings of shame and self-downing about practically *anything*. You can use REBT's shame-attacking exercises in this respect. At the same time, you can help your clients overcome their awfulizing and low frustration tolerance by showing them that remembering and facing painful experiences is indeed *uncomfortable,* but not *awful* and *horrible.* Moreover, by doing so, they will truly be able to live with them and stop obsessing about their "horror."

REBT also agrees with the psychoanalytic theory that many thoughts, feelings and behaviors are automatic and unconscious. But you can use REBT to show your clients that most unconscious thoughts and feelings are just below the level of conscious and not deeply hidden or repressed, as the psychoanalysts contend. Thus, when your clients are phobic about elevators, trains, or germs and they say they are unaware or unconscious of any thoughts that create these phobias, you can show them that they have unconscious musturbatory *Beliefs*—such as "I have a high degree of probability that no disaster will befall me if I ride in an elevator or train (or am in contact with some germs); but I *must* have a *perfect guarantee* that nothing dreadful will happen to me and since I can't have such a guarantee, I am *absolutely certain* that disaster will occur." Using REBT, you are pretty sure that your clients have *shoulds* and *musts* behind their anxiety, depression and rage, and if they are unconscious of these imperatives, you can easily figure them out yourself and with a few leading questions make your clients aware of their "deeply unconscious" horrifying thoughts.

Freudian theory holds that people's libidinal and death drives make people disturbed, which are quite dubious assumptions. But you can use, the more practical ego psychology hypothesis of Heinz Hartmann,

Ernest Kris, Erich Fromm, Harry Stack Sullivan, Karen Horney, Heinz Kohut, and other neo-Freudians—who were really neo-Adlerians—to help them see how ego problems, or self-depreciation, importantly lead to their disturbances.

Analysts emphasize transference and countertransference issues very strongly, reveal them to clients, and analyze them in detail. I have found this, even when I practiced psychoanalysis, to be too much of a "good" thing. But Freud, without quite realizing it, was on to something potentially valuable in his transference theories. For when a woman loves her father and transfers her love to her analyst, she is often inaccurately overgeneralizing. Her father may have some similar traits. So, she falls in love with her analyst—most of whose traits are probably quite *un*like those of her father. As Alfred Korzybski noted (1933/1991), overgeneralization is exceptionally common with humans, and leads to considerable misperception and disturbance.

Instead, then, of your obsessively (and probably fruitlessly) analyzing the transference and countertransference relationships between you and your client, you can more beneficially look at your clients and their tendencies to overgeneralize. Thus, your clients may love you or hate you because you resemble their father or mother in certain ways. If so, you can show them their strong tendency to incorrectly overgeneralize and to follow their early prejudices. You can also show your clients that you, too, may be attracted to them because you are overgeneralizing and following some of your early prejudices. But that hardly means that you are going to marry them or get rid of them as clients. Your goal is to minimize your overgeneralizations and narrow prejudices—and you hope they do the same!

INTEGRATING REBT AND CBT WITH ADLERIAN METHODS

The theory of REBT was distinctly influenced by Adlerian formulations—as were the theory of several neo-Freudian therapies that, as I mentioned in the previous section of this chapter, were largely neo-Adlerian. In one of my early papers on REBT, which was published in the Adlerian *Journal of Individual Psychology* (Ellis, 1957c), I showed how REBT and Adlerian principles significantly overlap. In one of his first books, *What Life Should Mean to You*, Adler wrote that our "meanings are not determined by situations, but we determine ourselves by the meanings we give to situations." His motto was *Omnia ex expinione suspense sunt*—everything depends on opinion. Right on!—as Epictetus would have said 2,000 years ago, and I say today. Because I follow this

Adlerian view, I have been a dues paying member of The National Society for Adlerian Psychology for over 30 years.

Some of the main propositions of Adlerianism that can be continually merged with REBT philosophies and methods include these:

- All behavior occurs in a social context. So, along with enlightened individual interest, you can encourage your clients to have deep-seated social interest—which in REBT terms is called unconditional other-acceptance (UOA).
- The life of people consists largely of their *chosen* goals—and is not a *being* but a *becoming*.
- To understand clients, you had better understand their *cognitive organization* and *lifestyle*.
- People do many "good" and "bad" acts—and you can help your client see that they and others are *not* good or bad *persons*.
- You can teach your clients that their anxieties do not notably stem from their libidinous urges but from their self-created *inferiority feelings* about sexual and nonsexual performances.
- Clients if you follow Adlerian principles, can be helped to overcome their feelings of inadequacy and also to strive for pleasurable self-realization and self-actualization.
- Adlerian methods are not merely useful for clients but can be successfully used by parents and teachers for child guidance.

In using REBT and CBT with regular and resistant clients, you can integrate into your methodology with the forgoing highly compatible Adlerian attitudes and practices.

INTEGRATING REBT AND CBT WITH JUNGIAN METHODS

Carl Jung was an unusual personality and a brilliant personality theorist, who I often find to be quite mystical and quite addicted to overgeneralizing. I have found that resistant clients—and particularly those with severe personality disorders—easily glorify his use of symbolism and archetypal images, and become more confused and disorganized than they were before they started Jungian therapy. So, I use some Jungianism with distinct reservations. Jung's hypotheses are often fascinatingly inventive, but not necessarily therapeutic!

You can use some aspects of Jungianism, however, and blend them with REBT and CBT Methods. Such as these principles:

- You can show your clients that people's quest for meaning and purpose are often much stronger than their libidinous "drives."
- Clients can be shown how to achieve holistic *individuation*—to reclaim their undeveloped and unused parts of themselves and to fulfill these aspects of their lives more completely.
- You can acknowledge the Jungian teaching that self-actualization is a very important and often neglected aspect of therapy. As you help your clients to be less disturbed, you can also encourage them to find goals and interests that are uniquely pleasurable and fulfilling and to broaden the meanings of their lives.
- You can use creative therapy, as Jung recommended, by including dance, art, and music therapy and other aspects of artistic involvement in your techniques. New effective philosophies that may help your clients can be incorporated in artistic and dramatic exercises.

INTEGRATING REBT AND CBT WITH PERSON-CENTERED METHODS

REBT, as I have been emphasizing throughout this book, strongly favors Carl Rogers' method of unconditionally accepting clients—especially those with personality disorders—just as they are, warts and all. This is possibly because Paul Tillich was one of Rogers' teachers when he studied at Union Theological Seminary; and I was greatly influenced by Tillich's book, *The Courage to Be* when it first was published in 1953. Tillich, though sexually profligate, was a good Christian in many ways, especially by endorsing the philosophy of accepting sinners in spite of their sins. Both Rogers and I highly endorsed this view.

REBT therefore strongly supports unconditional other-acceptance (UOA) and unconditional self-acceptance (USA). But having less faith than Rogers in most people's ability to easily achieve UOA, REBT gives it, models it, and especially *teaches* it—as Rogers did not. It agrees with Rogers that UOA and USA—as I pointed out in the previous chapter—interrelate and tend to reinforce each other. So it favors both kinds of unconditional acceptance.

Rogers also emphasized the value of the therapists being empathic, honest, congruent, open, and flexible, along with their fully accepting their clients. "Fine!" you will say, if you practice REBT and CBT. Your openness, congruence, and empathy will enhance your relationship with your clients and encourage them to be open and flexible themselves.

REBT and CBT however, are skeptical of Rogers' claim that your honesty and openness with your clients comprise the *necessary* and *sufficient* conditions for therapy. If you think about it, you will probably acknowledge that some clients—perversely?—improve when some of the open conditions Rogers strongly supported don't exist; and, indeed, quite a few people, including some resistant ones, significantly improve without a fine relationship with any therapist or therapeutic group—that is, they distinctly benefit from self-help materials. In fact, I dare say that many more people have improved their mental and emotional health by reading Rogers' (1961) book, *On Becoming a Person* than have been helped by many sessions with person-centered therapists!

Be that as it may, if you practice some important aspects of REBT and CBT, you can integrate them with person-centered therapy in the following ways:

- Fully recognize your clients' self-actualizing and constructivist abilities and steadily encourage them to extensively and intensively use them.
- Be as open, as listening, and as empathic to your clients as you can be; but also try to understand and empathize with their dysfunctional Beliefs that usually lie behind and help create their disturbed feelings. Figure out what their IBs are, check to see if you are accurate, and reveal them to your clients, so that they can recognize them and see for themselves how they lead to their disturbances. Try to be as REBT recommends, *doubly* empathic in this recognition.
- See that behavior change largely evolves from *within* the client, as well as partly from external conditions. Encourage your clients to strongly *want* to change, to be *determined* to change, to know that they *can* change, and to *push themselves* to think, feel, and act at changing.
- Your clients' close and trusting relationship with you will not by itself *make* them healthy, but your pronounced faith in and your mentoring of their constructive tendencies will frequently help them see that they *can* creatively change and that your expertise can *abet* their doing so. Your caring for them and encouraging their healthy motives to change can add to and reinforce their motivation to do so.
- Keep your clients mainly immersed in their *present* experiencing—including their close relationship with you and their *now* experiencing. Help them be more *aware* of what they feel. But also show them that you have great faith in their ability to live more fully in the *future*.
- Realistically recognize and help your clients see that they can function much *more* fully than they have been doing. But do not

unrealistically and romantically urge them to become *fully* self-actualizing people. Keep in mind, also, the possible conflict between their *fully* functioning for themselves and their also acquiring real *social* interest.

INTEGRATING REBT AND CBT
WITH GESTALT THERAPY METHODS

Fritz Perls (1969), like Carl Jung, had his own emotional problems, and was often hostile and unable to relate well with some of his clients—as he himself has noted. But his Gestalt Therapy is in many respects uniquely present-centered, quite active-directive, very experiential, and particularly oriented to clients' making themselves aware of—and undefensive about—their personal feelings. Gestalt therapy has its distinct hazards and can—like all extremist therapies—do as much harm as good, especially to resistant clients who have severe personality disorders. So, if you use it, I again warn: Do so with proper caution!

Many experiential and awareness-raising Gestalt therapy techniques, however, can be quite useful: so if you want to employ them with your resistant clients, you can integrate the following Gestalt therapy principles with REBT and CBT methods:

- By all means help your clients to be more aware of their feelings—especially, of feelings of guilt, shame, and self-downing that they may defensively suppress from their awareness. But also help make them much more aware of their Beliefs and behaviors that accompany and partly create their feelings. Their becoming more aware of their feelings and experiencing may well help them change themselves for healthier encountering. But awareness of their irrational thinking, which Gestalt theory often neglects, may be even *more* helpful!
- Gestalt therapy stresses that no one has a purely *objective* perspective on reality—as does constructivist, experiential, and Rational Emotive Behavior therapy. Show your clients that the way they see external events and their own behaviors include very subjective *biases* and are not always factual. Awareness of their own *biased* perceptions is important to self-change.
- Gestalt therapy holds that personal growth manly involves conscious awareness of people's present existence, including how they are affected by and how they affect others. REBT and CBT not only agree with this theory, but also help train clients to make

themselves consciously aware of intrapersonal and interpersonal feelings and to work for more effective methods of *improving* them. REBT and CBT therefore overlap with Interpersonal therapy (IP) by analyzing clients' relationships with the therapist and with other people and specifically showing them how to improve these relationships. *Action* about personal and interpersonal affect is thereby added to *awareness*. This particularly goes for resistant clients who often have serious problems in their interpersonal relations.

- Gestalt therapy tries to help clients become aware of their awareness. REBT and CBT specifically does this by helping them *think* about their awareness, to *assess* how effective it is, and to think about their thinking—which in large part is what awareness is.
- Gestalt therapy promotes an I-thou relationship in therapy and encourages therapists and clients to *work together* to co-direct their sessions. As noted throughout this book, REBT notably encourages both unconditional other-acceptance (UOA) and unconditional self-acceptance (USA)—so that its clients importantly collaborate to support each other and also to unconditionally (and unhostilely) accept other people *outside* of therapy. Again, like CBT, it provides problem-solving training in this respect.
- Gestalt therapy holds that therapists as well as clients can change themselves as they become truly aware of their feelings. Correct. I have particularly found, in using REBT and CBT, that clients are definitely helped—as scores of outcome studies show. But I also find that many therapists, as they persuade their clients to ameliorate their dysfunctional thoughts, feelings, and behaviors, also work at revising their own lives. They consciously and unconsciously say to themselves, "Let me face it. Just as my clients are largely creating their own disturbances and I am showing them how to uncreate them, I often do something similar. So let me look at *my* self-defeatism and use some of the same techniques that I use with clients to effectively work on myself." Consequently, after REBT and CBT trainees have spent some years showing their clients how to improve, I often note that they, too, are considerably less disturbed than they were before they became therapists. The Gestalt therapy notion that client and therapists interaction helps both of these participants to become truly aware of their feelings and to use this awareness to help each other is well borne out by REBT and CBT practitioners.
- Gestalt therapy sees people *in* their environment—*in* the external field in which they live. This gibes with the REBT concept that heredity *and* social learning, external Adversities (A) *times*

people's internal Beliefs and feelings (B) *equal* their behavioral Consequences (C). Gestalt therapy says much of the same thing—that disturbed people had better work on their internal perceptions *and* on the external field in which they reside in order to significantly change.

- Gestalt therapy, like constructivists and existential therapy, says that people are inherently *self*-regulating. Epicurus and Epictetus said the same thing; and REBT is fundamentally a *choice* therapy—as is William Glasser's cognitive-behavioral choice therapy. So REBT and CBT supplement Gestalt Therapy in this respect.
- Resistance, as some Gestalt therapists say, is a crucially important expression of the organism's integrity. But this is exactly what REBT says—that resistance is *natural* to humans and defends them against too abrupt and too risky changing (Ellis, 2001b). In a sense, resistance is "normal" and not "abnormal," and is widespread in many forms. You can help clients, and they can help themselves, to become less resisting by their being fully *aware,* of their *natural* proclivity to resist change and by seeing how "normal" this is.
- The only goal of Gestalt Therapy is awareness, Gary Yontef and Lynne Jacobs state. REBT and CBT practitioners would consider this an extreme, overgeneralized statement. But if you choose and their *multimodal* procedures with your regular and resistant clients, combined with Gestalt Therapy's awareness emphasis, you may help them to make unmiraculous changes.

INTEGRATING REBT AND CBT
WITH EXISTENTIAL THERAPY

REBT, as I said in *Reason and Emotion in Psychotherapy,* largely accepts the concepts and goals of the modern existentialists, such as Soren Kierkegaard, Martin Heidegger (1953), Jean Paul Sartre (1968), Martin Buber (1984), Paul Tillich (1953), and Robert Hartman (1967). It is somewhat skeptical, however, of the existential therapy of Rollo May and Irvin Yalom (2000) because they think that because people are innately free to choose their own destiny they can *easily* choose to be their existential selves and unfetter their acquired self-defeating limitations.

A noble philosophy!—but not exactly realistic. Yes, humans have a great deal of *potential* freedom—but they have to work damned hard to achieve it. They are naturally free—and also partly bound. They can mainly choose what to do and not to do—but they have their childhood training, their later-social learning, and their habituation tendencies to encourage them to make one choice instead of another—and even to stubbornly stay with behaviors that have been proven to be largely useless or handicapping. Consequently, their choices and the implementation of their choices are far from entirely free!

Existential therapists, therefore, can show their clients the possibilities of their making choices and changes, but unless they actively encourage them to keep working at changing, many clients—I would say the majority—will only sporadically do so. REBT realistically merges existential therapy with active-directive teaching and mentoring. It often *pushes* clients to take the freedom that they theoretically have and actively *use* it. Its famous PYA (Push Your Ass) slogan frequently has to be *sold* to clients before they will follow it and thereby *create* better thoughts, feelings, and behaviors to help themselves. Active-directive persuasion and instruction is (paradoxically) included in the REBT main therapy techniques.

In addition, REBT integrates the usual existential therapy theories and practices into its procedures. For example:

- REBT accepts the existential position that anxiety is a normal part of human existence, since all humans have to face considerable dangers and frustrations. Unless they are seriously *concerned* about how to deal with them, they can hardly survive. Their *existential concern*—or moderate anxiety—keeps them alive and kicking. It is when they are *over*-concerned, or see hassles and problems as *too much* to bear, that they become *neurotically* anxious. Then REBT (and some existential therapy) shows them that they are irrationally commanding that life's difficulties *absolutely must not exist* and thereby *making* themselves neurotics. REBT also shows them that they can *decide* to minimize their self-neuroticizing.
- Existential therapy indicates that people's capacity to transcend immediate (and future) unfortunate situations is *given,* as Irvin Yalom shows, in the ontological nature of being human; that people therefore can choose to use it. REBT agrees; but it also realistically shows that the human capacity to choose self-defeating behavior is also *given,* and that clients (and others) had better acknowledge and strongly choose to *resist* this aspect of "human nature." As a therapist, you had better acknowledge *both* these natural existentialist tendencies.
- Irvin Yalom and Rollo May (2000) state that person—centered therapy, "is not fully existential in that it does not confront the patient directly and firmly." REBT and CBT heartily agree. In fact, they go further and hold that unless you, as a therapist, *directly and firmly* show your clients the error of their ways, and *also*

show them some practical cognitive, emotional, and behavioral methods of *changing* their self-defeatism, they will again be "free" to change, but often will refuse to do so. Especially your resistant clients!

- Existential "truth" depends on individual clients existing in a given situation—the external world—at a given period of time. "Truth" is therefore relativistic rather than absolutistic. This is also the liberal postmodern philosophy that REBT partly holds. Absolute truth, which is true under all conditions at all times and places, doesn't seem to exist. Preferences—"I prefer to perform well at this time and place under these conditions "are reasonable human goals. But absolutistic musts—"I have to perform well under all conditions at all times and places"—are overgeneralizations that only supernatural "humans" can ever achieve. So REBT opposes absolution and favors probalistic and preferential goals and values, thus overlapping with existential therapy.
- Existential therapy holds that the human desire to have meaning is very powerful even though the world itself may have no intrinsic meaning. REBT agrees and also indicates that the creation of meaning considerably adds to life. It therefore favors you helping your clients to achieve a vital absorbing meaning or purpose that will enhance their lives and lead to greater self-actualization (Ellis & Harper, 1997).
- Existential Therapy deals with the most fundamental concerns *now* facing clients REBT and CBT also do. REBT particularly emphasizes helping clients to achieve a profound, meaningful philosophy—especially a preferential instead of a musturbatory ideology—that will help them cope adequately, without panic, with their most fundamental concerns, such as death, freedom, isolation, and meaningless.
- As in person-centered therapy, practitioners of existential therapy strive to be *fully present* with their clients and to achieve authentic, open encounter with them. REBT and CBT professionals strive for similar client-therapist relationships; but they also honestly acknowledge that their knowledge of human disturbance and its amelioration is usually more comprehensive than their clients' understanding. They therefore do not hesitate to explore with clients the specific use of many cognitive and emotive methods that regular existential therapists may neglect. At the same time, they are prone to encourage clients to take various homework assignments, where existential therapists may not suggest because they are not very behavioral.

INTEGRATING REBT AND CBT
WITH MULTIMODAL THERAPY (MMT)

Arnold Lazarus' (1997) Multimodal Therapy (MMT) is one of the main Cognitive Behavior therapies. Lazarus was one of the leading behavior therapists and in the 1950s actually coined the term Behavior Therapy. But in the late 1960s he began to see that cognition was very important, after he had taken a workshop with me on REBT in San Francisco. Being quite original and creative, Lazarus not only formulated one of the main Cognitive behavior therapies; but he also made sure that it included practically all the important aspects of therapy. Thus, where REBT was the first major system to emphasize cognition, emotion, and behavior, he went further and originated the BASIC ID of psychological treatment. B stands for Behavior, A for Affect, S for Sensation, I for Imagery, C for Cognition, I for Interpersonal Relationships and D for Drugs or Biological Aspects of Disturbance. So, although REBT definitely deals with all these seven problem areas under its three major headings, MMT is a little more specific in some respects. But Lazarus agrees that just as thinking, feeling, and behaving are all holistically integrated, as I noted in my first paper on REBT in 1956, all fields of personality described in the BASIC ID also inevitably affect and are connected with each other (Lazarus, 1997).

The main points of MMT that can be integrated with REBT and CBT include these:

- Some clients, and especially resistant ones, are more heavily inclined to and benefit from specific Modalities of the BASIC ID than your other clients. Therefore, you had better assess their personality and emphasize, with these particular clients, those modalities to which they are most likely to respond.
- MMT is largely a self-actualization or educational model of therapy and therefore, like REBT and CBT, you can use it with considerable direct teaching.
- MMT, again like REBT, has many specific therapeutic techniques. You can differentially apply these to clients with specific psychological problems—such as phobias or compulsions—with whom your general therapy techniques might not be as effective. You can also use some of the specific methods of MMT with resistant clients who are often unusual types of individuals.
- If you meticulously inquire, with each of your clients, into each modality of the BASIC ID you may uncover elements of behavior

that elude general diagnostic categories that you commonly employ. You may thereby turn up a useful, unique method of treatment for some of your clients.

- MMT, like REBT, is not just eclectic since it basically follows a social learning theory that includes general propositions about disturbed behavior. Like REBT, it eclectically uses several specific therapy techniques, in accordance with the unique problems of individual clients. But it also has a general theory of human disturbance and treatment that you may find useful.

- MMT uses *bridging,* a procedure in which you, as the therapist, deliberately tune in *first* to your client's preferred modality and *later* branch off into dimensions that seem likely to be more productive. Somewhat similarly, as an REBT practitioner, I first deal with what my clients are most distressed about *right now.* I relate this to some basic REBT principles, and then later may go into what I think are the clients' basic disturbances.

- MMT usually starts with a *Tracking Order* or *Firing Order* emphasizing the modalities that clients are primarily fixed upon, but you need not make these firing orders rigid procedures. REBT, too, has no fixed order in which the clients cognitive, emotional, and behavioral aspects of their disturbance *have to be* addressed. Whatever aspect of their disturbances you start from, you soon show them that its thinking, feeling, and behaving aspects are interrelated and that all three basic modalities are involved in the creation and maintenance of their symptoms.

- MMT teaches clients, cognitively, how to find and Dispute their Irrational Beliefs that lead to their emotional and behavioral difficulties and also works out with the clients rational coping self-statements that help provide a more effective and less disturbed outlook on life. You may therefore use MMT along with REBT and CBT.

- MMT deals with clients' interpersonal problems through giving them unconditional acceptance, through the therapist's acting as a good model, and through specific instruction in better human relationships. Again, these methods are similar to those you may use if you practice REBT and CBT and that may be very helpful when your clients have interpersonal relationship difficulties.

All told, MMT is one of the main cognitive-behavior-therapies, it adopts many REBT and CBT principles and techniques, and can significantly contribute to your therapeutic work with regular and resistant clients.

INTEGRATING REBT AND CBT
WITH OTHER FORMS OF THERAPY

REBT and CBT usually do not emphasize some of the methods of certain other modes of therapy—such as Reichian or bodywork therapy. They consider physical and physiological factors quite important to mental functioning and dysfunctioning but usually hold that the specific physical exercises espoused by Wilhelm Reich (1960) and other advocates of intensive bodywork may do little good and involve much sidetracking for some disturbed people. However some CBT practitioners have integrated Reichian with other CBT techniques and have claimed success in doing so. Therefore, REBT and CBT practitioners hold themselves open to use bodywork methods for some special clients who may respond well to them but not respond as well to the usual CBT techniques that they employ.

You may integrate REBT and CBT with several of the therapies considered in this chapter, as well as with some of the more unusual treatment methods. You can include a variety of other procedures that are used in some of the less conventional therapies. What works works. So, especially for resistant clients, you can experiment with unusual and unpopular therapy practices to see if they are effective with your unusual clients-—and, if they do, to possibly try them more often with your every day clients. Only by considerable trial and error will you really discover if they are worth using more than occasionally. Your watchword had better be, both conventionally and unconventionally, "Let me try this particular technique and see, for myself and for my clients, what results we get!" As I have repeatedly emphasized in my own practice and as I also emphasize in this book, your key directives to yourself can well be "Experimentation, flexibility, and checking on results!" Isn't that largely the essence of the scientific and pragmatic method?

How to Maintain and Enhance Your Rational Emotive Behavior Therapy Gains

If you work at using the principles and practices of rational emotive behavior therapy (REBT), you will be able to change your self-defeating thoughts, feelings, and behaviors and to feel much better than when you started therapy. Good! But you will also, at times, fall back—and sometimes far back. No one is perfect and practically all people take one step backwards to every two or three steps forward. Why? Because that is the nature of humans: to improve, to stop improving at times, and sometimes to backslide.

How can you (imperfectly!) slow down your tendency to fall back? How can you maintain and enhance your therapy goals? Here are some methods that we have tested at the Albert Ellis Institute's clinic in New York and that many of our clients have found effective.

HOW TO MAINTAIN YOUR IMPROVEMENT

1. When you improve and then fall back to old feelings of anxiety, depression, or self-downing, try to remind yourself and pinpoint exactly what thoughts, feelings, and behaviors you once changed to bring about your improvement. If you again feel depressed, think back to how you previously used REBT to make yourself undepressed. For example, you may remember that:

   a. You stopped telling yourself that you were worthless and that you couldn't ever succeed in getting what you wanted.

   b. You did well in a job or a love affair and proved to yourself that you did have some ability and that you were lovable.

c. You forced yourself to go on interviews instead of avoiding them and thereby helped yourself overcome your anxiety about them.

Remind yourself of past thoughts, feelings, and behaviors that you have helped yourself by changing.

2. Keep thinking, thinking, and thinking Rational Beliefs (RB's) or coping statements, such as: "It's great to succeed but I can fully accept myself as a person and have enjoyable experiences even when I fail!" Don't merely parrot these statements but go over them carefully many times and think them through until you really begin to believe and feel that they are correct.

3. Keep seeking for, discovering, and disputing and challenging your Irrational Beliefs (IB's) with which you are once again upsetting yourself. Take each important Irrational Belief—such as, "I have to succeed in order to be a worthwhile person!"—and keep asking yourself: "Why is this belief true?" "Where is the evidence that my worth to myself, and my enjoyment of living, utterly depends on my succeeding at something?" "How does failing at an important task make me totally unacceptable as a human?"

Keep forcefully and persistently disputing your Irrational Beliefs whenever you see that you are letting them creep back again. Even when you don't actively hold them, realize that they may arise once more, bring them to your consciousness, and preventively—and vigorously!—dispute them.

4. Keep risking and doing things that you irrationally fear—such as riding in elevators, socializing, job hunting, or creative writing. Once you have partly overcome one of your irrational fears, keep acting against it on a regular basis. If you feel uncomfortable in forcing yourself to do things that you are unrealistically afraid of doing, don't allow yourself to avoid doing them—or else you'll preserve your discomfort forever! Sometimes practice making yourself as uncomfortable as you can be, in order to eradicate your irrational fears and to become unanxious and comfortable later.

5. Try to clearly see the real difference between *healthy* negative feelings—such as those of sorrow, regret, and frustration, when you do not get some of the important things you want—and *unhealthy* negative feelings, such as depression, anxiety, self-hatred, and self-pity.

Whenever you feel overconcerned (panicked) or unduly miserable (depressed) acknowledge that you are having a statistically normal but a psychologically unhealthy feeling and that you are mainly bringing it on yourself with some dogmatic should, ought, or must.

Realize that you are capable of changing your unhealthy (or *musturbatory*) feelings back into healthy (or preferential) ones. Take your depressed feelings and work on them until you only feel concerned and vigilant. Use rational emotive imagery to vividly imagine unpleasant

Activating Events, even before they happen; let yourself feel unhealthily upset (anxious, depressed, enraged, or self-downing) as you imagine them; then work on your feelings to change them to healthy negative emotions (concern, sorrow, annoyance, or regret) as you keep imagining some of the worst things happening. Don't give up until you actually do change your feelings.

6. Avoid self-defeating procrastination. Do unpleasant tasks fast—today! If you still procrastinate, reward yourself with certain things that you enjoy—for example, eating, vacationing, reading, and socializing—only after you have performed the tasks that you easily avoid. If this won't work, give yourself a severe penalty—such as talking to a boring person for two hours or burning a hundred dollar bill—every time you procrastinate.

7. Show yourself that it is an absorbing challenge and something of an adventure to maintain your emotional health and to keep yourself reasonably happy no matter what kinds of misfortunes assail you. Make the uprooting of your misery one of the most important things in your life—something you are utterly determined to steadily work at achieving. Fully acknowledge that you almost always have some choice about how to think, feel, and behave; then throw yourself actively into making that choice for yourself.

8. Remember—and use—the three main insights of REBT that were first outlined in *Reason and Emotion in Psychotherapy* in 1962:

Insight No. 1: You largely choose to disturb yourself about the unpleasant events of your life, although you may be encouraged to do so by external happenings and by social learning. You mainly *feel the way you think.* When obnoxious and frustrating things happen to you at point A (Activating Events or Adversities), you consciously or unconsciously select Rational Beliefs (RB's) that lead you to feel sad and regretful and you also select Irrational Beliefs (IB's) that lead you to feel anxious, depressed, and self-hating.

Insight No. 2: No matter how or when you acquired your Irrational Beliefs and your self-sabotaging habits, you now, in the present, choose to maintain them—and that is why you are now disturbed. Your past history and your present life conditions importantly affect you; but they don't disturb you. Your present philosophy is the main contributor to your current disturbance.

Insight No. 3: There is no magical way for you to change your personality and your strong tendencies to needlessly upset yourself. Basic personality change requires persistent work and practice—yes, work and practice—to enable you to alter your Irrational Beliefs, your unhealthy feelings, and your self-destructive behaviors.

9. Steadily and unfrantically look for personal pleasures and enjoyments—such as reading, entertainment, sports, hobbies, art, science, and other vital absorbing interests. Make your major life goal not only the achievement of emotional health but also that of real enjoyment. Try to become involved in a long-term purpose, goal, or interest in which you can remain truly absorbed. A good happy life will give you something to live for; will distract you from many serious woes; and will encourage you to preserve and to improve your mental health.

10. Try to keep in touch with several other people who know something about REBT and who can help you review some of its aspects. Tell them about problems that you have difficulty coping with and let them know how you are using REBT to overcome these problems. See if they agree with your solutions and can suggest additional and better kinds of disputing that you can use to work against your Irrational Beliefs.

11. Practice using REBT with some of your friends, relatives, and associates who are willing to let you try to help them with it. The more often you use it with others, and are able to see what their IBs are and to try to talk them out of these self-defeating ideas, the more you will be able to understand the main principles of REBT and to use them with yourself. When you see other people act irrationally and in a disturbed manner, try to figure out—with or without talking to them about it—what their main Irrational Beliefs probably are and how these could be actively and vigorously disputed.

12. When you are in REBT individual or group therapy, try to tape record many of your sessions and listen to these carefully between sessions, so that some of the ideas that you learned in therapy sink in. After therapy sessions, play these tape recordings back to yourself from time to time to remind you how to deal with some of your old problems or new ones that may arise.

13. Keep reading rational writings and listening to REBT audio- and video-cassettes. Included in the instruction sheet you were given when you started therapy at the Institute is a list of some of the main books and cassettes giving the principles and practices of REBT. Read and listen to several of these and keep going back to them from time to time.

HOW TO DEAL WITH BACKSLIDING

1. Accept your backsliding as normal—as something that happens to almost all people who at first improve emotionally and who then fall back. See it as part of your human fallibility. Don't make yourself feel ashamed when some of your old symptoms return; and don't think that you have to handle them entirely by yourself and that it is wrong or

weak for you to seek some additional sessions of therapy and to talk to your friends about your renewed problems.

2. When you backslide, look at your self-defeating behavior as bad and unfortunate; but refuse to put yourself down for engaging in this behavior. Use the highly important REBT principle of refraining from rating you, your self, or your being but of measuring only your acts, deeds, and traits. You are always a person who acts well or badly—and never a good person nor a bad person. No matter how badly you fall back and bring on your old disturbances again, work at fully accepting yourself with this unfortunate or weak behavior—and then try, and keep trying, to change your behavior.

3. Go back to the ABC's of REBT and clearly see what you did to fall back to your old symptoms. At A (Activating Event or Adversity), you usually experienced some failure or rejection. At RB (Rational Belief) you probably told yourself that you didn't like failing and didn't want to be rejected. If you only stayed with these Rational Beliefs, you would merely feel sorry, regretful, disappointed, or frustrated. But if you felt disturbed, you probably then went on to some Irrational Beliefs (IB's), such as: "I must not fail! It's horrible when I do!" "I have to be accepted, because if I'm not that makes me an unlovable worthless person!" If you reverted to these IB's, you probably felt, at C (emotional Consequence) once again depressed and self-downing.

4. When you find your Irrational Beliefs by which you are once again disturbing yourself, just as you originally used Disputing (D) to challenge and surrender them, do so again—immediately and persistently. Thus, you can ask yourself, "Why must I not fail? Is it really horrible if I do?" And you can answer: "There is no reason why I must not fail, though I can think of several reasons why it would be highly undesirable. It's not horrible if I do fail—only distinctly inconvenient."

You can also Dispute your other Irrational Beliefs by asking yourself, "Where is it written that I have to be accepted? How do I become an unlovable, worthless person if I am rejected?" And you can answer: "I never have to be accepted, though I would very much prefer to be. If I am rejected, that makes me, alas, a person who is rejected this time by this individual under these conditions, but it hardly makes me an unlovable, worthless person who will always be rejected by anyone for whom I really care."

5. Keep looking for, finding, and actively and vigorously Disputing your Irrational Beliefs to which you have once again relapsed and which are now making you feel anxious or depressed. Keep doing this, over and over, until you build intellectual and emotional muscle (just as you would build physical muscle by learning how to exercise and then by continuing to exercise).

6. Don't fool yourself into believing that if you merely change your language you will always change your thinking. If you neurotically tell yourself, "I *must* succeed and be approved" and you change this self-statement to "I *prefer* to succeed and be approved," you may still really be convinced, "But I really *have to* do well and be loved." Before you stop your Disputing and before you are satisfied with your answers to it, keep on doing it until you are really convinced of your rational answers and until your feelings of disturbance truly disappear. Then do the same thing many, many times—until your new E (Effective Philosophy) becomes hardened and habitual—which it almost always will if you keep working at it and thinking it through.

7. Convincing yourself lightly or "intellectually" of your new Effective Philosophy or Rational Beliefs often won't help very much or persist very long. Do so very strongly and vigorously, and do so many times. Thus, you can powerfully convince yourself, until you really feel it: "I do not *need* what I *want!* I never *have to* succeed, no matter how much I *wish* to do so!" "I *can* stand being rejected by someone I care for. It won't *kill* me—and I *still* can lead a happy life!" "No human is damnable and worthless—including *me!*"

HOW TO GENERALIZE FROM WORKING ON ONE EMOTIONAL PROBLEM TO WORKING ON OTHER PROBLEMS

1. Show yourself that your present emotional problem and the ways in which you bring it on are not unique and that most emotional and behavioral difficulties are largely created by Irrational Beliefs (IB's). Whatever your IBs are, you can overcome them by strongly and persistently disputing and acting against them.

2. Recognize that you tend to have three major kinds of Irrational Beliefs that lead you to disturb yourself and that the emotional and behavioral problems that you want to relieve fall into one, two, or all three of these categories:

   a. I *must* do well and *have to* be approved by people whom I find important." This IB leads you to feel anxious, depressed, and self-hating; and to avoid doing things at which you may fail or avoiding relationships that may not turn out well.

   b. "Other people *must* treat me fairly and nicely!" This IB contributes to your feeling angry, furious, violent, and over-rebellious.

   c. "The conditions under which I live *must* be comfortable and free from major hassles!" This IB tends to bring about feelings of low frustration tolerance and self-pity; and sometimes those of anger and depression.

3. Recognize that when you employ one of these three absolutistic *musts*—or any of the innumerable variations on it—you naturally and commonly derive from them other irrational conclusions, such as:

a. "Because I am not doing as well as I *must,* I am an incompetent worthless individual!" (Self-downing).

b. "Since I am not being approved by people whom I find important, as I *have to* be, it's awful and terrible!" (Awfulizing).

c. "Because others are not treating me as fairly and as nicely as they absolutely should treat me, they are utterly rotten people and deserve to be damned!" (Damnation).

d. "Since the conditions under which I live are not that comfortable and since my life has several major hassles, as it *must* not have, *I can't stand it!* My existence is a horror!" (Can't-stand-it-it is).

e. "Because I have failed and gotten rejected as I absolutely *ought not* have done, I'll *always* fail and *never* get accepted as I *must* be! My life will be hopeless and joyless forever!" (Overgeneralizing).

4. Work at seeing that these Irrational Beliefs are part of your general repertoire of thoughts and feelings and that you bring them to many different kinds of situations. Realize that in most cases where you feel seriously upset and act in a self-defeating manner you are consciously or unconsciously sneaking in one or more of these IBs. Consequently, if you reduce them in one area and are still emotionally disturbed about something else, you can use the same REBT principles to discover your IBs in the new area and to minimize them there.

5. Repeatedly show yourself that you normally won't disturb yourself and remain disturbed if you abandon your absolutistic *shoulds, oughts,* and *musts* and consistently replace them with flexible and unrigid (though still strong) *desires* and *preferences.*

6. Continue to acknowledge that you can change your Irrational Beliefs (IB's) by rigorously (not rigidly!) using realistic and healthy thinking. You can show yourself that your Irrational Beliefs are only assumption or hypotheses—not facts. You can logically, realistically, and pragmatically Dispute them in many ways such as these:

a. You can show yourself that your IB's are self-defeating—that they interfere with your goals and your happiness. For if you firmly convince yourself, "I *must* succeed at important tasks and *have to* be approved by all the significant people in my life," you will of course at times fail and be disapproved—and thereby inevitably make yourself anxious and depressed instead of sorry and frustrated.

b. Your Irrational Beliefs do not conform to reality—and especially do not conform to the facts of human fallibility. If you always *had to* succeed, if the universe commanded that you *must* do so, you obviously *would* always succeed. But of course you often don't! If you invariably *had to* be approved by others, you could never be disapproved. But obviously you frequently are! The universe is clearly not arranged so that you will always get what you demand. So although your desires are often realistic, your god-like commands definitely are not.

c. Your Irrational Beliefs are illogical, inconsistent, or contradictory. No matter how much you *want* to succeed and to be approved, it never follows that therefore you *must* do well in these (or any other) respects. No matter how desirable justice or politeness is, it never has to exist.

Although REBT disputing is not infallible or sacred, it efficiently helps you to discover which of your beliefs are irrational and self-defeating and how to use realistic, pragmatic, and logical thinking to minimize them. If you keep using flexible thinking, you will avoid dogma and construct your assumptions about you, other people, and world conditions so that you always keep them open to change.

7. Try to set up some main goals and purposes in life—goals that you would like very much to reach but that you never tell yourself that you absolutely *must* attain. Keep checking to see how you are coming along with these goals, and at times revise them. Keep yourself oriented toward the goals that you select and that are not harmful to you or to others. Instead of making yourself extremely self-interested or socially interested, a balanced absorption in both these kinds of goals will often work out best for you and the community in which you choose to live.

8. If you get bogged down and begin to lead a life that seems too miserable or dull, review the points made in this pamphlet and work at using them. If you fall back or fail to go forward at the pace you prefer, don't hesitate to return to therapy for some booster sessions or to join one of the Institute's regular therapy groups.

References

Abelson, R. P. (1963). Computer simulation of "hot" cognition. In S. S. Tompkins and S. Messick (Eds.), *Computer simulation of personality* (pp. 51–63). New York: Wiley.

Alway, J. (1999). Can the Cognitive-behavioral therapies produce the kind and level of change which is measured by personality inventories? *Rational Emotive Behavior Therapist, 7*(1), 27–46.

Arnold, M. S. (1997, April). Oppression and multiculturism. *Counseling Psychologist,* 34–39.

Bandura, A. (1997). *Self-efficacy: The exercise of control.* New York: Freeman.

Bargh, J. A, & Chartrand, T. L. (1999). The unbearable automaticity of being. *American Psychologist, 54,* 462–479.

Beck, A. T. (1976). *Cognitive therapy and the emotional disorders.* New York: International Universities Press.

Beck, A. T., & Emery, G. (1985). *Anxiety disorders and phobias.* New York: Basic Books.

Beck, A. T., freeman, A. & Associates. (1990). *Cognitive therapy of personality disorders.* New York: Guilford.

Becvar, D. S., & Becvar, R. J. (1998). From subtraction to addition. In H. G. Rosenthal (Ed.), *Favorite counseling and therapy techniques* (pp. 40–41). Washington, DC: Accelerated Development.

Bernard, M. E. (2000). Common techniques for overcoming procrastination. In M. E. Bernard & J. L. Wolfe (Eds.), *REBT resource book for practitioners* (pp. III–38). New York: Albert Ellis Institute.

Bernard, M. E., & Wolfe, J. L. (Eds.). (2000). *The REBT resource book for practitioners.* New York: Albert Ellis Institute.

Betz, N. E., Wohlgemuth, D. S., Harshbarger, J., & Klein, K. (1995). Evaluation of measure of self-esteem based on the concept of unconditional self-regard. *Journal of Counseling & Development, 74,* 76–83.

Bishop, M. (2001). *Managing addictions: Cognitive and behavioral techniques.* Holmes, PA: Aaronson.

Bishop, W., & Fish, J. M. (1999). Questions as interventions. *Journal of Rational-Emotive and Cognitive Behavior Therapy, 17,* 115–140.

Brogan, M. M., Prochaska, J. O., & Prochaska, J. M. (1999). Predicting termination and continuation status in psychotherapy using the transtheorectical model. *Psychotherapy, 36,* 105–113.

Buber, M. (1984). *I and thou.* New York: Scribner.

Burns, D. D. (1980/1999). *Feeling good: The new mood therapy* (rev. ed.). New York: Morrow, Williams & Co.

Butler, M. H., & Bird, M. H. (2000). Narrative and interactional process for preventing harmful struggle in therapy. *Journal of Mental and Family Therapy, 26,* 123–142.

Chamberlain, J. M., & Haaga, D. A. F. (2001). Unconditional self-acceptance and responses to negative feedback. *Journal of Rational-Emotive and Cognitive Behavior Therapy, 19,* 177–189.

Clark, D. A. (2000). Cognitive behavior therapy for obsessions and compulsions. *Journal of Contemporary Psychotherapy, 30,* 129–147.

Clark, D. A. (2001). The persistent problem of negative cognition in anxiety and depression. *Behavior Therapy, 32,* 3–12.

Cloninger, C. R. (Ed.). (2000). *Personality and psychopathology.* Washington, DC: American Psychiatric Association.

Corsini, R. J. (1979). The betting technique. *Individual Psychology, 16,* 5–11.

Corsini, R. J. (1999). *The dictionary of psychology.* Philadelphia: Brunner/Mazel.

Counseling Psychologist (1996). Multicultural challenges: Theory, evaluation, and training. *Counseling Psychologist, 24,* 197–284.

Cowan, E. W., & Presbury, J. H. (2000). Meeting client resistance with reverence. *Journal of Counseling and Development, 78,* 411–419.

Csikszentmihaly, M. (1990) *Flow: The psychology of optimal experience.* San Francisco: Harper Perennial.

D'Andrea, M., Daniels, J., & Heck, R. (1991). Evaluating the impact of multicounseling training. *Journal of Counseling and Development, 70,* 143–150.

Deffenbacher, J. L. (1999). Cognitive-behavioral conceptions of anger. *Journal of Clinical Psychology/ In session: Psychotherapy in Practice, 55,* 295–309.

DeShazer, S. (1985). *Keys to solution in brief therapy.* New York: Norton.

Detwiler, R. A., & Whisman, M. A. (1999).

DiGiuseppe, R. (1991). Comprehensive cognitive disputing in RET. In M. E. Bernard (Ed.), *Using rational-emotive therapy effectively* (pp. 173–196). New York: Plenum.

DiGiuseppe, R. (2000). The top 10 reasons to give up your disturbed anger. In M. E. Bernard & J. L. Wolfe (Eds.), *REBT resource book for practitioners* (pp. III–62). New York: Albert Ellis Institute.

DiGiuseppe, R., Leaf, R., & Linscott, J. (1993). The therapeutic relationship in Rational Emotive Therapy: A preliminary analysis. *Journal of Rational-Emotive and Cognitive- Behavior Therapy, 11,* 223–233.

DiMattia, D., & Lega, L. (Eds.). (1990). *Will the real Albert Ellis please stand up? Anecdotes by his colleagues, students and friends celebrating his 75th birthday.* New York: Institute for Rational-Emotive Therapy.

Doyle, K. (2001). *Expanding your range of therapeutic techniques while remaining within the elegant solution.* Paper presented at the general session of the 45th anniversary conference on Rational Emotive Behavior Therapy. Keystone, CO. June 7.

Dryden, W. (2001). *Reason to change: A rational emotive behavior therapy (REBT) workbook.* Hove, East Sussex, England: Brunner-Routledge.

Dryden, W., & Matweychuk, W. (2000). *Overcoming your addictions.* London: Sheldon Press.

Dryden, W., & Still, A. (1998). REBT and rationality: philosophical approaches. *Journal of Rational-Emotive and Cognitive–Behavior Therapy, 16,* 77–97.

D'Zurilla, T. J., & Nezu, A. M. (1999). *Problem-Solving Therapy* (2nd ed.). New York: Springer.

Ellis, A. (1950). An introduction to the scientific principles of psychoanalysis. *Genetic Psychology Monographs, 41,* 147–212.

Ellis, A. (1955a). New approaches to psychotherapy techniques. *Journal of Clinical Psychology Monograph Supplement, 11.* Brandon, VT.

Ellis, A. (1955b). Psychotherapy techniques for use with psychotics. *American Journal of Psychotherapy, 9,* 452–476.

Ellis, A. (1956). An operational reformulation of some of the basic principles of psychoanalysis. In H. Feigl & M. Scriven (Eds.), *The foundation of science and the concepts of psychology and psychoanalysis* (pp. 131–154). Minneapolis: University of Minnesota Press. (Also: Psychoanalytic Review, 43, 163–180).

Ellis, A. (1957a/1975). *How to live with a neurotic: At home and at work.* Hollywood, CA: Wilshire Books.

Ellis, A. (1957b). Outcome of employing three techniques of psychotherapy. *Journal of Clinical Psychology, 13,* 334–350.

Ellis, A. (1957c). Rational-emotive therapy and individual psychology. *Journal of Individual Psychology, 13*(1), 38–44.

Ellis, A. (1958). Rational psychotherapy. *Journal of General Psychology, 59,* 35–49. Reprinted: New York: Albert Ellis Insitute.

Ellis, A. (1960). *The art and science of love*. New York: Lyle Stuart.

Ellis, A. (1962). *Reason and emotion in psychotherapy*. Secaucus, NJ: Citadel.

Ellis, A. (1963). *The intelligent woman's guide to manhunting*. New York: Lyle Stuart and Dell Publishing. Rev. Ed.: *The intelligent woman's guide to dating and mating*. Secaucus, NJ: Lyle Stuart, 1979.

Ellis, A. (1976a). The biological basis of human irrationality. *Journal of Individual Psychology, 32*, 145–168. Reprinted: New York: Albert Ellis Institute.

Ellis, A. (1976b). *Sex and the liberated man*. Secaucus, NJ: Lyle Stuart.

Ellis, A. (1977). Fun as psychotherapy. *Rational Living, 12*(1), 2–6. Also: Cassette recording. New York: Institute for Rational-Emotive Therapy.

Ellis, A. (1983). The philosophic implications and dangers of some popular behavior therapy techniques. In M. Rosenbaum, C. M. Franks, & Y. Jaffe (Eds.), *Perspectives in behavior therapy in the eighties* (pp. 138–151). New York: Springer.

Ellis, A. (1994). *Reason and emotion in psychotherapy*. Revised and updated. New York: Kensington Publishers.

Ellis, A. (1996). *Better, deeper and more enduring brief therapy*. New York: Brunner/Mazel.

Ellis, A. (1997). Postmodern ethics for active-directive counseling and psychotherapy. *Journal of Mental Health Counseling, 18,* 211–225.

Ellis, A. (1999). *How to make yourself happy and remarkably less disturbable*. Atascadero, CA: Impact Publishers.

Ellis, A. (2000a). *How to control your anxiety before it controls you*. New York: Citadel Press.

Ellis, A. (2000b). Rational Emotive Behavior Therapy. In R. V. Corsini & D. Wedding (Eds.), *Current psychotherapies* (pp. 168–204). Itasca, IL: Peacock.

Ellis, A. (2001a). *Feeling better, getting better, staying better*. Atascadero, CA: Impact Publishers.

Ellis, A. (2001b). *Overcoming destructive beliefs, feeling and behaviors*. Amherst, NY: Prometheus Books.

Ellis, A. (2001c). Rational and irrational aspects of countertransference. *Journal of Clinical Psychology, In session: Psychotherapy in Practice, 57,* 999–1004.

Ellis, A., & Becker, I. (1982). *A guide to personal happiness*. North Hollywood, CA: Melvin Powers.

Ellis, A., & Blau. S. (1998). (Eds). *The Albert Ellis reader*. New York: Kensington Publishers.

Ellis, A., & Dryden, W. (1997). *The practice of rational emotive behavior therapy*. New York: Springer.

Ellis, A., Gordon, V., Neenan, M., & Palmer, S. (1998) Stress counseling. New York: Springer.

Ellis, A., & Gullo, J. (1972). *Murder and assassination*. New York: Lyle Stuart.

Ellis, A., & Harper, R. A. (1997). *A guide to rational living* (rev. ed.). North Hollywood, CA: Melvin Powers/Wilshire Books.

Ellis, A., & Knaus, W. (1977). *Overcoming procrastination*. New York: New American Library.

Ellis, A., & MacLaren, C. (1998). *Rational emotive behavior therapy: A therapist's guide*. Atascadero, CA: Impact Publishers.

Ellis, A., McInerney, J. F., DiGiuseppe, R., & Yeager, R. J. (1998). *Rational-emotive therapy with alcoholics and substance abusers*. Needham, MA: Allyn & Bacon.

Ellis, A., & Tafrate, R. C. (1997). *How to control your anger before it controls you*. New York: Kensington Publishers.

Ellis, A., & Velten, E. (1992). *When AA doesn't work for you: Rational steps for quitting alcohol*. New York: Barricade Books.

Ellis, A., & Velten, E. (1998). *Optimal aging: Getting over growing older*. Chicago: Open Court.

Ellis, J. E., & Newman, C. F. (1996). *Choosing to live: How to defeat suicide through cognitive therapy*. Oakland, CA: New Harbinger.

Enright, R. D., & Fitzgibbons, R. P. (2000). *Helping clients forgive: An empirical guide for resolving anger and restoring hope*. Washington, D. C.: American Psychological Association.

Epictetus. (1890). *The Works of Epictetus*. Boston: Little Brown.

Erickson, M. H., & Rossi, E. L. (1979). *Hypnotherapy: An exploratory casebook*. New York: Irvington.

Falsetti, S. A., & Resnick, H. S. (2000). Treatment of PTSD using cognitive & behavioral therapies. *Journal of Cognitive Therapy, 14*, 261–285.

Field, T. F. (1998). Massage therapy effects. *American Psychologist, 55*, 1270–1281.

Firestone, R. W. (1998). Voice therapy. In H. G. Rosenthal (Ed.), *Favorite counseling and therapy techniques* (pp. 82–85). Washington, DC: Accelerated Development.

Flett, G. L., & Hewitt, P. L. (2002). *Perfectionism: Theory, research and treatment*. Washington, DC: American Psychological Association.

Foa, E., & Olasov, B. (1998). *Treating the theme of rape: Cognitive-behavior therapy for PTSD*. New York: Guilford.

Frank, J. (1994). Effective components of psychotherapy. In J. D. Corsini, *Encyclopedia of psychology*, 2nd ed. (pp. 464–465). New York: Wiley.

Frank, J. D., & Frank, J. B. (1993) *Persuasion and healing* (3rd ed.). Baltimore, MD: Johns Hopkins University Press.

Frankl, V. (1960). *Man's search for meaning.* New York: Pocket Books.

Fredrickson, B. L. (2001). The role of positive emotions in positive psychology. *American Psychologist, 56,* 218–226.

Freeman, A., & Dolan, M. (2001). Revisiting Prochaska and DiClemente's stages of change. *Cognitive and Behavioral Practice, 8,* 224–234.

Garfield, S. L., & Bergin, A. E. (1994). *Handbook of psychotherapy and behavior change.* New York: Wiley.

Gendlin, E. (1999). Implicit entry and focusing. *Humanistic Psychologist, 27,* 79–88.

Glasser, W. (1999). *Choice theory.* New York: Harper Collins.

Golden, W. (1983). Resistance in cognitive behavior therapy. *British Journal of Cognitive Therapy, 1*(2), 33–42.

Gollwitzer, P. M. (1999). Implementation intentions: Strong effects of simple plans. *American Psychologist, 56,* 493–503.

Haley, J. (1998). *Strategies of psychotherapy.* New York: Grune & Stratton.

Hall, C. C. I. (1997). Cultural malpractice. *American Psychologist, 52,* 642–651.

Hanna, F. J. (2001). *Therapy with difficult clients. Using the precursors model to awaken change.* Washington, DC: American Psychological Association.

Harvard Mental Health Letter. (2000). Personality Disorders, Parts I and II. *Harvard Mental Health Letter, 11*(9), 141.

Hauck, P. A. (1974). *Overcoming frustration and anger.* Philadelphia: Westminster.

Hauck, P. A. (1991). *Overcoming the rating game: Beyond self-love— beyond self-esteem.* Louisville, KY: Westminster/John Knox.

Hayes, S. C., Strosahl, K., & Wilson, K. G. (1999). *Acceptance and commitment therapy.* New York: Guilford.

Held, B. S. (1995). *Back to reality: A critique of post modern theory in psychotherapy.* New York: Norton.

Herzberg, A. (1945). *Active psychotherapy.* New York: Grune & Stratton.

Hollon, S. D., & Beck, A. T. (1994). Cognitive and cognitive-behavioral therapies. In A. E. Bergin & S. L. Garfield (Eds.), *Handbook of psychotherapy and behavior change* (pp. 428–466). New York: Wiley.

Horney, K. (1950). *Neurosis and human growth.* New York: Norton.

Horvath, A. T. (1998). *Sex, drugs, gambling & alcohol.* Atascadero, CA: Impact Publishers.

Hovland, C. I., & Janis, I. L. (1959). *Personality and persuasibility.* New Haven, CT: Yale University Press.

Irwin, J. F., Bowers, C. A., Dunn, M. E., & Wong, M. C. (1999). Efficacy of relapse prevention. *Journal of counseling and clinical psychotherapy, 64,* 563–570.

Ivey, A. E. (1998). Community genogram: Identifying strengths. In A. G. Rosenthal (Ed.), *Favorite Counseling and therapy techniques,* (pp. 109–111). Washington, DC: Accelerated Development.

Ivey, A. E., Ivey, M., & Simek-Morgan, L. (1997). *Counseling and psychotherapy: A multicultural perspective.* Boston: Allyn & Bacon.

Jacobson, E. (1938). *You must relax.* New York: McGraw-Hill.

Kahneman, D., & Tuersky, A. (2000). *Choices, values, and frames.* New York: Cambridge.

Karen, R. (2001). *The forgiving self.* New York: Doubleday.

Kelly, G. (1955). *The psychology of personal constructs.* New York: Norton.

Kierkegaard, S. (1953). *Fear and trembling* and *The sickness unto death.* New York: Doubleday.

Kinney, A. (2000). The intellectual-insight problem: Implications for assessment and rational-emotive behavior therapy. *Journal of Contemporary Psychotherapy, 30,* 261–272.

Kirsch, I. (1999). *How expectations shape experience.* Washington, DC: American Psychological Association.

Kirsch, I., & Lynn, S. J. (1999). Automaticity in clinical psychology. *American Psychologist, 54,* 504–518.

Knaus, Bill. (2000). *Smart recovery: A sensible primer* (4th ed.). Mentor, OH: SMART Recovery.

Korzybski, A. (1933/1991). *Science and sanity.* Concord, CA: International Society for General Semantics.

Kuehlwein, K. T., & Rosen, H. (1993). *Cognitive therapies in action.* San Francisco: Jossey-Bass.

Kwee, M. G. T., & Ellis, A. (1997). Can multimodal and rational emotive behavior therapy be reconciled? *Journal of Rational Emotive and Cognitive-Behavior Therapy, 15*(2), 95–132.

Lange, A., & Jakubowski, P. (1976). *Responsible assertive behavior.* Champaign, IL: Research Press.

Langer, E. (1997). *The power of mindful learning.* Reading, MA: Addison-Wesley.

Langer, E. J., & Moldoveneau, M. (2000). The construct of mindfulness. *Journal of Social Issues, 56*(1), 1–9.

Lazarus, A. A. (1997). Brief but comprehensive therapy. New York: Springer.

Lazarus, R. S. (2000). Toward better research on stress and coping. *American Psychologist, 55,* 665–673.

Leahy, R. L. (2001). *Overcoming resistance in cognitive therapy.* New York: Guilford.

Lejuez, C. M., Hopko, D. R., LePage, J. P., Hopko, S. D., & McNeil, D. N. (2001). A brief behavioral activation treatment for depression. *Cognitive and behavioral Practice, 8,* 164–175.

Linehan, M. (1992). *Cognitive behavioral treatment of borderline personality disorder.* New York: Guilford.

Lyons, L. C., & Woods, P. J. (1991). The efficacy of rational-emotive therapy: A quantitative review of the outcome research. *Clinical Psychology Review, 11,* 357–369.

Mahoney, M. J. (1974). *Cognition and behavior modification.* Cambridge, MA: Ballinger.

Mahoney, M. J. (1991). *Human change processes.* New York: Basic Books.

Mahrer, A. (1998). Personality change. In H. G. Rosenthal (Ed.), *Favorite counseling and therapy techniques* (pp. 127–130). Washington, DC: Accelerated Development.

Malkinson, R., & Ellis, A. (2001). The application of rational-emotive behavior therapy (REBT) in traumatic and non-traumatic loss. In R. Malkinson, S. S. Rubin, & E. Witztom (Eds.), *Traumatic and non-traumatic loss and bereavement: Clinical theory and practice* (pp. 173–195). Madison, CT: Psychosocial Press.

Marlett, G. A., & Gordon, J. R. (Eds.). (1989). *Relapse prevention: Maintenance strategies in the treatment of addictive behaviors.* New York: Guilford.

Maultsby, M. C., Jr. (1971). Rational emotive imagery. *Rational Living, 6*(1), 24–27.

May, R., & Yalom, I. (2000). Existential psychotherapy. In R. V. Corsini & D. Wedding (Eds.), *Current psychotherapies* (pp. 273–302). Itasca, IL: Peacock.

McMullin, R. E. (2000). *The new handbook of cognitive therapy.* New York: Norton.

Meehl. P. E. (1962). Schizotaxis, schizotypy, schizophrenia. *American Psychologist, 17,* 827–838.

Meichenbaum, D. (1997). Evolution of Cognitive Behavior Therapy: Origins, tenets and clinical examples. In J. K. Zeig (Ed.), *The evolution of psychotherapy. The second conference* (pp. 114–128). New York: Brunner/Mazel.

Miller, I. W. (1984). Strategies for maintenance of treatment gains for depressed patients. *Cognitive Behaviorist, 6*(1), 10–13.

Mills, D. (2000). Overcoming self-esteem. In M. E. Bernard & J. L. Wolfe (Eds.), *REBT resource book* (2nd ed., II 14–15). New York: Albert Ellis Institute.

Moore, R. H. (1983). Inference as "A" in RET. *British Journal of Cognitive Therapy, 1*(2), 17–23.

Moreno, J. L. (1990). *The essential J. L. Moreno.* New York: Springer.

Najavits, L. M. (2001). Helping "difficult" patients. *Psychotherapy Research, 11,* 131–152.

Neenan, M., & Dryden, W. (1999). When laddering and the downward arrow can be used as adjuncts to inference chaining in REBT assessment. *Journal of Rational-Emotive and Cognitive Behavior Therapy, 17,* 95–104.

Nelson, R. C. (1998). Creating SPA in counseling. In H. G. Rosenthal (Eds.), *Favorite counseling and therapy techniques* (pp. 109–111). Washington, DC: Accelerated Development.

Nielsen, S. L., Johnson, W. R., & Ellis, A. (2001). *Counseling and psychotherapy with religious persons: A rational emotive behavioral approach.* Mahwah, NJ: Erlbaum.

Norcross, J. C., & Beutler, L. E. (1997). Determining the therapeutic relationship of choice in brief therapy. In J. N. Butcher (Ed.), *Personality assessment in managed health care.* New York: Oxford.

Overholzer, J. C. (1993). Elements of the Socratic method. I. Systematic questioning. *Psychotherapy, 30,* 67–74.

Overholzer, J. C. (1994). Elements of the Socratic method: III Universal definitions. *Psychotherapy, 31,* 286–293.

Paris, J. (1999). *Nature and nurture in psychotherapy.* Washington, DC: American Psychiatric Association.

Paul, G. L. (1967). Strategy of outcome research in psychotherapy. *Journal of Consulting Psychology, 31,* 109–118.

Perls, F. (1969). *Gestalt therapy verbatim.* New York: Delta.

Persons, J. B., Davidson, J., & Tompkins, M. A. (2001). *Essential components of cognitive-behavior therapy for depression.* Washington, DC: American Psychological Association.

Phadke, K. M. (1982). Some innovations in RET theory and practice. *Rational Living, 17*(2), 25–30.

Pietsch, W. V. (1993). *The serenity prayer.* San Francisco: Harper San Francisco.

Powers, W. T. (1999). *Making sense of behavior: The meaning of control.* New Canaan, CT: Benchmark Publications.

Prochaska, J. O., DiClemente, D.C., & Norcross, J. C. (1992). In search of how people change: Application to addictive behaviors. *American Psychologist, 47,* 1102–1114.

Redding, R. E. (2001). Sociopolitical diversity in psychology. *American Psychologist, 56,* 205–215.

Reich, W. (1960). *Selected writings.* New York: Farrar, Straus and Cudahy.

Reis, B. F., & Brown, L. G. (1999). Reducing psychotherapy dropouts. *Psychotherapy, 36,* 123–136.

Reiss, S., & McNally, R. J. (1985). Expectancy model of fear. In S. Reiss and R. R. Bootzin (Eds.), *Theorectical issues in behavior therapy.* New York: Academic Press.

Richards, P. S., & Bergin, A. E. (2000). *Handbook of psychotherapy and religious diversity.* Washington, DC: American Psychological Association.

Rigazio-DiGilio, S. A., Ivey, A. E., & Locke, D. C. (1997). Continuing the post-modern dialogue. *Journal of Mental Health Counseling, 19,* 233–255.

Robb, H. B. (2001). Facilitating Rational Emotive Behavior Therapy by including religious beliefs. *Cognitive and Behavioral Practice, 8,* 29–34.

Robin, M. W., & Balter, S. (1995). *Performance anxiety.* Holbrook, MA: Adams.

Rogers, C. R. (1961). *On becoming a person.* Boston: Houghton Mifflin.

Rohrbaugh, M. J., & Shohan, V. (2000). Brief therapy based on interrupting ironic processes. *Clinical Science, 86,* 66–80.

Rorer, L. G. (1999). Dealing with the intellectual-insight problem in cognitive and rational emotive behavior therapy. *Journal of Rational-Emotive and Cognitive-Behavior Therapy, 17,* 217–236.

Salter, A. (1949). *Conditioned reflex therapy.* New York: Creative Age.

Sartre, J. (1968). *Being and nothingness.* New York: Washington Square.

Schneider, S. L. (2001). In search of realistic optimism. *American Psychologist, 56,* 250–263.

Seligman, M. E. P. (1991). *Learned optimism.* New York: Knopf.

Seligman, M. E. P., & Cziksentmihali, M. (2000). Positive psychology: An introduction. *American Psychologist, 2000, 55,* 5–14.

Shelley, A. M., Battaglia, J., Lucey, J., Ellis, A., & Opler, L. A. (2001). *Symptom-specific group therapy for inpatients with schizophrenia.* Bronx, NY: Bronx Psychiatric Center.

Sue, D. W., Bingham, R. P., Porche-Burke, L., & Vasquez, M. O. (1999). The diversification of psychology. *American Psychologist, 54,* 1061–1069.

Thorne, F. C. (1950). *Principles of personality counseling.* Brandon, VT: Journal of Clinical Psychology Press.

Tillich, P. (1953). *The courage to be.* Cambridge, MA: Harvard University.

Turkat, D., & Meyer, V. (1982). The behavior approach. In P. H. Wachtel (Ed.), *Resistance* (pp. 157–184). New York: Plenum.

Urdang, N. S. (2000). Tips for motivating clients to do homework. In M. E. Bernard & J. L. Wolfe (Eds.), *The REBT resource book for practitioners* (pp. I-83–84). New York: Albert Ellis Institute.

Vriend, J., & Dyer, W. W. (1977). Counseling reluctant clients. *Journal of Counseling Psychology, 20,* 240–246.

Walen, S., DiGiuseppe, R., & Dryden, W. (1992). *A practitioner's guide to rational-emotive therapy.* New York: Oxford University Press.

Watson, J. B. (1919). *Psychology from the standpoint of a behaviorist.* Philadelphia: Lippincott.

Watzlawick, P., Weakland, J., & Fisch, R. (1974). *Change.* New York: Norton.

Wegner, D. M., & Wheatley, T. (1999). Apparent mental causation. *American Psychologist, 54,* 480–492.

Weinrach, S. G., & Thomas, K. R. (1996). The counseling profession's commitment to diversity-sensitivity counseling: A critical reassessment. *Journal of Counseling and Development, 74,* 472–478.

Weinrach, S. G., & Thomas, K. R. (1998). Diversity-sensitive counseling today: A postmodern clash of values. *Journal of Counseling and Development, 76,* 115–122.

Weinrach, S. G., & Thomas, K. R. (2002). A critical analysis of the multicultural counseling competencies. *Journal of Mental Health Counseling, 24,* 20–35.

White, M., & Epston, D. (1990). *Narrative means to therapeutic ends.* New York: Norton.

Wilde, J. (1992). *Rational counseling with school-aged populations: A practical guide.* Muncie, IN: Accelerated Development.

Wolfe, J. L. (1992). *What to do when he has a headache.* New York: Hyperion.

Yeh, C. J., & Hwang, M. Y. (2000). Interdependence in ethnic identity and self: implications for theory and practice. *Journal of Counseling and Development, 78,* 420–429.

Yochelson, S., & Samenow, S. E. (1977). *The criminal personality.* New York: Aronson.

Yontef, G., & Jacobs L. (2000). Gestalt therapy. In R. Corsini & D. Wedding (Eds.), *Current psychotherapies* (pp. 303–339). Itasca, IL: Peacock.

Young, H. S. (1974). *A rational counseling primer.* New York: Albert Ellis Institute.

Young, J. E. (1990). *Cognitive therapy for personality disorders.* Sarasota, FL: Professional Resources Exchange.

Zettle, R. D. (1994) Discussion of Dougher: On the use of acceptable language. In S. C. Hayes, N. S. Jacobson, V. M. Fonnette, & M. J. Dougher (Eds.), *Acceptance and change: Content and context in psychotherapy* (pp. 46–50). Reno, NV: Context Press.

Ziegler, D. J. (2001). The possible place of cognitive appraisal in the ABC model underlying Rational Emotive Behavior Therapy. *Journal of Rational-Emotive and Cognitive Behavior-Therapy, 19,* 137–152.

Ziegler, D. J., & Hawley, J. L. (2000). The Relationship between irrational thinking and the pessimistic explanatory style. *Psychological Reports, 88,* 483–488.

Zilbergeld. B. (1983). *The shrinking of America*. Boston: Houghton, Mifflin.

Zuckerman, M. (1999). *Vulnerability to psychopathology*. Washington, DC: American Psychology Association.

Index

Springer Publishing Company

Brief But Comprehensive Psychotherapy: *The Multimodal Way*

Arnold A. Lazarus, PhD, ABPP

"...substantially advances the practice of short-term psychotherapy. Dr. Lazarus distills his many years of experience as a master clinician and teacher and outlines the fundamentals of multimodal therapy in an exciting and readable fashion. I highly recommend this volume to everybody in the mental health field, from students to advanced psychotherapists."

—**Aaron T. Beck,** Univ. Professor Emeritus University of Pennsylvania

The current healthcare environment has created a need for short-term and cost-effective forms of psychotherapy, emphasizing efficiency and efficacy. The central message is "don't waste time." But how can one be so brief and also comprehensive?

Using his traditional acronym — BASIC ID — Dr. Lazarus stresses the assessment of seven dimensions of a client's personality: behavior, affect, sensation, imagery, cognition, interpersonal relationships, and the need for drugs. Featuring distinctive assessment procedures and therapeutic recommendations, this volume enhances the skills and clinical repertoires of every therapist.

Contents:
- Let's Cut to the Chase
- Elucidating the Main Rationale
- What is the Multimodal Way?
- Theories and Techniques
- Multimodal Assessment Procedures: Bridging and Tracking
- Multimodal Assessment Procedures: Second-Order Basic ID and Structural Profiles
- Some Elements of Effective Brevity
- Activity and Serendipity
- Two Specific Applications: Sexual Desire Disorders and Dysthymia
- Couples Therapy
- Some Common Time Wasters

Springer Series on Behavior Therapy and Behavioral Medicine
1997   192 pp   0-8261-9640-3   hard

536 Broadway, New York, NY 10012• (212) 431-4370 • Fax (212) 941-7842
Order Toll-Free: (877) 687-7476 • *www.springerpub.com*

Springer Publishing Company

Journal of Cognitive Psychotherapy

An International Quarterly

Robert L. Leahy, PhD, Editor

E. Thomas Dowd, PhD, International Editor

William Lyddon, PhD, Assistant Editor

Since 1987 this journal has been devoted to the advancement of the clinical practice of cognitive psychotherapy in its broadest sense. As the official publication for the International Association of Cognitive Psychotherapy, this journal seeks to merge theory, research, and practice—providing an international forum to investigate clinical implications of theoretical developments and research findings.

Each issue offers a variety of case studies, in-depth analyses, and literature reviews of clinical topics. Also included are reviews and abstracts of books, tapes, films, and other clinical resources.

SAMPLE ARTICLES:

- Cognitive Vulnerability to Depression: Theory and Evidence, *Lyn Y. Abramson, Lauren B. Alloy, et al.*
- Cognitive Styles and Life Events in Subsyndromal Unipolar and Bipolar Disorders: Stability and Prospective Prediction of Depressive and Hypomanic Mood Swings, *Lauren B.Alloy, and Noreen Reilly Harrington, et al.*
- Specific Cognitive Content of Anxiety and Catastrophizing: Looming Vulnerability and the Looming Maladaptive Styles, *John H. Riskind and Nathan L. Williams*
- Response Modulation Deficits: Implications for the Diagnosis and Treatment of Psychopathy, *John F. Wallace, Jennifer E. Vitale, and Joseph P. Newman*

Volume 16, 2002 • 4 issues annually • ISSN 0889-8391

536 Broadway, New York, NY 10012• (212) 431-4370 • Fax (212) 941-7842
Order Toll-Free: (877) 687-7476 • *www.springerpub.com*

DATE DUE

NOV 0 9 2005			
NOV 0 8 2005			
JUL 0 5 2007			

GAYLORD   PRINTED IN U.S.A.